A MAN'S BOOK

A MAN'S BOOK

edited by jane waller

duckworth

To *The Tailor and Cutter*

First published 1977 by
Gerald Duckworth & Co. Ltd,
The Old Piano Factory,
43 Gloucester Crescent, London NW1

Book design by Alphabet and Image,
Sherborne, Dorset
Designer: Jamie Hobson

ISBN: 0 7156 1019 8

Printed and bound in Great Britain by
Redwood Burn Limited, Trowbridge & Esher

Contents

THE KING TAKES THE WHEEL

Introduction

A Man's Book is concerned with the world of the middle-class man—his pleasures and his preoccupations, and above all his fashions—as prescribed and preserved in the mass circulation magazines of the period. The Prince of Wales is the hero of the book, for it was he whom the young men took as their ideal. As a 'working man' he worked hard for his country both at home and as an ambassador abroad, his motto being 'I Serve'. He set new social standards by breaking many of the stuffier traditions so rigidly adhered to by his father, King George V. In the world of fashion he was considered the best-dressed man in the world, setting the trend for soft shirts in dress wear, Fair-Isle pullovers for sport and his very own Prince of Wales check for suiting, a firm favorite today, used to clothe the modern man and reproduced on the end-papers of this book.

The fashions of the twenties and thirties man are described in detail and illustrated with many plates taken from *The Tailor and Cutter*, the magazine of men's tailoring. Authentic knitting patterns have been included which can be knitted up today using modern yarn and needle equivalents.

I have tried to avoid treating a change in fashion as an isolated occurrence, but to set it instead in the light of other factors, social, political and personal. To illuminate the background, the changing image of the twenties and thirties man has been revealed through extracts and articles written by the 'brilliant young men' of the times. Beverley Nichols writes on 'The Life I Lead'; Godfrey Winn on 'Why I will not share a home with my wife', and Cecil Beaton on 'Behind the Scenes at Hollywood'. Through these articles by writers both distinguished and popular we are able to recreate a man's love life or his taste in women; his leisure and home life; to help him to choose a car, or to share his growing fears for the future of England during the Depression and the events leading up to the outbreak of war.

In an age where women were challenging the male's superiority as a sex, rivalry between them was active on all fronts. Women accused their husbands and boyfriends of being weak and effeminate. The men accused the women of taking over their roles. Through necessity, women had filled the men's jobs during the First World War, and they found that they were not only competent at them but enjoyed working and sometimes even excelled the men in their jobs. But there were compensations for the men. The working girl made an exciting companion for a man who had grown tired of the lady of leisure; she shared his sports, his interests and came unchaperoned to the talkies.

Even in the world of fashion, the twenties woman had tried to be dominating. She had, it seemed, actually tried to swop silhouettes with the man: her hair had been cut short and straight, and she wore flat-chested, straight-sided suits that were shapeless and tom-boyish. The man, on the other hand, wore skirt-like garments like plus-fours and the Oxford bags. His suits were shapely and fitted close to his body, and he grew his hair right down below his ears! Not until the thirties did women feel the inclination to revert to their curves, wearing long fitted dresses with frills, whilst the men bolstered their forms with padded shoulders and 'a lot of chest' in order to epitomize the healthy, virile, athletic man.

In 1929 'The Men's Dress Reform Party' was formed. Its members' aims were to try and establish some kind of 'Unisex' by advocating for men the same comfortable fashion that women had already favored. They suggested shorts, sandals and loose open-necked blouses in bright colors. They attempted to abolish trousers and replace them with tunics or one-piece suits with zips. Although many changes were made as a result of this movement, especially in sports clothes—where shorts became acceptable for tennis instead of trousers, or a daring pair of trunks were allowed on the beach instead of the one-piece costume—men on the whole preferred to be conservative in dress. They only changed into something bizarre if the Prince of Wales took the lead . . . as he often did.

In 1936, when the Prince of Wales first became Edward VIII and then abdicated in the same year, the country was shocked into silence. His brother George VI could not hold the eye of fashion nor break with traditions in the same way, but he gave the country what it needed: stability and security. It was America that took over the lead in fashions, imparting a colorful 'sporty' look to clothes, but by the time war broke out again in 1939 the men went back into a uniform that was little different from that of 1918, and the wheel of fashion had turned full circle. The skirmishes and competitiveness of the sex war since 1918 were forgotten in a new world conflict. The man returned willy nilly to a masculine, protective and aggressive role, and women were content once again to be feminine in a man's world.

The 20s

PLAIN HELMET (or BALACLAVA CAP)

MATERIALS REQUIRED.—4 ozs. (1 Cut) J. & J. BALDWIN'S "White Heather" Wheeling (or "Beehive" Double Knitting Wool). Four No. 8 Celluloid Knitting Needles.

Cast on 100 stitches, 36 on to one needle and 32 on to each of the other two needles.

Work, in rounds of ribbing (knit 2 and purl 2), until the fabric measures 12 inches.

Cast off 24 stitches loosely to make the opening for the face.

Work backwards and forwards (in the rib) for 2 inches.

Cast on 24 stitches again and join up the round.

Work 4 more inches in the rib.

Finish the cap in plain knitting and decrease as follows:

1st round. — Knit each 19th and 20th stitch together.

Knit 1 round plain.

3rd round. — Knit each 18th and 19th stitch together.

Knit 1 round plain.

5th round. — Knit each 17th and 18th stitch together.

Knit 1 round plain.

Decrease in this manner until only 25 stitches remain. Run a thread through these and fasten off securely. M.T.

The Returning Soldier

'We have seen a devastating war in which the victors have gained little; and we have watched civilized people competing with one another in aeroplanes, submarines and other armaments.' *Lady Asquith*

The soldiers returning from the war were disillusioned, demoralized and without the feeling of victory and peace that they had expected. They came back to a 'victorious' country with a housing shortage, poverty and unemployment when they hoped for a secure job, a home of their own and some material comforts. The old order that they had fought to preserve was gone, for the Edwardian age had been swept away by the economic necessities of the war itself. What post-war prosperity there was in Britain during the years 1918–20 quickly collapsed, and unemployment with over a million people out of work brought considerable distress, and remained a problem throughout the twenties. 'After the war, the sick soul of man wanted nursing; it wanted to lie on a soft breast and be won to

SEAMAN'S JERSEY

MATERIALS REQUIRED.—1½ lbs. (6 Cuts) J. & J. BALDWIN'S "White Heather" 3 ply Wheeling (29 shade—an absolutely fast and reliable Navy Blue, stands sea-water). Two No. 7 Celluloid Knitting Needles and four No. 8 (pointed at both ends),—a loose knitter should use needles a size finer, i.e. Nos. 8 and 9.

For a really excellent Jersey, in a smoother finish than can be obtained from any Wheeling Yarn, BEEHIVE DOUBLE KNITTING WOOL is recommended. In 1334 shade, a pure Indigo Blue, it is of particular interest for Jerseys.

THE BACK.

Cast 96 stitches on No. 7 needles.

1st row. — Knit 4, * purl 2, knit 2, repeat from * to the end of the row.

Always slip the first stitch throughout.

Repeat this row 20 times.

22nd row.— Knit plain.

23rd row.—Knit 2, purl to the last 2 stitches, knit these.

Repeat these last 2 rows until the work measures 30 inches from the commencement.

Cast off 30 stitches at each end for the shoulders, and leave the 36 stitches at the centre on a No. 8 needle for the collar.

THE FRONT.

Work exactly like the back.

THE SLEEVES.

Cast on 76 stitches.

1st row.—Knit 4, * purl 2, knit 2, repeat from * to the end of the row.

Repeat this row 30 times.

32nd row.—Knit plain.

33rd row.—Knit 2, purl to the last 2 stitches, knit these.

Repeat these last 2 rows throughout the sleeve and increase at the beginning and end of the 7th, then every 6th row, until there are 7 increasings at each side of the work. Then knit without shaping until the under-arm seam measures 18 inches (without cuff).

Cast off loosely.

TO MAKE UP SWEATER.

Sew up th shoulder and side seams, leaving 9 inches for the armhole. Sew up the seams of the sleeves and fix the latter in the armholes, placing seam to seam.

THE COLLAR.

With the No. 8 needles, knit 1 and purl 1 into each of the stitches that were left at the neck, work (in rounds) in rib of knit 2 and purl 2 for 6 inches. Cast off. M.T.

---

forgetfulness . . . instead of that slow gentle process, the men were flung against the problems of how to live.'

Both the older and younger generation wanted to forget the horrors of the war as soon as possible. The older men were eager to return to an approximation of their old way of life, tending to ignore the immediate past and the unpleasant present, and by working hard hoped for economic recovery in the future. But the younger generation ignored the past and the future and chose to live only in the present. In reaction they wanted variety instead of stability, 'dangerous living' instead of a peaceful existence, and freedom instead of security.

Many older men whose feeling of duty and self-sacrifice was strengthened during the war found hard work much easier than the young things, whom they accused of having no staying power. But there were youngsters who wanted to get on in life: those who had won newly-available scholarships for places at univer-

During the year the Prince of Wales, in order to gain first-hand knowledge of the prevailing conditions in the coal mining industry, made tours of the distressed areas. He is here seen at the house of a Durham miner during one of his visits.

sity, who could not have afforded a place previously; those who had put their heart into a career of their own choice and were no longer expected to 'follow in their father's footsteps'; or 'those who had taken one of the many opportunities open to hard-working youths who wanted to work their way up to a good position through their own enterprise.'

These young men took as their hero the Prince of Wales—the 'work-a-day prince', the 'Empire's young man'. For it was he who worked harder than anyone else for the nation's welfare. He always put his whole soul into the job . . . took risks if they were needed, though he was never allowed to make a mistake.

'Their mores are lax and promiscuous, their manners at the best casual and the worst abominable. They live on cocktails, never answer letters, wreck borrowed cars, make apple-pie beds for honoured guests in historic houses, spend their nights in night-clubs, believe in nothing, and mock and ill-use their parents.' *Lady Violet Bonham-Carter*

The younger generation sought to start a fresh new world and gain a social dominance they had never achieved before. The war brought about a rapid expansion of technology and scientific discovery, and this provided the tools with which the younger generation built their new life.

They drove around in fast cars, danced to the excited strains of jazz and the Charleston, played energetic games of tennis and flew planes. Likewise, their heroes were the lone aviator, the record-breaker, the explorer or anyone who represented 'the spirit of heroic youth'. They lived life fully and spontaneously, 'burning the candle at both ends' at gay parties, and indulging in wild affairs. Life was filled with the urgency of the moment, and by living in the present instead of dwelling on the past it was easy for the gay young things to weather a disappointment. If a love affair went wrong, it soon blew over and they would be in love again.

Unlike those of the older generation who tended to harbour their frustrations, the young things preferred to air their discontents, give vent to their feelings and overcome restlessness with activity. They grabbed at opportunities, dared new adventures and changed things that seemed stuffy and outmoded. Perhaps the art of letter-writing had died with the invention of the telephone; etiquette and manners had given way to lax behavior, and opinions were given instead of asked for; but the new youth was certainly spirited and the generation an evolving rather than a static or retrogressive one.

The Bright Young Things

The young no longer seemed to rely on their parents —or even need them—in fact they referred to them as 'old thing' and 'old stick' as if they were some relic of antiquity. An 'unnatural antagonism' had created a schism between the old and the young. Many of the older generation felt that youth had become flippant, and that its need for entertainment all the time made life superficial and meaningless. 'Our youth appear to know nothing that happened before 1914, and do not want to know. Their wits are quick but small, and their thoughts though active are almost empty. They are impatient and unwilling to make long efforts; everything must be peptonized for them. They are obsessed with excesses of all kinds. They drink too much, talk too much and rush about too much.' The new ideas of youth about how to live shocked the old generation, and their ideas about love and what they thought it meant were original to say the least. Matters of sex were discussed openly and birth-control was an accepted thing. They had a tendency to look at everything from the point of view of sex, and the older generation wondered if perhaps the game might not have become less exciting now there were next to no rules. The young, extremely outspoken about matters of sex and religion, emerged from a generation in which it was considered 'indecent' even to mention appendicitis in public.

Many older people admitted to being jealous of the new liberties of youth because they themselves had not had the freedom or the means to do the same themselves. Some tried to emulate youth. In fashion women copied the 'flapper' by shedding half their clothes and wearing dresses that were short, tubular and straight. The men copied the boys by wearing school-boy shorts and sandals; they became clean-shaven, smooth-skinned and more healthy looking. Fashions generally went the way of youth, and were dictated by youth, which in turn followed the glamorous figure of the Prince of Wales.

Youths

A youth who possesses the best qualities of youth-hood is one of the most delightful creatures in creation

By

Magdalen King-Hall

*T*HE motoring youth pretends to admire the slim type of girl who will fit into the cockpit of his racing car.

*A*T a highbrow luncheon that I attended recently, a well-known writer propounded the theory that there were too many unmarried women in England, that they were all " sex ridden and starved," and that they ought forthwith to be massacred.

He then turned and looked at me in such a peculiar way, that I could only conclude that, had circumstances permitted, he would have offered me up as the first victim in this proposed holocaust of spinsters !

Mildly I pointed out to him that to be unmarried did not necessarily imply a desire to die, and that anyhow, as far as girls of my own age were concerned, they suffered not so much from a scarcity as from a surfeit of youthful male society, and that far from being " starved," they were often in danger of being " fed up." This discussion led my thoughts to the subject of " Youths " — (a sweeping designation that includes young men between the ages of seventeen and twenty-five). I have felt for some time that it is a topic that lends itself to considerable comment, and one that might well replace the threadbare problem of the " Modern Girl."

What is wrong with the Modern Youth ? Nothing very serious as far as I know, but I realise that this is the recognised *cliché* with which to begin an article on the younger generation.

Let us grant, however, for the sake of argument, that modern youths have faults, and surely the most infatuated mother of sons will admit that no youth is blameless. At the risk of living a wallflower and dying a spinster, I make bold to state that in my opinion their chief defect lies in a tendency to over-rate their own value.

Youths have read and have been told that there is a shortage of men (the subject of superfluous women threatened at one moment to become a perfect obsession with the Press), their fond mothers have informed them

that young men are worth their weight in gold. Not realising that these statistics and remarks apply only to their elder brothers who have been spared by the War, they have conceived the erroneous notion that *they* are rare, that *they* are precious, that *they* are golden (and many of them act accordingly !). My experience of English society convinces me that they are misguided ; as there are girls everywhere, so there are youths everywhere, of all sorts, shapes and sizes. Why should it be otherwise ? The war did not take toll of them, and the post-war influenza plagues claimed victims impartially from either sex. On the face of it I cannot understand why the youth of to-day should imagine that he is a *rara avis*, a kind of human phœnix !

If youths would only disabuse themselves of this lamentable delusion and resolve to stand upon their own merits, there would be an end, I think, to the hard and unfriendly things that are said about them in the privacy of girls' luncheon and tea-parties.

A young man said to me the other day—" I suppose you girls talk about us the whole time ? "

Had politeness permitted I might have replied : " Yes, but not always in a very complimentary manner."

I think I must have a sympathetic nature ; at all events I am the recipient of endless confidences from my girl acquaintances on the subject of their admirers !

" My dear, I'm absolutely fed up with Jack "—" Really, I almost hate

A UKELELE is the favourite instrument of the night club youth.

Timothy at moments "—" I must tell you how badly that beast Osbert has behaved "—and so on. Can one wonder that the divorce courts are crowded when sex warfare is rampant even between youths and *débutantes* ?

Reviewing mentally the list of my young men acquaintances, I find that youths, like girls, can be fitted more or less accurately into various types. There is the Motoring Youth, for instance. His hands reek of motor-oil, his hair stands on end, one of his fingers is usually bandaged with a dirty rag. His car is his divinity ; Brooklands his idea of Paradise. His conversation is all of petrol tanks, carburettors, front axles, magnetos, cylinders, exhaust pipes, overhead valves and leaking radiators. His reading is confined to motoring magazines, and his pet hobby, when he is not raising the dust on the King's high road, is to retire into a garage with a congenial companion and " hot her up." With that single-minded fervour that distinguishes lovers and poets, he will stand for hours on a deserted road, tinkering with a recalcitrant carburettor by the light of an electric torch—oblivious to wind, rain, cold and hunger.

Walking is an exercise that he holds as demeaning and despicable in the extreme. Pedestrians and bicyclists in his eyes are " less than the dust."

It is the Motoring Youth who has inspired the older generation's gloomy prediction that the younger generation are losing the use of their legs !

When the Motoring Youth falls in love, his soul is torn between the allegiance due to his car and to his lady. Fortunately, he generally manages to combine his two loves—his cup of happiness brims over as he crouches over the wheel of his machine, his lady love (probably rigid with apprehension !) seated, wearing a jaunty leather cap, by his side.

The Motoring Youth naturally tends to admire the slim *petite* type of girl who will fit easily into the cramped cockpit of a racing car ! Though a lover of few words, his attention being engaged in steering clear of destruction, he is not unskilled in the gentle art of flirtation. Cars possess the same quality of inconsistency as the fair sex, and the Motoring Youth is a coaxer *par excellence*. Whatever his shortcomings may be, I maintain that he is hearty, courageous and impetuous. England looked to him to man her deserted trains and 'buses in a not far distant crisis and he responded gallantly.

A T the opposite end of the pole stands the Social Youth. I know him well ; we have panted together in the crush of many a London dance. He is immaculate and elegant with carefully oiled hair and irreproachable socks. The hand that he lays on my back as we dance is gloved in white kid. *He* will not leave the marks of damp hands on my dress ! His voice is faint ; faint not from shyness, but from weariness. He has been out to a dance, he tells me, every night this season ; not *any* dance, but dances cautiously selected from a pile of invitations. He owes it to himself not to be seen at the wrong places. He does not go to dances for pleasure he may confide to me in a moment of expansion. "What for, then ? " He smiles pityingly at my ignorant question. He is a walking Who's Who and Peerage. He knows instinctively that I am a gossip, and as we gyrate together he informs me discreetly who everyone is, whom they married, whom they hope to marry, their social advantages and disadvantages, their past scandals and present incomes. Above all, he has penetrated that mystery of social life : he knows "who the people are who matter."

I am a little afraid of the Social Youth. He suspects me of having a strain of deplorable unconventionality in my nature, due, no doubt, to my Irish blood. I should not like him to discover that I was so shockingly unfashionable as to spend a week of August in London.

As far as I know the Social Youth never indulges in flirtation—or not what I would call flirtation ! He falls in love, if his discreet passion can be termed love, with heiresses. He reminds me of the insect in "Alice in Wonderland," who lived on wedding

T HE youth who is both affected and supercilious is a bad specimen of his kind.

cake. His chief merit is politeness—a quality not to be despised nowadays. If he is my escort for a dance I know that as far as partners, refreshments and taxis are concerned, I am safe.

Since I have taken to writing I have suffered considerably from what one might call the highbrow or *precieux* Youth. His voice is also practically inaudible ; weak with the burden of

A TYPE of youth which can be seen everywhere writhing in the coils of the Charleston.

his culture and superior knowledge. He has an excellent plot for a realistic novel or Grand Guignol play, and he relates it to me at length. Unfortunately he cannot find time in which to write it. He is quick to point out the errors in my own humble literary efforts. "Didn't you know that the word ' donkey ' was never used in the eighteenth century ? " No, I didn't, and am properly ashamed !

I see plainly written on his face the thought, " Why was this girl a best seller ? She looks to me a perfect fool ! " The highbrow youth's spiritual home is Oxford, his hobby is collecting books on witchcraft and

seeking out quaint little restaurants in Soho. He will probably end in the Foreign Office.

When a young man is dark-eyed, slim, long-legged, with sleek black hair and forward drooping shoulders, looks as if he might do well on the films and asks me if I can dance the Tango, I know that he is a Night Club Youth.

This particular species of terpsichorean performer can be seen in shoals at any dancing resort, writhing in the coils of the Charleston. He falls in love only with a lady whose steps suit his own. The greater part of his leave or vacation he spends on the Riviera. He was doing the Charleston before his benighted fellow-countrymen had even heard of it. The ukelele is his favourite instrument, a cocktail his only form of nourishment. It was a Night Club youth who announced to me during the Great Strike that he " would like to go to bed and stay there till it is all over ! "

I have come to the conclusion that it is a great mistake to imagine that every male creature takes to work as gleefully as a duck takes to water.

Youths also have their troubles. The delightful " Serena Blandish " experienced the " difficulty of getting married." We may be sure that her brother, if she had one, suffered from the " difficulty of getting a job." Job-hunting plays the same anxious part in the lives of most modern youths as husband-hunting does in those of their feminine contemporaries. Mothers of girls may be anxious to get their daughters "off the shelf." Mothers of youths are harassed by the no less pressing problem of how to get their sons " settled down." Their maternal conversations it would seem turn constantly to the merits and demerits of various professions. Is there money in shipping—or Angora rabbits ? Is Archibald clever enough for the Diplomatic ? Is it true that Uganda is a white man's grave ? Would Lord Thingmejig be able to get Ambrose anything? What is Chris thinking of doing ? *I* could tell them that Chris is thinking of nothing but motor bicycles !

The Girlfriend

When the young man returned from war, he found that the woman who had taken over his job had proved herself more than adequate at it, and had kept things going with great efficiency. After the war was over, although the majority of women went 'quietly and with dignity', some, particularly the older girls, had for the first time in their lives known the sweetness of earning money and the independence that it brought.

At the same time, men were at a premium. Although London in 1919 seemed packed with men, there was a man shortage. There were now two million more women than men, and matters were not helped by the fact that many young men, finding no employment for themselves in England, had escaped abroad and taken off for the colonies. The supernumerary women saw to it that they made themselves very attractive, and

'never before were there so many beautiful girls as there were after the war'. As a result, many young men were spoilt. This was partly the fault of their mothers: they had already fostered their 'male superiority' at an early age by continually reminding them that they were special and more important than girls. 'The mothers fawn on their sons, and cherish this vile weed of sex-superiority instead of rooting it out, so that now the spoiled boy looks on spoiling as a tribute to his own indescribable magnificence.' After the war mothers told their sons that there was a shortage of men. This emphasis on the man's value to society had been aimed at those of their older brothers whom the war had spared, but the result was to 'spoil' the upcoming generation. The young man was no longer content with a girl who was delicate and precious, dependent and perdurable; he looked for one who was exciting and unrestrained, one who knew her own mind and had something to say, and one who was capable and could keep up with him. The girlfriend took on a new shape to meet these requirements. She was youthful and boyish-looking; active, healthy, flat-chested and athletic—rather like himself in fact. And with her lack of frills and corsets, her hair shortened and her skirts shortened too, she could share all his activities and give him fair competition on the courts. She arrived unchaperoned, and he did not have to protect her. She was emancipated and knew all there was to know about love. She was independent and skilled in the art of business matters and she had taken up smoking and golf, cricket and motoring, and could sometimes fly a plane.

The spoilt young man soon found that his girlfriend beat him at some games and excelled him in other things. All in all she was becoming dangerous, and by

"I'LL TAKE THIS ONE."

showing equality with him in matters of sex, hadn't she challenged his supremacy and even threatened his manhood? Some girls even did the proposing! The girlfriend was no longer inferior, she was more of a rival. Was she now the stronger and he the weaker sex?

It was as if the sexes had swopped roles, for she was 'masculine' in her approach to love, and he feminine. The ideal girlfriend was boyish-looking with her short hair and determined face, and the 'ideal' young man looked rather effeminate with his soft, clean-shaven face and his hair fixed down with perfumed oils. He was sentimental, too. He would send flowers in the most touching manner, write messages of love in flowery language, and turn his hand to poetry when the occasion demanded. Love for him was rash, foolish and gay.

15

Masculinities for the Car

Here are some practical and ingenious ideas for the car which cannot fail to appeal to the male enthusiast.

Right : A veritable "multum in parvo," this Lighthouse Mascot serves a triple purpose. It carries a radiator thermometer. It is a striking ornament. Its lantern lights (green or purple) are wired in connection with the rear light. If this fails your lighthouse lamps go out and you know you are on the rocks—in time. (Harrods.)

P. ROSSI. EASTBOURNE. PAT. No 297004

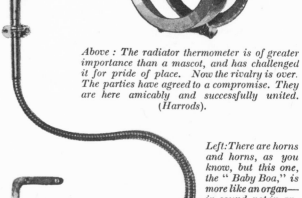

Above : These 'cute little lamps (two wing and one rear) dispel the fear attendant on the battery giving out. They carry enough petrol to ensure you emergency lights for three hours. Standard fittings. (Harrods).

Right : This more than useful little driving mirror has a convex surface and is made of black glass. It serves the usual purposes by day, but as night falls its previously undetected virtues are revealed. Gone is the glare in your eyes from the reflected lights of an overtaking car ; instead, just steady points of light and undistorted relationships. (Smith's).

These "Gaunt-lite" driving gloves are signally effective. Has a back-handed punch in the shape of two lights—red and white—the red to warn the following car, and the white for use as a spotlight. Contact is effected by metal plates on finger tips and thumb, and the current is derived from small battery in the flap. Cape tan—all sizes. (Harrod's).

On a dark night or a foggy day, you cannot tell whether you are on rising or falling ground. This little calibrated spirit level (1 in 30, 1 in 15, etc.), lies along the top of the off-side door and gives you the lie of the land. Tells you when to gear down on the up-grade —which is a boon to the engine under any conditions—and gives you brake warning on the down-grade. (Smith's).

Left : This Car Lighter is wireless to the weed ! Any time is lighting-up time with this little fellow. Cigarette, cigar or pipe (special cone-shaped element for pipe)—a red-hot glow—perfect ignition—contentment, and no wobbling on the road. (Smith's).

Above : The radiator thermometer is of greater importance than a mascot, and has challenged it for pride of place. Now the rivalry is over. The parties have agreed to a compromise. They are here amicably and successfully united. (Harrods).

Left : There are horns and horns, as you know, but this one, the "Baby Boa," is more like an organ— in sound, not in appearance. Its appearance and fittings are in keeping with its tone. It warns but never frightens. (Smith's).

The Motorist

In 1920 the first filling station in England was opened at Aldermaston. In 1921, with 873,700 cars on the road, such amazing standards of reliability had been reached that a business man could say: 'Gone are the days when breakfast had to be hurried over in order to catch the 9.05 train to the city. Instead, one can have an extra five or ten minutes in the house, the meal in comfort and arrive at one's destination in time. And instead of starting work with a headache and temper ruffled, one commences it with a freshness and with an energy that only a pleasant run in the car can supply.'

King George officially opened the Great West Road at Brentford in 1925. In 1926 the number of cars had doubled that of 1921, and by 1928 there were some two million motorized vehicles on the roads. Traffic problems were beginning to increase in London, and by the end of the decade many motorists lacked the courage to drive there. Pedestrians in London whose nerves were already overwrought with the rush and hurry of everyday life found that the extra never-ending roar of traffic became so bad that they had to plead with Mr Winston Churchill to put a tax on noise. This he did by the simple process of giving a 'remission' to the owners of motor lorries with pneumatic tyres.

The Motor Show, at Olympia in London, showed all the latest models which were reputed to be 'docile yet dashing, capable of flying like the wind, yet smooth and almost silent. There is a sleekness and gleam which marks them as being well-groomed, for some of the coach work is suave as a West End suit, chic as the latest Paris gown. Today, power goes in hand with comfort, and great trouble has been taken to ensure that the lines are as pleasing as the colours attractive.' The gentleman now found that the upholstery on the inside of his new car matched the exterior two-tone color-scheme: cream and crimson; deep blue and black; light blue and dark fawn or apple green and dark green. On show too were countless accessories which could not fail to appeal to the male enthusiast. Radiator thermometers in the form of mascots; calibrated spirit levels that told you whether you were on rising or falling ground, or the latest novelty of brown leather gauntlets which boasted a bright red light on the back of the right hand glove.

Many people thought that mechanical transport had brought its horrors, and in moments of extreme exasperation declared that it had robbed life of all its pleasures, but they could not deny that the motor had been instrumental in 'enlarging and extending the outlook of millions'. On the outskirts of the manufacturing towns, for example, thousands of workers enjoyed fresh air and sunshine instead of smoke and grime by being able to live further away from their work. By the end of the twenties petrol was cheaper than at any period for over twenty years, and 'there seem to be no fears for the supply of petrol . . . when oil wells fail, shale areas can be developed. Wood alcohol is becoming a commercial possibility. The earth has many fruits in store, and the pessimist has to take the back seat.'

THE RICHMOND SALOON, £530
(Sliding roof, £15 extra)

VAUXHALL

The Sport

The great move towards 'health and hygiene' had started. The outdoor life was encouraged and enjoyed as recreation: golf, tennis, cricket, football, rowing, rugger, bicycling, walking and climbing were the favorite pastimes, and the outdoor look was achieved with tweed plus-fours, a Fair-Isle jumper and a pair of stout brown 'brogues'. Health-giving activities were enthusiastically endorsed by the nation. Keep-fit classes were popular, youth centres increased, and scouting was much admired. As a man could not start too young in his efforts to develop outdoor success, he became a scout at an early age, and youth movements in Britain were connected with other youth movements all over the world in a framework of international strength by Lord Baden-Powell.

Owing to an increase in the popularity of *watching* tennis and soccer matches, it became imperative that more accommodation be arranged for spectators, and in 1922 a new stadium was opened at

WEMBLEY'S FIRST CUP-FINAL

1923

ON April 28 the Cup Final between Bolton Wanderers and West Ham United was played for the first time in the new Wembley Stadium. Bolton Wanderers won by 2 goals to nil. The crowds were so enormous that they broke down the barriers and the police had to form cordons to prevent spectators overflowing on to the ground. *Above :* the police endeavouring to keep the crowd back, and the lower picture shows Joe Smith (*right*), the Bolton Wanderers' captain, shaking hands with George Kay, captain of West Ham United, before the kick-off.

Wembley. In 1923 the Cup Final between Bolton Wanderers and West Ham was played for the first time in the stadium to a packed audience—some spectators wearing bowler hats.

Hunting was very popular, probably made more so by the Prince of Wales, who loved the sport. But he had the habit of falling off and injuring himself, and as he was the heir to the throne his father forbade him to ride to hounds. So he grew to prefer golf, which became more and more popular as a sport for everyone. The King himself was a 'sailing man', and was happiest when sailing his yacht *Brittania* at Cowes.

EPIC
OF THE
ATLANTIC

CHARLES LINDBERGH, a young American aviator, was the first man to fly the Atlantic alone. He received a tremendous reception both in Paris—where he landed at 10 p.m. on May 21, at the conclusion of his flight—and also later in London. He is seen above being congratulated on his arrival in France by a famous French aviator Rene Fonck, and below arriving at Croydon in his 'plane *Spirit of St. Louis*.

Shooting was, as always, the favorite sport for the gentleman, and if he was 'asked down' for a large shoot he was expected to have a pair of guns and his own cartridges. He did not need to bring with him a 'loader' other than his valet, who would act in this capacity.

Rules of etiquette applied as equally in sport as in any other activity, and a gentleman had to observe strict rules of conduct. For example, if a man were invited fishing, shooting or whatever in the country, and he found himself with an interval of one or two days between two sporting visits that were in the same neighborhood, he was on no account to ask his hostess if he could remain for that extra time unless she was a relation or an intimate friend. Nor could he spend it at an hotel in the adjacent village or town, as that would be a reflection upon the hospitality of his hostess. He should rather return to London or stay somewhere outside the immediate neighborhood— and remember that a man never breakfasts in his room unless he is ill.

If a man were on board a cruiser, he often found that with standards not quite the same as they had been before the war, he had to exercise the utmost control over his patience on deck with all the modern 'organized games' that now took place to amuse the passengers. But he did take the trouble to see that he himself was correctly dressed. The plus-four was the popular

Col. Sir Albert Bingham partridge shooting on his estate, Ranby Hall, Notts.

garment for 'promenading' during daylight hours. Flannels were also *de rigueur*, since they looked 'very doggy' for deck quoits, croquet and shovelboard.

ENTERTAINMENT

'They wish to have gaiety, excitement. They are incessantly in search of diversion.... One finds the bridge tables deserted for the ballroom nowadays, so compelling is this craze for dancing.'

Dancing was the universal pursuit of the younger generation, and everyone was eager to learn the latest steps. The jazz-step, the one-step, the fox-trot and the Boston; all went like hot cakes. Jazz from America had already captured every section of London society by 1919, and there was a wild rumour that it had even reached Glasgow.

Although it was obvious that an early training would produce the more perfect dancer, the young man who had not received the advantages of a 'liberal education' during his youth did not need to despair. If he possessed moderate qualifications and intelligence and placed himself under the instruction of a good dancing master he could soon learn to take his place on the floor of the ballroom with tolerable grace. The further practising of intricate steps could be carried out at home with the aid of a wireless or phonograph, and with the addition of a book of instructions 'the Prince of Wales fox-trot' or the tango 'as danced by Rudolph Valentino' could be mastered. Self expression and improvization were encouraged whenever possible, especially in the dancing of ragtime, an exhausting Charleston or an exhilarating quickstep.

The adept young man of the day carried round a banjo or ukelele with which he could provide 'Dixie', the 'Blues' or 'hillbilly' serenades on every available occasion to help life go by in an enjoyable type of frenzy. At night, if a young man was going to a party, he was sure to be wearing fancy dress. If he had seen Rudolph Valentino's costume in his film 'The Sheik' then he would try to imitate it, or if he had been thrilled by the 1923 excavations of the tomb of Tutankhamen he might prefer to be an ancient pharaoh.

On board the cruisers the propriety of pre-war days frequently gave way to instances of quite horrifying behavior: there upon the ballroom floor of the new 'one class' tourist ship some young men of college type danced indecently with 'bobbed flappers' who themselves boasted of a high-school education. They held each other 'familiarly', sometimes with their heads together, and charged all over the floor.

More and more did a young man take his girlfriend to the movies for the evening to see the sentimental Lillian Gish, to laugh at slapstick or marvel at Clara Bow. The film stars were copied in every action, and the young man was encouraged to believe that if he could only look the slightest bit like Ramon Novarro, Ronald Colman or Ivor Novello he would be able to steal any woman's heart away.

Neither the Prince of Wales nor his father King George were serious playgoers, and they did not pretend to be. They preferred to see Harry Lauder at the music hall, reviews and musical comedies. The King's royal laughter at light fare was most infectious, but often continued after that of the audience had ceased.

The LIFE I LEAD

By Beverley NICHOLS

I SOMETIMES wake up in the middle of the night to the loud clamour of imaginary bells pealing through the darkened room. They die away almost at once, but their echoes linger on, filling me with unrest; for I have a sense that they are summoning me to some shadowy rendezvous—with whom, or for what purpose, I do not know. But one day, I feel, they may go on ringing and ringing and ringing until I have to follow, and then——

I expect no sympathy for this confession. We live in a chemical age. Love is a formula, Genius a glandular secretion, Terror a stomachic order. To deny these things is to proclaim oneself a heretic, yet I choose to deny them. For I believe that those bells are, in some way or other, a warning. It sounds very naïve and unsophisticated to say so; but, then, you have never heard them. Nor will you, too, ever hear them unless you, too, drift into the sort of life that I lead.

Only Picasso could paint that life, because Picasso is the only ultra-modern artist who has ever been able to take a wild kaleidoscope of forms and colours and weld them into a rational design.

Consider my programme for 1928. I welcomed the New Year from the top of a sky-scraper in New York, drinking a toast of bootleg gin to the freezing stars. I was on a lecture tour. It took me, night after night, to the gigantic cities that sprawl across the Middle West. I have a vision of endless halls filled with strangers, and the only thing which links them together is the sound of my own voice talking, desperately talking, into space.

The tour comes to an end. I accept an invitation to go to Hollywood. There I wander through studio after studio, while the great arc lamps beat down upon me, blinding and pitiless. It is no city for those who are in danger of losing their sense of values. It is a city of millionaires who yesterday were beggars, of palaces where yesterday the weeds were growing, of the hum of motor-cars over streets which yesterday were only tracks for covered wagons. I act in a movie, I write a scenario, and I fly away.

I come back to England. I have a new book that must be finished, but I cannot finish it. The telephone rings incessantly. "We are putting on a new revue at —— Theatre. Will you write some music for it?" And for two days I sit at the piano, hammering out tunes which by now will certainly have echoed into the ultimate silence. The telephone goes on ringing. "The English-Speaking Union would like you to address their monthly meeting next Tuesday. Will you do it?" I say that I will. Still the telephone rings. "Is that Mr. Nichols? Yes? Well, you wouldn't know who I am; I just rang you up for a bet. Good-bye."

In despair, I go to Paris. I *must* finish my book. I find a room which looks out on to a garden. A great chestnut tree spreads green arms outside my window. There is no sound except the chattering of sparrows and the distant roll of traffic. Here at last I might get some peace. I sit down at the table, pen in hand. Nothing happens.

And here I come to the first of my two complaints against the life I lead—that I am one of those writers who are utterly incapable of writing to order. As a result, half of my life is wasted. People say to me, "What an enchanting life you lead! No office hours. No need to stay in the same place. Merely a pen and a piece of paper, and there you are!"

Yes; there you are. The paper is blank. Your mind is a riot of fancies. Maybe a moon is shining somewhere in your head. You half-close your eyes. You want to darken the paper, to throw across it a silver, tenuous thread of words. They are all there—dancing, tiny, ethereal words—to be spun into that thread. Here is one, and here is another; slowly your pen begins to write. Then suddenly it stops. The moon of your delight is being covered with clouds. The words are flying away swiftly, disdainfully, over the hills of Thought. Your eyes open. You look down at the sheet of paper. You read a few faltering, leaden sentences. In an agony of irritation, of remorse—yes, and of wounded vanity—you crumple up the sheet of paper in your fist. You remain staring at the opposite wall. Thus do the hours pass.

And each of those hours, remember, is a fragment of your life.

Winston Churchill once said to me that a writer ought to be able to discipline himself to work as regularly as any business man. He proclaimed that you should shut yourself up in a room from nine to one every morning, and say to yourself, "Here is a job of work to be done," and do it. Being rather young at the time, I expressed myself somewhat freely upon this theory. I asked: "How can you make love to order every morning between the hours of nine and one?" He wanted to know what I meant. I replied that all good writing is a form of love-making, whether you are wooing the summer wind, or painting the shadows in a woman's hair, or toying with a purely abstract theory for the mere exhilaration of pursuing it. Mr. Churchill did not agree with me. I have often wondered why, because his recent Budgets have been as unworldly and as opulently phrased as the love-letters of a crazy poet. Perhaps Mr. Churchill *is* a—— But that would be rude, would it not?

However, I finish my book. I come back to London. I have all the summer and the early autumn before. I return to New York to produce my first play, edit for a short time a magazine, and indulge in the luxury of another lecture tour. These months will not be exactly months of leisure, and, obviously, I should go to the country to work. But I dare not go to the country. Because I am alone in the world, and when I am lonely I hear those damned bells.

And that is my second complaint against the life I lead.

Why, then, do I remain alone? God knows. And if I ever meet God, I shall ask Him why He has put the curse of loneliness upon some of His creatures, why He has forced them to greet the morning sun alone, to watch the stars fade in solitude. You may think me a blasphemer, or merely a bore. You may say that loneliness is easily remedied, that there are plenty of nice, bouncing girls who would be willing to cure me of it; or that if I didn't, for the moment, wish to marry, I could at least induce a friend to take the house next door. If you *do* say those things, you will utterly misunderstand me. By loneliness I do not imply being alone. One can sit on a desert island and people it with enchanting figures, just as one can sit at a crowded party and feel that the world is empty of human life. Loneliness is not a result of selfishness, nor even of bad management. It is in oneself.

I am throwing all discretion to the winds, but I believe that honesty is the best policy. And if you would know what loneliness means, you should stand opposite a little house in Chelsea towards midnight. If you are patient enough, you will see a taxi drive up to the door, and a figure will step out

" A queer young man." " A very frivolous young man." " An original young man." All these and more are said of Beverley Nichols. But—we venture to add —such a very interesting, tantalising and young young man !

of it. But the figure does not go into that house ; it hesitates and then walks quickly down the street. A few minutes pass. The figure is back again, turns, and is off once more. Another interval and the figure has returned. It stands on the steps. There is the sound of a latchkey. I have come home.

I have come home. To what ? To a dying fire, a softly lit room, a clock ticking silently. To quiet and peace, the companionship of books, the soft delight of sleep. So you may say. To blackness and desolation, to ghosts of the past and the future ; so say I. That is why I walked up and down the street. I fear this solitude. Nothing can cure it. I scan a row of books; they seem to me like tombstones. In this one a man has buried the story of his love. In that one a man has enshrined the memory of his mate.

And there, I think, we had better stop. This is the most difficult article I have ever had to write, because one's outlook on life varies from moment to moment. When I began to write rain was falling and the skies were overcast ; but now the rain has stopped and the sun is filtering on to my desk, and I shall be able to play tennis this afternoon. And if you ever saw me play tennis you would agree that I was best fitted for a life of solitary confinement. At least, that is what my partners always tell me.

THE PRINCE IN INDIA

FASHION

1919

'A man can't make love with any kind of conviction unless he is wearing a coat cut within half a mile of Piccadilly.' *The Tailor and Cutter*

Piccadilly was still the most fashionable place for the gentleman to order his suit, and it was the center of the post-war boom in the trade for tailor-made suits for those able to afford them. Tailors found that they had to alter the measurements for some men who appeared to have become more 'manly' during their years of fighting. 'Tailors generally are discovering that the discharged soldiers among their customers have developed quite a different attitude of figure, and undergone a change of physique during their time in the army. The drill, physical exercise and open-air life have developed particularly the muscles of the chest and arms and upper part of the body.'

For the majority, who were not able to afford a tailor-made suit, the Government instructed the Board of Trade to adopt a clothing scheme, and gave financial support to a project that provided clothing of standard quality and price for men's, women's and children's ready-made wear, as well as hosiery and blankets. A ready-made suit could be produced for 43/6 (£2.17) and retailed at 57/6 (£2.75), and at this fixed price 'British Standard' suits were available to all soldiers upon demobilization. In 1919 the money granted to discharged soldiers in lieu of civilian clothes was increased to 30/- (£1.50) per soldier with a further 30/- for an overcoat.

Meanwhile, the suit worn by the middle-class man at the office was the same as it had been before the war: the anonymous jacket and matching baggy trousers, the discreet tie and plain socks, and the respectable business hat, either bowler or trilby. For the man returning from the battlefield it was simply a swop from one uniform in khaki to another in gray. In reaction, advocates of brighter color in men's civilian clothes became more active, and the depressing effect of khaki upon its wearers, and upon others not condemned to wear it, even received the attention of the medical men, one of whom wrote in the *Lancet*: 'After more than four years of war the prevalence of this dim tint has a malign influence. The introduction of color would dispel any depression caused by the war.' One only had to be reminded that 'drab' or khaki serge

was dyed with a color originally designed to merge with the landscape, and that the word khaki came from India and meant 'dusty' or 'dirty'.

There was a theory that one of the reasons for the lack of color in cloth was because England before the war obtained her dyes from German factories and had only just begun to produce her own. But even with a dull-colored suit it was thought that men could at least be a little more adventurous in the style of their clothes. 'It is the man who is the real slave to fashion, and not women. Woman is governed by individual caprice; there is no order or system in feminine fashions today. Man's dress is almost a uniform; what diversity there is trifling and concerned with trifles.'

There were those, of course, who defended the uniform itself. It seemed that it was almost too difficult for some men to stop wearing uniforms in peacetime. A number felt that a uniform gave prestige; others wished to get full wear from any uniform they may have had in their possession on demobilization. The Secretary of War announced that all military buttons on uniforms used in civilian life had to be replaced by plain ones, and all badges and shoulder straps removed from service dress jackets, greatcoats and pea-jackets within one month from the date of demobilization.

After the war, the Government found itself over-stocked with military garments and put vast amounts of ex-army wear on the market. Working men often preferred to buy this as it was not only very cheap but warm and durable for work in the factories and on the building sites. Even the ex-army officers said that they could find no substitute for their uniform trench coats or the 'British Warm'. Both garments were not only sturdily made but well lined. The 'British Warm', or drab pea-jacket (from sea-pilot's jacket), as it was officially known, was a short double-breasted coat or reefer cut on comfortable lines and generally made of Melton cloth. It made its first appearance when the British troops had to face the rigors of a winter in the Indian Frontier during the Tirah Campaign. The coat was knee-length, and cut easy-fitting so as to allow a fleece lining to be inserted. The trench coat or officer's top coat (overleaf) was full-cut, belted and had a deep collar and reveres. This garment reached to just below the knees, and was lined with a check waterproof material and interlined with oilskins, or alternatively wholly lined with fleece. The addition of pockets and storm cuffs with wrist-straps or elasticated insets also helped to keep out the wind and rain.

2337

1920

To cope with the post-war obsession with sport and outdoor activities, plenty of specialized sports clothes were designed. The most popular garment chosen for outdoor wear generally was the sports jacket, for it was this garment that so admirably fitted man's increasing desire for comfort and a more relaxed and informal atmosphere in his clothing. The sports jacket was usually single-breasted with patch pockets and a half-belt at the back. A soft tweed was preferred in a pattern of herringbone, stripes or tiny checks, and the favorites in the shops were described as: 'some a symphony in brown; others a symphony in grey'.

The business man, needing a garment that was casual and easy-fitting to wear at home, also chose the sports jacket, for he had discovered that 'in casting away clothes worn during working hours, the cares and worries of the daily round fly with them: a change of raiment makes a new man of one.'

The sports jacket made a casual outfit with the addition of flannel matching trousers or knickerbockers. Beneath the jacket the choice of a canary yellow-colored knitted waistcoat was now frequently superseded by a sleeved or sleeveless vee-necked pullover.

The Prince of Wales was reputed to have been able to knit his own, and delighted in wearing a Fair-Isle patterned one, so most other men could not but delight to wear one too. With added accessories like a cloth cap on the head, two-toned shoes on the feet, a stick in the hand and perhaps one of those new wrist-watches, 'as used by men on active service', the outdoor man felt not only comfortable but smart and handsome in his sports outfit. In order to be handsome, the average young man now presented to the world a clean-shaven face, and whilst a few ex-officers still retained their short 'toothbrush' moustaches, beards were decidedly confined only to the 'elderly, literary, artistic and eccentric'.

For the motor car and motor cycle enthusiast the walking stick was already quite out of fashion. Motoring had become a most popular activity, and to go for a 'spin' in the open air with the wind rushing past at 25 mph was for some 'the only sport'. For this activity the motoring coat was coming into its own, and with the coat a pair of breeches or leggings was invariably worn.

Other popular coats were the single-breasted raglan (see left), long, full in the back and sometimes with patch pockets. This was used as a raincoat and came in drab, khaki, dark blue gaberdine and sometimes in tweed. To wear in town, the Newbury with its velvet collar, fly-front and half-belt and inverted pleat at the back, was affected by the smart set. The 'Macintosh', named after its Scottish inventor in the nineteenth century, was becoming increasingly worn for rainwear, especially a lightweight model with a belt, all of which could be folded up and conveniently stored in the pocket.

A FAIR-ISLE JUMPER

For Golf Or Walking This Pullover Is So Comfortable.

The pullover is made on very simple lines that can easily be adapted for either a man or a girl.

15th and 16th rounds: K. 2 mottle and 2 dark alternately.

17th and 18th rounds: K. 2 light and 6 dark alternately. Repeat the first 12 pattern rounds.

Next round: While working the 13th pattern round work as follows: K. 14, slip the next 30 st. on a spare needle for pocket top, and in place work 30 pocket-lining stitches from spare needle, work next 34 st., slip next 30 on spare needle, and in place work 30 pocket-lining stitches, work to end of round.

Work the 14th to 18th rounds in-

Continued overleaf

THIS pullover is constructed on very simple lines, with straight arm-hole and short V neck, so that it is easily adaptable for either sex. The pattern is so simple (although it looks elaborate) that the beginner will not have any difficulty in following it, even on the short rows at the neck. Up to the armholes it is worked in rounds, and only two colours of wool are in operation at the same time. The colour not actually in use along the row is twisted once over the working thread, so that there are no loose threads at the back of the work.

MATERIALS: Templeton's " Ayr " " F " Fingering, 4-ply, in the following quantities : 6 oz. of mottle, 6 oz. light and 4 oz. dark ; 4 bone knitting needles No. 9, with double points, and four No. 10.

ABBREVIATIONS: K., knit plain ; p., purl ; tog., together ; s.s., stocking-stitch, which is k. on the front of the work and p. on the back.

TENSION AND MEASUREMENTS : Worked at a tension of 6 st. to the inch in width, the following measurements will be obtained after light pressing : From shoulder to hem, 25½ inches ; width all round body at underarm, 38 inches ; underarm-seam of sleeve, 20½ inches.

To Work

BEGIN with pocket linings and, using light wool and No. 9 needles, cast on 30 st. Work 30 rows in s.s., then cut wool and slip these stitches on a spare needle. Work a second lining exactly the same and put both aside for the present.

THE BODY OF PULLOVER : Begin at the lower edge, using mottle wool and No. 9 needles. Cast on 232 st., arranging 72 on the first needle, 88 on the second, and 72 on third needle. Join into a round and work 20 rounds of k. 2 and p. 2 alternately for the ribbed hip-band. It is now ready to begin the multi-colour pattern.

The Colour Pattern

FIRST *and 2nd rounds:* K. all light.

3rd and 4th rounds: K. 2 light and 2 mottle alternately all round.

5th and 6th rounds: K. 2 mottle and 2 dark alternately.

7th and 8th rounds: K. 2 dark and 2 mottle alternately.

9th and 10th rounds: K. 2 mottle and 2 light alternately.

11th and 12th rounds: K. all light.

13th and 14th rounds: K. 2 light and 6 dark alternately.

Continued from page 29

clusive. Repeat the 18 pattern rounds 4 times more, when armhole opening is reached.

Next round : With light wool cast off 2, k. 59 for left front ; on a second needle k. 59 for right front ; cast off 2, k. remaining 110 all on one needle for back. The work now proceeds in rows, so back or alternate rows will be purled, in pattern.

THE BACK.—Continue with 2nd pattern row, and on every row work items in reverse order to that given, for instance the 3rd and 4th rounds will be " 2 mottle and 2 light alternately," which is simply continuing the pattern.

Repeat until the 18th row has been worked for the third time from the armhole. Work the first 6 pattern rows, then cut threads and leave these stitches until fronts have been worked.

RIGHT FRONT.—Join light wool to purl row and continue with 2nd pattern row. K. 2 tog. at beginning (neck opening) of two k. rows out of every three (that is, 2 decreasings in every 6 rows) until 40 st. are left for shoulder. Work until 2 rows longer than back. Hold needle with these stitches in front of the matching 40 st. from end of back with the right sides of knitting together. K. tog. 1 from front and 1 from back needles and cast off at the same time.

LEFT FRONT.—Work as described for right front, except that decreasings are at end of k. rows instead of beginning.

THE NECK.—With mottle wool and No. 10 needles pick up 47 st. down left front of neck (taking 3 st. to every 4 rows) for first needle ; on second needle pick up 47 st. at right-front neck ; on third needle k. 30 back neck stitches. Work 1 round of k. 2 and p. 2 rib, then work 6 rounds, decreasing at centre front, thus : Sl. 1, k. 1 and pass sl.-stitch over on the last 2 st. of first needle, and k. 2 tog. at beginning of second needle in every round. Cast off rather loosely.

POCKET TOPS.—With mottle wool and No. 10 needles k. 8 rows and cast off.

Sleeves

WITH light wool and No. 9 needles cast on 88 st., 32 on first needle, 24 on second needle, and 32 on third needle. Join in to a round and work in pattern, decreasing on every 4th round. To decrease on first needle, k. 2, k. 2 tog., work to end of needle, work the 2nd needle to within 2 st. of end of 3rd needle, then sl. 1, k. 1, pass the sl.-stitch over. After the 5th decrease round, decrease every 8th round until 56 st. remain. Work for length required, then with No. 10 needles and mottle wool k. 1 round and k. 2 tog. at beginning of first and second needles, also at end of second and third needles (52 st.). Work 22 rounds of k. 2 and p. 2 rib, cast off.

TO MAKE UP.—Sew sleeves to armholes with join of rounds to under-arm. Sew pocket linings to wrong side of pullover, and darn in all ends. Press all, except ribbing, with a damp cloth over knitting.

2351

2352

The chesterfield, with its single-breasted, slightly waisted fit, full-length and fly-fronted, was the most accepted style for every social occasion—except when the weather became cold and inclement. Then the double-breasted Ulster was preferred.

FOR THE MENFOLK

A Crochet Tie Or a Knitted One—Take Your Choice!

A KNITTED TIE

THIS tie is worked in a flat piece on two needles, and is afterwards sewn up the long edge to form a circular tie.

MATERIALS : 1 ball (50 grammes) of Clark's Anchor Stranded Cotton and a pair of No. 14 steel knitting needles make a double tie 2 inches wide.

ABBREVIATIONS : K., knit ; p., purl ; tog., together ; m., make.

TO WORK

CAST on 43 stitches and do 3 rows of plain knitting, working into the back of stitches on first row.

4TH ROW : K. 3, p. 4, * k. 2, p. 4, repeat from * to end.

5TH ROW : K. 3, * m. 1 (by bringing the thread to the front of the needle for an open stitch), k. 2 tog., k. 4, repeat from * until 4 remain, m. 1, k. 2 tog., k. 2.

Repeat the 4TH and 5TH Rows 3 times more, then work the 4TH Row.

13TH, 14TH and 15TH Rows : All plain knitting.

16TH Row : P. 4, * k. 2, p. 4, repeat from * until 3 remain, k. 3.

17TH Row : K. 6, * m. 1, k. 2 tog., k. 4, repeat from *, finishing with k. 1.

Repeat the 16TH and 17TH Rows 3 times more, then work the 16TH Row. This completes one pattern.

Repeat the pattern 7 times more for the long end. Work the first 12 rows of next pattern.

NEXT Row : (K. 3, k. 2 tog.) 3 times, k. 13, (k. 2 tog., k. 3) 3 times (37 stitches).

Work the 2ND Row, and continue pattern up to and including the 12TH Row.

NEXT Row : (K. 4, k. 2 tog.) 6 times, k. 1. You have 31 stitches.

K. 2 rows and p. 1 row.

NEXT Row : (K. 2 tog., k. 2) 7 times, k. 2 tog., k. 1.

There are now 23 stitches, on which p. 1 row and k. 1 row alternately for 13½ inches, finishing with a purl row.

NEXT Row : (K. 1 into front and 1 into back of same stitch, k. 2) 7 times, k. 1 into front and 1 into back, k. 1 (31 stitches).

P. 1 row and k. 2 rows.

NEXT Row : (K. 4, k. 1 into front, and 1 into back of next stitch) 6 times, k. 1, giving 37 stitches in the row.

Begin pattern with 4TH Row and work up to and including 14TH Row.

NEXT Row : (K. 3, k. 1 into front, and 1 into back of next stitch) 3 times, k. 13, (k. 1 into front, and 1 into back of next stitch, k. 3) 3 times.

Continue pattern from 4TH Row then work 4 repeats of pattern and one more repeat to the end of 15TH Row.

The Crochet Tie

K. one plain row and cast off.

Press well on wrong side and sew together the long edges for back of tie with sewing silk of the same shade. Press seam to flatten.

THE CROCHET TIE

MATERIALS : One ball (50 grammes) of Clark's Fil D'Ecosse No. 20 will make two of these ties, with a steel crochet hook No. 1.

ABBREVIATIONS : Ch., chain ; d.c., double crochet , tr., treble.

The groundwork of tie is worked in d.c., putting the hook into the front loop only of the two at the top of stitch on previous row. The raised stitches are tr. worked thus : Miss next stitch on last row and into front loop of stitch on the row before last, work 1 tr., then continue on last row again, and work the number of d.c. given. Every tr. thus spans 2 rows of d.c. The first d.c. on every row is worked on the second d.c. of last row, the 2 turning ch. forming the first d.c. At the end of the row work the last stitch into the top of the 2 ch.

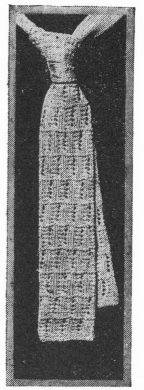

The Knitted Tie

Make 23 ch., and work 1 d.c. into the 3rd ch. from hook, 20 more d.c., 2 ch., turn.

NEXT 2 Rows : 21 d.c., 2 ch., turn.

* NEXT 12 Rows : 2 d.c., 1 tr., (4 d.c., 1 tr.) 3 times, 3 d.c., 2 ch., turn.

NEXT 2 Rows : 1 d.c., (1 tr., 1 d.c., 1 tr., 2 d.c.) 4 times, 2 ch., turn. Repeat from * 9 more times for long end of tie.

TO DECREASE FOR NECK

1ST Row : 2 d.c., 1 tr., (miss 2 stitches, 3 d.c., 1 tr.) 3 times, miss 2 stitches, 2 d.c., 2 ch., turn.

2ND Row : 1 d.c., 1 tr., (miss 2 stitches, 2 d.c., 1 tr.) 3 times, 2 d.c., 2 ch., turn.

NEXT 2 Rows : 1 d.c., (1 tr., 2 d.c.) 4 times, 2 ch., turn.

NEXT Row : 3 d.c., (miss 1 stitch on last row, 4 d.c.) twice, 1 ch., turn.

Now, for neck band work 13½ inches with 11 d.c. in each row, 2 ch., turn.

TO INCREASE

1ST Row : 2 d.c., 2 d.c. into next stitch, 4 d.c., 2 d.c. into next, 3 d.c., 2 ch., turn.

Work 2 rows of 13 d.c., 2 ch., turn.

NEXT 2 Rows : 1 d.c., (1 tr., 2 d.c.) 4 times, 2 ch., turn.

For next 2 rows work into every d.c. to increase.

6TH Row : 1 d.c., (1 tr., 3 d.c.) 4 times, 2 ch., turn.

7TH Row : 2 d.c., 1 tr., (4 d.c., 1 tr.) 3 times, 3 d.c., turn.

Work to match long end for 6 patterns.

Work 2 rows d.c., and fasten off end.

Press very lightly with a warm iron.

1921

A sudden slump in the tailoring trade caused by wage reductions and rising costs was driving bespoke tailoring in 1921 into the hands of the 'ready-made' or 'reach-me-down' clothier. High-class tailors were appalled at a current air of 'clothes carelessness' at various social functions held during the London season. At the opening of the Royal Academy Exhibition at Burlington House—usually an event of tailoring elegance—the sartorial spies observed a state almost approaching slovenliness. 'Where was the trimness and elegance we wished to applaud? Where was the grace of garb on the well-groomed man? Where the suits that deserved sonnets? One looked in vain for the style and shapeliness of Schott, the prestige of Poole, the hall-mark of Hills, or the bold and handsome lines of Lovegrove. Can it be that men are turning to false gods and are lured by the slogan of mass-production?' This mediocrity of dress was echoed in the subjects of the canvasses, where the careless painting too, offended the tailors. 'If artists would only gain a little first-hand knowledge of dress, they wouldn't paint such shabby second-hand clothes.'

At Henley Regatta, however, 'the great river carnival of the year, where everybody who *is* anybody fore-gathers', the sparklingly-dressed people presented one of the most glorious sights of the year. 'The multi-colored dresses and sunshades of the ladies, the colored costumes of the competitors and the blue and white flannels of the gentlemen altogether present a picture resembling fairyland.' The correct habiliment at Henley was unmistakably flannel, as there was 'a veritable riot of flannel garments on the towing path'. Straw boaters with a fancy band of stripes or the wearer's club colors were worn as smart headgear to top the outfits.

The view that man actually preferred the drab and sombre in clothing instead of showing a love of color was refuted upon occasions like Henley, when he was allowed openly to indulge in a splash of color and was expected to show flamboyant taste. It must have been the conventions of everyday life that forced him to suppress his natural sartorial lusts. In the daytime one was only occasionally given a glimpse of man's secret yearning for color by the appearance of a tartan tie or a pair of checkered socks.

Beau Brummell was really responsible for this, for it was he who first realized that the psychology of the Englishman was best interpreted in subdued colors. He relied on the elegance of line and cut rather than the brilliance of color and trappings to express and enhance the physical perfections of the 'English Adonis'.

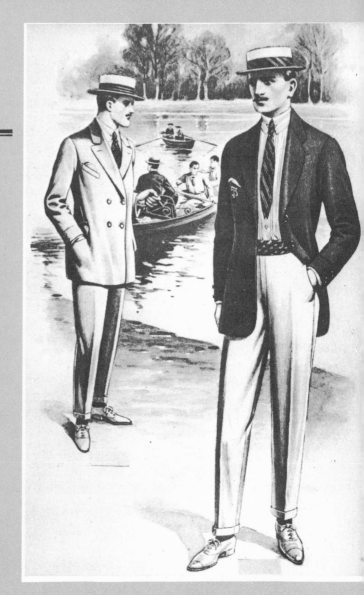

Even in the city the morning coat had by now been replaced by the lounge suit. It was more informal and comfortable to wear, and owing to a noticeable decrease in the weight of the cloth the fit was lighter and less bulky. The jacket could be single or double-breasted and the matching trousers had either plain or turn-up bottoms. America, however, had a style of lounge that was not 'chaste and reticent' like the British version, 'for the American tailor is influenced by the clothes sense of many people; a hint from the East, a suggestion from the Southern States; a little semitic emphasis, and a little yankee restlessness: all these things help to shape American styles, and the finishing touch is often a negro jazziness.' In fact the Americans had just produced a garment which they called 'the young men's four-buttoned Novelty Sac Coat of the jazz variety'. The English tailors enquired into the meaning of the word 'jazz' and found it was a slang word for something that was bright, lively and up to date, and of rather extreme character. The novelty jacket certainly suited the definition, for it had narrow shoulders, a fitted waist and very heavy round lapels. It outraged the English sense of good taste, and it was thought unfortunate that the interest of many a young Englishman was being caught by the coat—which was 'rather effeminate' in appearance. Apparently the wearing of it in England could 'change the whole manliness of a man and encourage other bad habits'. Some students in America had the same idea, and formed themselves into a club 'for the combating of effeminate appearance'. The rules were that 'wasp-waists, decolleté collars and all such signs of weakness are to be taboo. The penalty for powdering the face after shaving is a fine of 50 dollars—the use of scented hair-wash is equally banned, and all members of the club must smoke pipes.' Had a similar society been formed in England it would have had plenty of scope and a large field from which to draw its members.

The Prince of Wales set another fashion by reverting to flaps for the lower pockets of his coat, and he had his lounge suit trousers all permanently 'turned up and cut wide'. His waistcoat was finished with a boldly shaped vee-opening, and the last button was left undone. 'As worn by the Prince' was a phrase much used to advertise lounges in West End shops. Among all classes the Prince was admired for his way of dressing with 'that little bit of individuality which pleased but which was not at all outrageous'—not yet, anyway. He had shown a liking for check lounge suits and check neckties . . . 'what the Prince wears today his numerous admirers will wear tomorrow . . . the vogue of check is assured.'

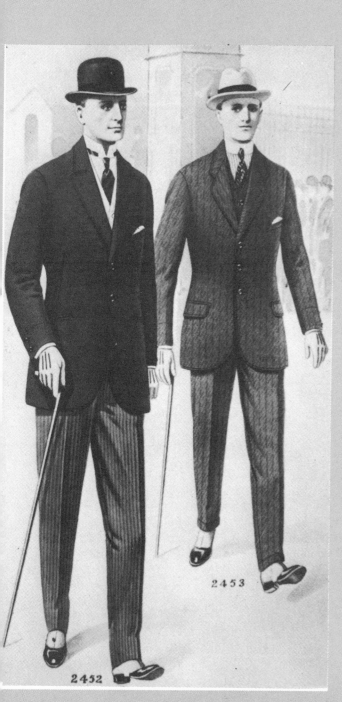

2453

2452

wear, 'now that khaki has been discarded it is the most stately garment worn in everyday life.' Even some of the younger men adopted it to give them 'age and an appearance of respectability', but it was undoubtedly the King who really kept alive that dressy and dignified garment, and at functions such as Royal Garden Parties he would be seen wearing a dark or light gray frock coat.

The King was very conservative; but because everything he wore was so well styled and in such excellent taste he was much admired and very often copied. His personality 'peeps forth in little touches which doubtless please him'. As well as his liking for the frock coat he favored trousers which had a side-crease to them, being a 'sailing man' at heart. His tie was often slipped through a golden ring, and his gloves always had black 'points' to them. He carried a stick and liked to use a long cigarette holder. On his head he wore a very pale gray 'topper' with a distinctive light gray band to match, and over his shoes he wore spats.

Spats were fashionable wear for most formal occasions. When the King attended the Chelsea Flower Show 'it was a great day for spats, mostly gray with a few white ones. In fact spats were in spate, they foamed all over the ground.' Spats even found popularity in the House of Commons, although apparently not always for decorative purposes but 'as a protection against the hurricane which was constantly blowing round their feet and legs.'

The top hat was still *de rigueur* in the Temple and the Stock Exchange and at certain of the Public schools, and the topper was still recognized as a sign that the wearer was 'one of those who toils not, nor spins'. It was worn too, of course, at weddings, when it accompanied the two-button morning coat suit. The morning coat was styled on beautiful lines, with its 'cut-away' skirts of ample length and a waist made very short and straight above the normal waistline to give the wearer the appearance of having long elegant legs. The shoulders and chest were made wide to enhance this slimness below, and the waistcoat fitted the figure quite closely, and was worn single-breasted with four pockets. The trousers, held up with braces, were in dark gray and white striped cashmere, and starting full in the thigh swept downwards towards a pair of black shoes and white spats.

So fitted and curved had the male silhouette become in comparison with the female one, which was flattened, straight and masculine-looking, that they seem to have changed places. At the Derby it was reported that 'Man is shapely. Woman is shapeless.' At Ascot there was no doubt about it: 'The most noticeable paradox was that man's dress showed form and corsetry, while woman's form was loose and non-commital'; and 'whilst woman's waist is slipping downwards, man's is creeping upwards.'

Man's formal evening dress wear was a swallow-tail coat made of thin black cloth known as dress-coating. The front dipped just to cover the waistcoat, and the

At court functions medals and decorations were required to be worn, and it was a matter of courtesy and grace that they should be correctly displayed in the right order, beginning with the Victoria Cross and the British orders of Knighthood. His Majesty, King George, was most meticulous in preserving the formal court dress of black knee-breeches and evening dress coat, white waistcoat and silk stockings. Such Levée dress was correct for civilians, but full dress uniform had to be worn by members of the forces.

Although the frock coat with its double-breasted front and knee-length skirts was not so dominant in the fashion world as in former years, there were still a few men of maturer years who found it a valuable and comely garment for ceremonial and even for business

9653

9652

9654

1923

long tapering tails just covered the back of the knee. The coat was cut double-breasted but always worn open, and the waist again was on the short side. It was fashionable to have braiding on the side seams of the trousers, but on no account were there turn-ups on the trouser legs. Silk hat, white muffler and gloves were standard accessories. A black or white waistcoat according to taste was worn with a bow tie and wing collar. An innovation of the past year or so had been a backless waistcoat held with a strap at the waist and a strip at the neck. This was more comfortable and helped to keep a slim contour down the back.

The dinner jacket, dress jacket or tuxedo was worn for less formal occasions and was cut on the lounge style and had 'jetted' or bound slit-pockets. This was also a shapely garment, defining the waist and fitting closely over the hips. Shoulders and breast were again made to look as broad as possible. Although this

jacket was single-breasted and worn with a single-breasted waistcoat, some 'slim men about town' were ordering double-breasted waistcoats, perhaps to give them broader-looking chests. Black or white waistcoats were worn, with neckties to match, and the trousers, neatly pleated at the waistband at the front, always had to have turn-ups. Dinner jackets, always black, were usually made in vicuna, angora, hopsack or twilled worsted cloth. This costume was becoming more popular, vying with the tail coat for formal occasions. Once again the Prince of Wales had set the example. At a certain function where dress coats were *de rigueur* the Prince and several guests had turned up in dinner jackets. Many people were shocked and annoyed with the Prince because they knew others would follow his example, and standards would be 'let down'. The Vicar of Mansfield was amongst those who expressed displeasure.

35

The Duke and Duchess of York
putting on the private course
at Polesdon-Lacey during their
honeymoon

A MAN'S GOLF STOCKINGS

MAKE THEM FOR THREE SHILLINGS— OR A LITTLE OVER!

A pair of hand-knitted stockings is a gift any man will love

These stockings can be made to fit any sized foot

THESE stockings are worked in a very easy style, because the shaping of the leg is done by changing the needles only, so as not to interfere with the rib.

MATERIALS : 7 ozs. of grey Sirdar Coronation Wool, equal in thickness to a good 4-ply fingering; a set of 4 steel needles No. 12, and a set of No. 13.

TO KNIT

CAST 28 stitches on each of 3 No. 12 needles, so that there are 84 stitches altogether, and do 50 rounds of single ribbing, that is, 1 plain and 1 purl alternately. In the last round decrease 4 stitches at equal distances apart. There should now be 80 stitches.

Work 56 rounds of k. 4 and p. 1 alternately.

Change to No. 13 needles and work 72 rounds, when the stocking should be long enough to begin the heel, but, o course, more rounds can be worked for any length.

THE HEEL

KNIT the first 20 stitches of the round on one needle, slip the last 20 stitches of the round on the other end of the same needle. These 40 stitches are for the heel. The remaining 40 stitches are for the instep or front needle.

Purl and knit alternate rows on the heel stitches. Always slip the first stitch. Work for 39 rows, the last of which should be a purl row.

The heel has now to be turned. K. 25, k. 2 tog. Turn. P. 11, p. 2 tog. Turn. K. 12, k. 2 tog. Turn. P. 13, p. 2 tog. Turn. K. 14, k. 2 tog. Turn. Continue thus until the row p. 23, p. 2 tog. is worked, and then purl the remaining stitch. There are now 26 stitches on the needle. Turn, and knit the first 13 on one needle. Take another needle, and knit the remaining 13 stitches on it. This is now the first foot needle.

THE INSTEP

ON the first foot needle, knit 19 stitches at side of heel. Turn, and purl back along this needle, and along the needle with the 13 stitches upon it. On this needle pick up purlwise the 19 stitches at the other side of heel.

There should be 64 stitches altogether on the 2 needles. Pass the 40 instep stitches on one needle, and keep these stitches in the rib pattern up the foot, the other 2 needles in plain knitting.

1ST INSTEP ROUND : K. in rib across front needle ; on the second needle k. 2, k. 2 tog., then knit plain until within 4 stitches of end of 3rd needle ; here k. 2 tog., k. 2.

2ND ROUND : Knit without any decreasing.

Repeat these 2 rounds until there are 40 stitches only on the plain knitted needles.

Continue on these stitches until the foot piece measures 6½ inches for a 10-inch foot, 7 inches for a 10½-inch foot, 7½ inches for an 11-inch foot, measuring from the side of the heel where the stitches were picked up. The shaping of the round toe makes another 2¼ inches.

THE TOE

TO work this, the stitches should now stand, the first or front needle, 40 stitches, the second and third plain needles, 20 stitches each, 80 stitches in the round.

1ST ROUND : K. 8, k. 2 tog. all round.

Do 2 rounds without decreasing.

4TH ROUND : K. 7, k. 2 tog., all round.

Now work 2 rounds without decreasing, and then knit a round with 6 stitches between the decreases.

Continue thus, with 2 rounds without shaping, then a round which has one stitch less between the decreases than the previous decreasing round. When 16 stitches remain, cut off the wool and run it through the stitches. Fasten off securely.

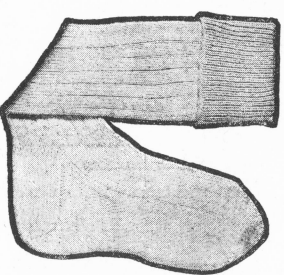

The shaping of the leg is done by changing the needles

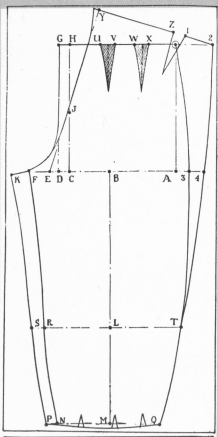

DRAFT OF PLUS-FOURS.

The measures are: 42 side, 30 leg; 30 waist, 36 seat, knee 23.

Draw line O A 1½, and square from A.

A to B (please note) is one-third scale less ½in.   A to C half scale.

C to F one-sixth scale plus ½in.

Square up from C to H and from H to O. Add 1 inch at D and G and draw fly-line. H to U 2½ inches.   U to V 1½in.

V to W 1¾in.   W to X 1¼in.

Square down from B, and make B to L half leg less 2 inches.

L to M 8 inches (more or less according to overlap).

L to T and L to R are one-fourth knee; if there is any difficulty in getting a run, add at little at T.

M to Q and M to N are about 1¼in. less than at knee.

Add 1 inch from A to 3, and a little round at bottom.

For the undersides make F to K 1¾in., R to S 1 inch. and N to P 1 inch.

From C mark up to J one-fourth scale plus ½in.

Point E is midway between C and F.

Rule a line from E through J.

Measure up waist, adding sufficient for seams and pleats, and a cut in underside, and locate 2.

Rest square against seat-line and draw from Y to 2.

2 to 1 is 2½ inches; add 1 to 1½in. from 3 to 4, and complete.

'Plus-four knickers have become quite popular of late, and every tailor is called upon to make these fashionable nether garments.'

1924

The plus-four trousers were cut eight inches below the knee and fell in baggy fashion over a narrow garter fitting. The fullness above was taken in as pleats into the front waistband. In 1924 it was fashionable to have these knickers cut very full, sagging well below the knee and pouching voluminously over the calf. Although the plus-four was really a variation or evolution from the knickerbocker, the origin of the name was a matter of some controversy. Some said that the plus-four was merely the result of the instruction given to the tailor to cut the overlap four inches longer, but others said it was derived from the golfing term: 'A golfer who is first class would often be plus four in a handicap, and the familiar term 'plus-four' as a mark of quality was in time transferred to the swagger knickers with which the young bloods at first startled the more sedate golfer in close knickers or long service flannels.'

The extreme length of plus-fours as a distinctive feature was probably introduced into knickers for stalking, the object being that the length would save strain or split when the sportsman slipped. Whatever the origins, the plus-four had become a tremendous vogue; 'they are to be seen on every golfing course and at every sports meeting, and also may be met occasionally in town.' Plus-fours were worn together with a matching jacket, a tweed cap and brown brogues on the feet—especially those types with the fringed tongues so favored by the Prince. Below the knee were stockings, usually with fancy tops, kept up with elastic garters with the stocking tops turned down over them.

In matters of dress a man tended to have an 'ideal' to follow and copy; and whether the ideal was a film star, a writer or a politician, if he set a new fashion trend it immediately became the vogue. The Empire Exhibition in 1924 attracted people from all over the world, and the Prince of Wales found he was not only advertising the Empire in general but advertising British clothes in particular. With sanguine alliteration, *The Tailor and Cutter* declared 'the lounge suit is first favorite with prince and peasant, duke and dustman'. It was every-man's wear. The 'lounge' advertised by the Prince in particular was the 'London cut', a new type of high-waisted, close-fitting lounge suit and body coat. These had double-breasted lapels and fastened with one button only or else were made to link at the waist.

One of the leaders of fashion in England was the writer Arnold Bennett. His clothes had to be made by a first-class tailor, and he liked to renew his wardrobe twice a year. Another was the politician Austin Chamberlain, for he was 'debonair, well turned out, and wears his clothes with an air'.

Just as the fashion-conscious had heroes in dress, so too there were anti-heroes, especially those in 'high up' places who should have known better and were letting the good name of tailoring down. 'He who is in the public eye should see to it that there is nothing un-sightly in his garb.' This reproof was directed to almost all the members of Prime Minister Baldwin's cabinet, who did not seem to realize that 'the way to a lengthy stay at Westminster lies through Savile Row, Bond Street and the Burlington Arcade. One would have thought that respect for a great assembly and for its ancient tradition should have kept down the practice of making speeches in lounge suits. It would be infinitely preferable, for example, if ministers came down to the House after dinner in full evening dress. The Prime Minister himself is the worst offender. He has a liking for being unbuttoned. Whether it be overcoat, frock coat or jacket, it is usually undone . . . if only he would put his coats on properly and fasten them up he would enjoy that well-dressed feeling which helps to surmount obstacles.' The second offender was Mr Winston Churchill, then Chancellor of the Exchequer. He was charged with 'eccentricity' in his vesture. His Astrakhan-trimmed overcoat suggested the impresario rather than the statesman. Worse was to come, sartorially speaking, from Churchill in the next decade.

Jack Buchanan

The English stage star Jack Buchanan spent much of his time in America, and was greatly admired for his style. He wrote articles on fashion for magazines and off the stage as well as on he was exceptionally smartly dressed. Just as a well-dressed gentleman in England is sometimes spoken of as a 'Brummel', in America the same type of man was referred to as a 'Buchanan'. Jack Buchanan liked to wear the new dinner jacket, a double-breasted jacket with silk-covered lapels which 'rolled' to the waist. The fronts were quite square at the bottom, and though two buttons were shown on each forepart, only one fastened

For months, stories of a weird movement in dress in Oxford had been going around. The smart young men were having their trousers made wide—in some cases very wide indeed, with forty inch bottoms—and these baggy trousers in conjunction with a jacket fitted closely round the hips gave a very strange line. During Oxford 'Eights' week one could see the undergraduates in their 'bloated bags' along the towing-path and in the beautiful meadows. Not content with appearing in these ballooning trousers in shades of lavender, cinnamon, mauve, sand and delicate green, they outraged even further with ribbed and patterned cloth. The fashion flickered briefly outside Oxford, reaching Oxford Circus in London, and 'they have even caught the Speaker's eye' in the House of Commons.

At the opera there were no signs as yet of any such Oxford liberties, but 'tweeds' had been worn there, which is disgraceful enough; but how could a man be criticized, for example, if he wore tweeds in the stalls of a West End theatre, when *Hamlet* had been produced in modern dress with Hamlet himself wearing plus-fours? Women were perhaps to blame for ideas like these, for they were pleased by any 'sartorial daring' shown by men, and encouraged them to be adventurous in fashion. It had already been suggested that women should be invited to design men's clothes: 'as a man's best valet was his wife, why could she not be his

1925

dress designer too?' The answer could be that women were apt to overdo things a trifle. One prominent woman said, for example: 'I would like to be appointed Mistress of the Robes for all men all over the world. What materials I could gather together! I would make good use of armour and jerkins and hose and togas and kilts and satin waistcoats.'

With golf rising in popularity, new links were being opened up all over the country, and this year the 'golfing rig' of plus-fours, colored and patterned jumpers and socks was seen everywhere. When playing golf one could be as conspicuous as one liked, and if the actual knickers were not brightly-hued and patterned, color and contrast could be added with a startling jumper or hose. Both cardigans and pullovers fought one another for supremacy, and appeared in colorful Fair-Isle and diamond and check patterns. Popular, too, for golf were the wind-jammers and macintosh blouses. A neat and novel style was for the golfer to have his sweater or pullover tucked inside the knickers.

In the hot weather of June 1925, flannels which were cool and comfortable were in great demand. In fact flannels were associated with some of the 'happiest moments' in men's lives. Although for the older men flannels would more often than not be gray, many of the 'young bloods' were asking for flannels in biscuit and in various pastel shades.

OXFORD BAGS
HAVE THEIR DAY

ABOVE are examples of "Oxford bags" which, though "freaks" or "stunts" in themselves, have influenced the width of the modern trouser.

Charming hat in Petersham, with smart quill at side-back.

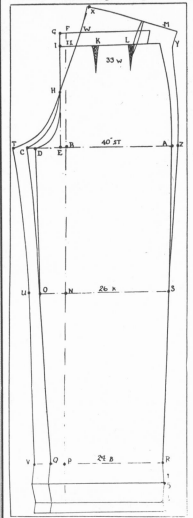

DRAFT OF OXFORD "BAGS"

We are giving a draft of these wide trousers as, in all probability, many of our readers may have to execute such orders. The measures are: 33 waist, 40 seat; 32 leg, 43 side; 26 knee, 24 bottom.

THE DRAFT.

A to B 11 inches.   B to C 4 inches.
B to E and F to G ½in.
B to F the rise plus ½in.
11 to side 10 inches, which allows for two small pleats.
F to 11 the width of band desired.
B to P 32 inches, length of leg.

B to N half leg less 1 inch, 15 inches.
N to O 2½ inches.
O to S half knee measure.
P to Q 1½in.
Q to R half bottom measure less ½in.; add 5 inches for p.t.u.
C to T 1½in.   O to U 1 inch.
Make up size of bottom plus 1 inch at V.
E to H 5 inches; go back 1 inch from 11 and shape seat-seam as diagram.
W to X 2½ inches.
Measure up the waist plus 2 inches to Y, after allowing for the pleats in fronts, add about ½in. from A to Z, and complete as diagram.

The game of tennis was at the peak of its popularity, and the thing to wear on the courts was a blue jacket to accompany the white tennis bags. Perhaps because of the red rubble—now used as a surface on 'hard' tennis courts—which quickly soiled long white flannels some men were taking to golf attire, and it was thus that plus-fours invaded the courts.

Cricket was second only to tennis as the most popular summer sport. The cricket outfit was the result of a long process of evolution. The cricketer in the days of Fuller Pilch and Alfred Mynn wore a top hat, a check shirt, high collar and braces, etc. But in 1925 he was garbed in ideal fashion—given a fine summer: easy-fitting white flannel trousers, a loose and sometimes billowing shirt, white boots and peaked hat sporting his 'colors', and of course the gorgeous blazer for strolling around the grounds between innings. This added more color and distinguished club or college.

43

1926

At the 1926 Royal Academy Exhibition, a fashion parade as well as a picture parade, Mr Arnold Bennett gave 'distinctive encouragement' to the vogue for brighter men by wearing 'a symphony in mauve', even to the tie and handkerchief, and to complete the assemblage he flaunted a brown bowler hat. *The Tailor and Cutter* pandered to his self-indulgence: 'he who loves life will love fine clothes, and will regard

G. 7.

a tinge of dandyism as a debt he owes himself and those around him.'

Never before in the history of the tailoring trade were such brightly-colored cloths for suits being made. Brown and mauve mixtures were much in demand and patterned cloths were good sellers. White shirts had practically disappeared except for formal evening wear, and there was a huge color range to choose from—putty shades, cedars, cinnamons, fawns, blue-gray, mauve and flesh-color. Modern man was eclipsing women in the brightness of his clothes.

Sadly, a great fashion idol much admired for, amongst other things, his great 'passion' for clothes, died this year. This was the well-loved star Rudolph Valentino. He dressed with 'the grace and distinction of an eighteenth-century courtier', wearing clothes that were different.

The tailoring press urged that with all the standardization of sizes, mass-production and uniformity in ready-mades, it was even more important for a man to have a good-fitting suit of choice material, for this would give the increased confidence and sense of well-being necessary for him to get through his working day. Perhaps the conservative business man should have followed more the example of fashionable youth and have chosen the new-styled trousers that were wider in the leg. These were undoubtedly a development from the Oxford bags. 'Fashions were never launched from Oxford or Cambridge, but freakishness has often stalked by the Cam and Isis and left its mark on the world!' In March, the catastrophic collapse of Oxford in the Boat Race was thought by some to be been entirely the fault of the 'bags'.

At the Chelsea Flower show, breeches appeared in a smart blue and white check and were worn with a blue lounge jacket. But they were by no means the exclusive garment on view, for trousers in brown and white check worn with a brown jacket were highly fashionable and these outfits had obviously taken over in popularity from the black and white check worn with a black jacket.

King George alarmed the fashion world twice this year. Not only did he favor a morning coat instead of his usual frock coat at the self-same Chelsea Flower Show, but he upset all the Americans who came to his Garden Party by a sudden disfavoring of spats. It was related that 'after the Garden Party at Buckingham Palace the shrubberies were snowed under with white spats discarded by Americans who showed enterprise at the last moment.'

When a man decided to shed the smooth urban character of the worsted and the vicunas of town clothing for the rough homespun or hardy tweed of his sports suit, he became another being. Such country suits were being made up in fragrant tweeds with attractive patterns in check or shepherd's plaid, and

PRINCIPAL EVENTS OF 1926

JAN. 4. Death of Queen Margherita of Italy.

,, 21. Lord Lloyd, High Commissioner of Egypt, opens the Sennar Dam.

,, 31. Evacuation of Cologne by the British troops.

FEB. 17. Alan Cobham reaches the Cape, after flight of 8,000 miles.

MAR. 6. Shakespeare Memorial Theatre at Stratford-on-Avon burnt down.

,, 13. Alan Cobham lands at Croydon, concluding a flight of 16,000 miles from London to Capetown and back.

,, 20. Death of Louise Josephine Eugenie, Dowager Queen of Denmark.

,, 27. Cambridge win the Boat Race.

,, 29. C.O.D. parcel service came into operation.

APR. 3. Lord Irwin took office as Viceroy of India.

,, 19. Death of Sir Squire Bancroft—actor-manager.

,, 21. Birth of a daughter to Duchess of York (Princess Elizabeth).

,, 24. Russo-German Treaty signed.
,, Bolton Wanderers beat Manchester City in Cup Tie Final (1—0).

,, 30. Stoppage of work in coal mines.

MAY 3. National Strike Begins.

,, 9. Commander Byrd and Floyd B fly over North Pole.

,, 12. National Strike Ends.

JUNE 2. Lord Woolavington wins Derby with Coronach.

,, 4. French Senate ratifies Locarno Pact.

,, 24. Jubilee of the telephone.

,, 30. Alan Cobham leaves for Australia and back.

JULY 2. Death of Emile Coué, auto-suggestionist.

,, 12. Caillaux and Churchill sign an agreement for funding of French War Debt.

AUG. 1. Death of Izrael Zangwill, Jewish author.

,, Death of Desire Joseph Mercer, Belgian Prelate.

,, 6. Miss Gertrude Ederle of New York, first woman to swim channel. Also beat fastest time by two hours.

,, 15. Alan Cobham arrives at Melbourne.

,, 18. England wins final Test Match of the season at the Oval, wresting championship from Australia.

,, 23. Rudolph Valentino dies.

SEPT. 10. Germ ns.

,, 11.

OCT

'the peaty reek of homespun, the heartiness and toughness of buff, tan, lovat Shetlands and tweeds are so good by swirling stream, on the moors and for the ardors of golf.'

On the moors the shooting jacket was worn. This sometimes had a special seam at the waist neatly covered by an all-round belt. The intention was to cater for the mammoth size of the pockets and the additional weight carried in the way of cartridges and game. Moderate breeches, too, were more suitable to wear with the jacket than loose knickers, and with them gaiters or canvas leggings were eminently useful. The materials used for making the shooting outfit were tougher and more closely woven than those used for the golfing suit, and the wise sportsman also selected cloth which 'toned in' with his surroundings—it was not considered good form to look conspicuous in the country landscape.

'It may almost be said that sex is departing from modern clothes, which are becoming interchangeable. Many women wear plus-fours, pyjamas and dinner jackets, while their suits follow closely the lines of man's.'

The bobbing of women's hair, which was primarily a war-time convenience to save time, was now cultivated for its own particular beauty, and today the coiffures of both men and women were identical. Women were wearing flat-chested, waistless tubes, and men wide skirt-like garments such as plus-fours or 'bags'.

In the homespuns, the limit in loud checks appeared to have been reached, particularly in cloths for plus-fours. Never before had the Harris tweed industry been so popular, and so great was the demand that the crofters could not produce enough. Checks of all sizes, ranging from gun club or dog's tooth varieties up to bold Glen styles, were favored by leading men in society, and the ordinary lounge had undergone a change, for now many fancy patterns were being woven into the cloth. However 'fanciful' the lounge may have been, it was the fashionable 'Jacquard' jumpers that outrivalled all other clothes in brightness and pattern design, and they became the most popular style of knitwear for everyone. Large diamonds, big Argyll checks, lozenges and all manner of bold geometric patterns in 'joyful' colors were sought after, and it seemed that never had men been so gay in their dress.

For his evening wear, when color was kept within bounds, a man compensated by wearing the most 'shapely' garments. His dinner jacket or dress lounge suit of the latest style was cut to give the figure a broad-chested, 'waisted' appearance. It followed the outline of the body quite closely and there was no superfluous material on the hips. So conceited had man become that he wore monogrammed scarves with his evening wear—one man boasted of having the tweed for his suits specially woven so as to bring in his initials. He decided to wear a particular shade of dark blue for his dinner and dress clothes because he discovered that in a brilliantly illuminated room blue looked more black than black itself, which tended to appear green in artificial light. This fashion came from America, and was soon adopted by the Prince of Wales and other leaders of fashion.

In the daytime a navy-blue suit was coming into favor for the man who needed one suit as a bridge between the formal and the informal. He chose this color because he learned that nothing showed off the average man to better advantage. 'I like you in blue serge' was said to be the most frequent compliment that women paid to a man's appearance. This suit could be recommended for town wear; and with a

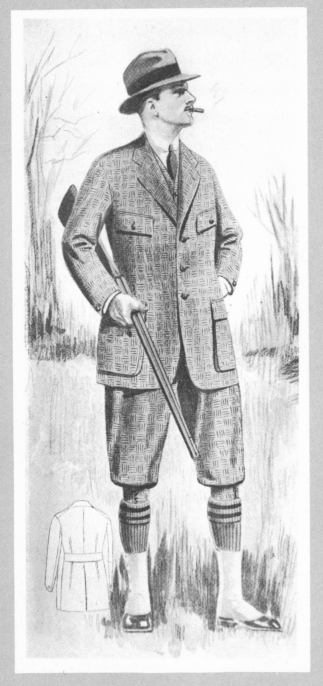

WOMAN and HOME

APRIL 1927 · Monthly

A Magazine of Delightful Suggestions

bowler hat it would be spruce enough to wear to take a lady to a concert matinée.

Having 'accessories to match' was a mode that man had adopted from women. Handkerchiefs exactly to match the tie in pattern were quite the newest vogue. Socks, if not actually matching the suit, should at least harmonize with it; but if possible, the tie, socks and handkerchief should all correspond in color. This new awareness of harmony in dress caused more men to frown heavily when they was a person wearing a brown suit, a grey overcoat and a green hat, all with the first tie that came to hand: 'a study in sartorial discord'. Even more men realized that the fashionable 'reptile' ties could not possibly be worn with anything but a plain dark lounge suit, because the markings of lizards, pythons and chameleons were too realistic and startling to be confused with other patterned effects. Many such ties were made of the real thing.

Boots and shoes were now of prime importance in appearance, for although shoes or boots in either brown or black could accompany a lounge, no smart man nowadays chose a light brown leather. Black patent Oxford shoes were correct for evening wear, but for morning dress, with spats out of fashion, the black boot with a contrasting upper was much worn. This decorative upper section was made of tan leather, cloth or buckskin, and the 'daintiest' variety of all for a man was a special patent leather boot fastening with buttons, and with the uppers in a pale shade of cloth.

Hats had to be as smart as the shoes in appearance and every man needed to own not only a bowler to wear with a suit and overcoat but a soft hat or two in either the popular curl-brim or snap-brim style. These had to match the suit if possible, in a light gray or fawn. A silk hat was needed for formal wear and, of course, a cap for informal wear. It was not so long since the cap had been regarded as suitable only for the artisan, but now rich and poor favored this form of headgear, especially for sports wear, and there were new designs and colorings in the most attractive weaves, as the Prince of Wales was to show (page 53). The top hat had fallen from grace for wear in the streets, and was now sported on formal occasions only. This was because the lounge suit had taken over from the morning frock coat for everyday outdoor use, and it was probably an incompatibility with the motor car which finally sealed the topper's fate.

The motor car was having a devastating effect on smart dressing and formal clothes. The increase in the number of those who owned motor cars, and the growing popularity of the 'sporting and motoring week-end' made many think that the world was going a little mad. At the Motor Show at Olympia in London in 1927 people were 'almost giving themselves up to the worship of the car'. The cars were beautifully upholstered and decorated, but where were the clothes to harmonize with all this color and style? One tremendous truth emerged—'clothes do not matter to the motorist.' The motorist, 'swathed to the chin, goggled and lumbering', had unwittingly dealt the death blow to many formal

STORM COAT L3018/2.

(The Ledux Company, 19 Nassau Street, London, W.1., and Leeds.)

and stately types of garments. Exposure to the weather, the possibility of the car breaking down and an 'undignified but necessary grappling with the engine' all helped to give an unbecoming attire a measure of popularity. The motorist's overcoat was often a clumsy leather affair or uncouth cloth garment, but men's fashion designers, seeing the car as an inflexible pointer to the future, endeavored to put some style into the motorist's appearance. They came up with the 'storm coat', the 'original furry warm'. This new overcoat, illustrated above, was warm and quite light in weight for motoring, travelling or ordinary wear in cold weather. The lining, although not real fur, was an excellent imitation, and it was very stylish.

Choose the best—within your reach

Let your final choice be the Bean—a car into whose every feature quality is built.

With ample power at his command, the seat and pedals adjusted to suit him exactly, the owner of a Bean "Twelve" or "Fourteen" can drive for hour after hour with only the pleasant fatigue of health at the end of a day enjoyed.

Each passenger is completely at ease, obviously comfortable, sure to reach the journey's end as fresh as at its beginning. Should it rain, the Calso one-man hood is true to its description, while the clear vision side screens are truly weatherproof and free from rattles.

The equipment includes everything you can desire.

A. HARPER SONS & BEAN, LTD.
DUDLEY, WORCESTERSHIRE

LONDON: 11a Regent Street, S.W.1.
'Phone: Gerrard 7672-3.

MANCHESTER: Wood Street, off Deansgate.
'Phone: Central 1016.

AUSTRALIA: . . . . 517/519 *Little Collins Street,* **MELBOURNE.**

Four wheel brakes—Perrot-Servo type. Four speed gear box, right hand control. Exceptionally roomy four door body. Front seats and all controls adjustable. Spare wheel and tyre. Dunlop Cord Balloons.

"Twelve" 2-seater	-	- £298
,, 4-seater	-	- £298
,, Saloon	-	- £375
"Fourteen" 3-seater	-	- £395
,, 5-seater	-	- £395
,, Saloon	-	- £450

BEAN CARS

Motoring Mittens

Materials Required.

To obtain the best results use 3 oz. of "Viyella" Yarn, 4-ply, in fawn, and 1 oz. in brown; also a set of No. 14 knitting needles.

The mittens should fit over gloves up to size 6¾. For a smaller size shorten the straight part after working the thumb.

The work is done at a tension of 10 sts. to 1 in.

Begin at the top of the gauntlet by casting on 112 sts. with brown wool, 36 sts. on each of the first 2 needles, and 40 on the third.

Work in a rib of K. 3, P. 1, for a depth of 12 rounds, working into the backs of the sts. on the first round.

Change to the fawn wool and work

10 rounds, then work
8 „ in brown,
6 „ „ fawn,
4 „ „ brown,
4 „ „ fawn.

Should a longer gauntlet be desired work

2 rounds in brown,
2 „ „ fawn,
1 „ „ brown,
4 „ „ fawn.

From here complete the mitten in fawn wool.

On the next round decrease in every knit rib by knitting the 2nd and 3rd sts. together all round—84 sts. remain.

The rib is now K. 2, P. 1. Continue without further alteration for a depth of 12 rounds.

On the next round again decrease by knitting together the 2 K. sts. in every knit rib. 56 sts. remain on the needle.

The rib is now K. 1, P. 1. Continue in this rib for a depth of 2 in.

Change to stocking st. and on the first round work 2 sts. into every 4th st. all round.

There are now 22, 22, 26 sts. on the needles.

Work a depth of in. without alteration.

On the next round commence the thumb increases.

On the first needle K. 2 sts. into the first st., K. 1, then K. 2 sts. into the next st., then complete the round.

These would make an opportune Gift for your Motoring Friend.

Work 1 round without alteration.

On the next round K. 2 sts. into the first st., K. 3, then K. 2 sts. into the next st. and complete the round.

Work the next round without alteration.

Continue increasing on every alternate round with 2 sts. extra between the increases each time till there are 42 sts. on the needle.

Now knit the first 23 sts. on the first needle of the round, and pass these sts. to a piece of wool.

There are now 19, 22, 26 sts. on the needles.

Complete the round and cast on 5 sts. at the end of the third needle.

Continue across the 19 sts. of the first needle, then pass the 5 cast on sts. on the previous needle to the beginning of the first needle of the round.

There are now 24, 22, 26 sts. on the needles.

Pass 2 sts. of the needle holding 26 sts. to the one with 22 only, making 24 sts. on each needle.

Continue quite straight for a depth of 3 in.—or more or less as required—then shape for the tip.

On the next round K. 2 tog., K. 34 K. 2 tog., K. 34.

Work 3 rounds without alteration.

On the next round K. 2 tog., K. 33, K. 2 tog., K. 33.

Work 3 rounds without alteration.

On the next round K. 2 tog., K. 32, K. 2 tog., K. 32.

Work 3 rounds without alteration.

On the next round K. 2 tog., K. 31, K. 2 tog., K. 31.

Work 3 rounds without alteration.

On the next round * K. 2 tog., K. 14, and repeat from * all round.

Repeat the decreases on every round always with 1 st. less between the decreases on every round till 28 sts. remain.

On the next round K. 2 tog. all round.

Arrange the remaining sts. on 2 needles and graft together.

The Thumb.

Pass the sts. of the thumb to 2 needles, then pick up and knit through the 5 cast on sts. on the hand, and also 1 on each side—the edge of the row on both sides—making 30 sts. on the needles.

Work over all sts. for a depth of 1¼ in.

The top shaping takes about ¾ of an in. in depth, so try on the thumb to be sure of the right length.

To shape the top :

1st round.—Knit tog. every 9th and 10th sts., then work 2 rounds without alteration.

4th round—Knit tog. every 8th and 9th sts., then work 2 rounds without alteration.

7th round.—Knit tog. every 7th and 8th sts., then work 2 rounds without alteration.

10th round.—Knit tog. every 6th and 7th sts., then work 2 rounds without alteration.

13th round.—Knit tog. every 5th and 6th sts., then work 2 rounds without alteration.

On the next round K. tog. 2 sts. all round.

Draw the wool through the remaining sts. and fasten off firmly.

The second mitten is made in the same way.

Press out carefully on the right side with a hot iron over a damp cloth, without opening the ribbing at all.

1928

The English tailoring trade was so renowned that the writer Tom Moore remarked: 'A trade that can sell an English morning suit to Harold Lloyd for £27 and a tweed suit to Ronald Colman for £19 is the calling for an ambitious young man. I shall give up journalism.'

The Prince of Wales still led most of the changes in fashion, and popularized them abroad. He not only put on several different outfits in a day, but kept it up week after week. The Prince also brought great reforms to men's clothes in the way of comfort and color. Following his diatribe against the 'hard-boiled' shirts for double-breasted dinner jackets, perfectly plain soft white shirts 'sans starch' were now accepted. At Ascot he continued his crusade against the 'un-relieved dullness' in formal dress, wearing a blue shirt with a double collar to accompany his black morning coat—and so a blue shirt is all the rage. For a few years now the Prince, together with the Duke of York, Lord Lascelles and many other leaders of fashion, had adopted the double collar for formal day wear. Indeed King George himself had grown so partial to the double shape that he wore one with a frock coat at Lady Mary Crichton's wedding.

There was a certain informality of attire that was not sanctioned by the Prince and which bred a lack of courtesy. Made-up evening bows, for example, were supposed to rank for sheer ignorance with the circula-tion of the port the wrong way round the table. One had to be sorry for the womenfolk in this respect, for how many pleasant evenings must have been spoiled by the tie which would not 'go'. How many outfits, too, had been spoiled by the accessories 'going too far'? Ties that jarred with the suit, or went ill with a man's complexion.

There was often a great lack of tact shown when men in power chose what to wear on special occasions. Last year, Mr Baldwin presided over the Imperial Con-ference wearing a lounge suit, and other statesmen addressed the House in all sorts of promiscuous apparel. Mr Baldwin and Mr Ramsay MacDonald made the grave mistake of always wearing clothes of the same style and color. 'They spring no surprises, and create no sensations, and are day in day out sombre and without point . . . and still unbuttoned.'

The wrong thing was often worn at a wedding, and now and again a bridegroom and his best man donned flannels! Many people had thought that the first signs of such decadence occurred when the morning coat was substituted for the frock coat at weddings. Even more horrifying, therefore, when invitations to the country wedding of Lord Saye and Sele's daughter Cicely were inscribed 'lounge suits'. Such garb had often been noted at country weddings, yet it is doubtful if official prescription had ever been given before, especially from such a source.

The rumour that Oxford men were reviving Oxford bags had sent a shudder through England. But the rumour was not true, though everyday trousers became more easy-fitting; they were, however, slightly on the long side, and many had plain bottoms. The plus-four suit was still patronized, the baggiest ones especially by youth: 'At their biggest we may smile, for youth will have its fling.' Plus-fours appeared in dashing gun-club checks, fancy checks, Glen Urquhart squares and many other designs and weaves. Rich browns, grays and beige were the popular colors, and green too was making an appearance. But when a man chose to wear his plus-fours to work, and introduced a feverish note into a quiet commercial house, he could not be looked upon with favor, 'for dull of soul, and lacking in response . . . or blessed with powers of concentration is he who is able to harness his attention to a ledger or a counter while clad in baggy knickers and a pullover of colored wools!'

For golf, jazz and Jacquard in knitwear continued to thrive without opposition, and the 'pullover cult' was universal. At its most outlandish it startled every-one. One young man at the golf club caused general panic by wearing a white pullover with a broad zig-zag line in bright yellow on the front. 'He looked for all the world as if he had been struck by lightning!'

Golf stockings matched the pullover in color, pattern and weave. Plain self-colored hose with fancy tops, or fancy hose with plain tops appeared in diamonds, squares and checks of all sizes, in colors of gray, fawn, blue, biscuit and brick. This year, some golfers were adopting the American plan of having a belt or side-buckles in lieu of braces, but Harry Varden's opinion was: 'once you have found a pair of braces that really suit your play ... neither too stiff nor too elastic ... keep them for golf only. Never change them, and never wear them except when you are going to the links.'

In the spring of 1928 the smart set wore red carnations and thus revived a fashion for button-holes, and at the 'varsity match held at Lords the younger fry wore really fancy waistcoats with either dark blue cornflowers or dyed light blue carnations in their coats. Stripes this year were fighting for supremacy with checks, and smart tie and handkerchief sets in an all-over pattern of stripes were worn by many young men with studied elegance. At Oxford, the undergraduate's newest idea was to wear a decorative stripe down the side-seam of the trousers. This fashion came from America, and when Mr Hennessey came over to play at Wimbledon, he appeared on Court No. 1 in white flannel trousers with black stripes down the sides. Another young American caused a sensation at

For instructions for knitting the pullover on the right, see foot of page 160.

53

three buttons and jetted pockets the sleeves had turned-back cuffs. The Prince of Wales and Mr Austin Chamberlain each had one. Another accessory only to be found in very smart circles was a revived fashion for carrying an evening dress walking stick made of Malacca cane with a plain, gold or ivory top.

1929

In 1929 a party was formed which called itself 'The Men's Dress Reform Party'. Its sole aim was 'to discuss the means whereby men may reform their clothes with as much profit to health and appearance as women have recently achieved'.

At the first meeting the signatories included such famous names as The Very Reverend W. R. Inge, CVO, Dean of St Paul's; Dr C. W. Saleeby, President of the Sunlight League; Mr Richard Sickert, artist; Mr Ernest Thesiger, actor; Dr Leonard Williams, physician and author; Dr Alfred C. Jordan, CBE, acting Honorary Secretary; Mr Guy Kendall, headmaster of University College School. The first object of man's apparel to come under attack was his business suit: 'boring, uneventful, uncomfortable and tedious'. It was felt that trousers could be abolished altogether, and men could revert to either knee-breeches or shorts. Many attacks were made on trousers, especially by the Dean of St Paul's, who thought them ugly and unhygienic. Because trousers hid the natural line of the limbs, they were considered unaesthetic; because they restricted the legs and were often too hot to wear in summer they were thought uncomfortable, and because they were stuffy and dust collected in the turn-ups they were labelled unhygienic. Mr Guy Kendall and Mr Richard Sickert were in favor of replacing trousers with some sort of kilt. This would be a romantic and exciting garment for a man to wear: 'the Highland dress is a goodly sight: give a man the dress of a hero and he walks proudly in the light; clothe him in many a modern suit and he creeps in the shadows.'

One of the bitterest cries of the modern reformer was aimed at the tight collar. Mr Bernard Shaw, as was well known, had all his life been a consistent critic of the white collar. He inveighed against what he termed 'the white cliffs of Old England's necks'. The Dean of St Paul's disliked the collar and tie combination, and pleading for freer necks thought that the tie should be sacrificed altogether, or if the tie were used, it should be a hanging tie with the knot much lower than at present, when it could be worn with a Byron collar. A loose-fitting blouse of silky material could be worn instead of the shirt. Many ridiculed the Dean, and remarked sarcastically: 'is not example better than precept? If he would bare his neck with a Byronic

Wimbledon by wearing flannel knickerbockers and jazzy stockings.

Evening dress clothes had also achieved a remarkable degree of decoration. The white bow tie, which was smaller this year, had acquired a narrow black edge; the white dress scarf had been checked with black and white or had figured bars at both ends. Some smart men had jewelled, and what appeared to be platinum, buttons on their waistcoats. It also seemed that man had at last realized that it was considerably better to wear a waistcoat that had a line gently dipping down at the front rather than one which had a straight line at the base. This was particularly so for the fat man, for 'look at a fat man in a double-breasted dress waistcoat with a straight line at the base: the picture is that of a jelly trying to escape from a mould!'

Astrakhan now decorated the collar and lapels of the shapely evening dress overcoat, and in addition to the

MERE MAN in UNIFORM

By Dr. A. C. JORDAN

(From "New Health" by courtesy of the Editor).

A woman's "Ideal" uniform for soldiers—not Ouida's "Guardsman" but Dr. Marian Thornett's.

How Dr. Jordan would dress our Telegraph Boys.

FOR THOUSANDS of years men have been marshalled and drilled. Since the dawn of history, and, no doubt, before, nations have struggled for the upper hand; and it has been the men that have borne the brunt of the fighting while the women have borne the fighters of the next generation. Each nation has had its army and each soldier has worn his nation's uniform, whether war-paint or khaki. Without a uniform an army would be little better than a mob.

THE SOLDIER'S LOT.

But need a soldier be swathed in thick, close-fitting cloth, leaving no outlet for his pent-up vapours? The Army Council, I am glad to know, is at last beginning to realise the need for reform and is to consider recommendations that have reached it "from within." How far will these reforms go? Will the Army Council dare to go back 2,000 years and clothe the soldiers as Julius Cæsar had them clad—and as Hannibal had them clad for the arduous journey across the Alps? Dr. Marian Thornett has designed an "ideal" uniform for marching, and I cordially invite the Army Council to adopt it as the healthy ideal and to approach it as nearly as they dare. If an army is to be healthy and efficient, it must live and work under the best conditions. Dr. Thornett's uniform consists of a cotton tunic and shorts with shoes (or sandals) and a cloak of waterproof material to act as a windscreen in cold weather and as a ground sheet when required. In cold weather the cotton tunic and shorts are worn as underclothing with a similar suit (tunic and shorts) of a woollen material over them.

THE POLICEMAN.

Whenever there is a spell of hot weather the plight of the policemen excites the pity of the man (and woman) in the street. *Must* they wear those terribly thick clothes and those hard helmets and chin-straps? And with policemen rank park-keepers. The difficulties in the way of reform are not quite so easily overcome as in the case of the soldiers. Our policemen are unarmed (except with the baton), and must be ready for a rough-and-tumble with an ugly customer at any time. A uniform of a flimsy material, suitable for hot weather, might be torn off the policeman's back in such an encounter. The helmet, while affording some slight protection in case of attack, has a moral effect inasmuch as it adds inches to the (apparent) height of its wearer and gives him a more formidable appearance than he would have in a flat hat such as is worn by superior officers and by the armed police of other countries; a gun is, in itself, a begetter of respect!

Still, when all these matters have been taken into account, there is a good deal of relief that could safely be provided for policemen in hot weather. The summer uniform could be made of a strong washable material; this would be very much less thick and heavy than the serge now in use, and would afford all the protection necessary in case of attack; and if a helmet is considered essential it could be made of loosely-woven straw such as is actually worn by the police in some towns.

THE POSTMAN.

For the last three years the postmen have begged for permission to wear open-neck shirts during hot weather; each year this has been refused by the Postmaster-General on the ground that such a reform would detract from the smart appearance of uniform that is associated—in the public mind —with efficiency. What an argument for perpetuating an unhealthy and unsuitable dress! The Postmaster-General and his advisers are clearly not in touch with to-day's outdoor conditions; except in Government and City offices and behind the counters of shops and stores, men of all classes are now free to adopt the open neck, and thousands do so without any suggestion that the style is a slovenly one; if it looks slovenly that is the wearer's own fault. The postman's dress is an ordinary lounge suit; it is a " uniform " only in the sense that it is made of a thick serge such as few private citizens would care to wear, and that it has a border of red and a special hat. Far better would it be for postmen to wear washable suits made of a strong blue " holland " and designed for perfect freedom at the neck. There could be a red border as at present. The overcoats at present provided would furnish the warmth needed in cold weather; a scarf could be added if desired.

TELEGRAPH BOYS.

In hot weather telegraph boys suffer even more than postmen (who have permission to leave off the waistcoat), for the boys' thick serge uniform is applied closely to the body from neck to ankle; those who cycle have to clamp their trousers round the ankles, thus cutting off the last chance of body ventilation. This serge suit cannot be worn without a complete layer of underclothing. The only way to a little relief is by the untidy expedient of leaving the upper buttons of the tunic undone, displaying a not too sightly shirt. Why not give the boy a washable suit with zipp fastening for the neck, so that it can be thrown open as far as desired without loss of neatness, and open at the knees so that he can be healthy and free? No cyclist messenger should be asked to wear trousers; they are utterly unsuitable. As with postmen, the red border to the blue holland could be retained, and the complete uniform could present a far neater and smarter appearance than the present mummy-like garb. In cold weather the overcoat gives all the warmth necessary; in the case of cyclists, however, a woolly cardigan (blue with red border) might be considered; it would be far more suitable, and would be worn over the uniform.

PORTERS.

Scene: A railway terminus in August; taxis arriving in dozens, all laden with heavy trunks; porters struggling with them, sweating profusely into thick and filthy corduroys; even the (wholly unnecessary) waistcoats have long sleeves. Why cannot porters have brown washable overall suits as (for instance) in Sweden at the steamer piers? Knee-caps and shoulder-pads can be added.

collar and expose his knees in shorts, no more would the unjust dub him as the "gloomy Dean" but rather "the gay Dean".'

The substitution of jumpers and cardigans for waistcoats as being more informal and comfortable to wear was put forward by Mr Thesiger. He also attacked unnecessary buttons and ridiculous pockets. But Mr Thesiger himself was criticized: 'by dispensing with the pockets one would have to carry around . . . a handbag.'

Although opinions differed over these proposed reforms, the majority of people was united in agreement that shorts were certainly the most suitable nether garment for sporting purposes, and wished that they could soon be adopted for tennis, walking and cycling. This vital reform was already being fiercely fought on the continent, where the hot weather—92°F in Paris—

made it an increasing necessity to discard some of one's clothing in summer. They discovered that no man looked a hero in braces, and as these could not easily be discarded the French were asking the reformers for 'tight-fitting trousers that needed no braces or belt, and a really chic shirt'. In Germany a craze for nudism had developed. This 'bathing in sunlight' was held to be a very healthy activity, and it was hoped by some that the craze would reach England, and that people would be less afraid of revealing their bodies.

It was clear that The Men's Dress Reform Party was not a young man's party: the young dandies did not regard a collar stud as torture, nor trousers as a tragedy, and actually liked dressing up smartly. It was formed instead by middle aged and elderly gentlemen who wished to dress like little boys, for substitute shorts for

A glimpse of
experimental male modes
at a Dress Reform Dance.

trousers and you suggest juveniles, or wear sandals or the sandal-shaped shoes, which were considered healthier and more comfortable than ordinary shoes, and you go back to school! It was ironic that little boys wished avidly to be clad like their fathers, while older men lost all their dignity when imitating the dress of schoolboys.

Amongst the hatters, however, it was the younger generation who were causing some resentment; they had taken to walking down the street hatless. Hats were considered no longer necessary except as protection against rain or excessive sun. But if a man did not wear or even carry a hat, how was he to salute a lady? Such a decay in dress observances was inevitably followed by a lapse in morals. Some young men nowadays had hair 'which would wave in the wind if it were not securely held down by cosmetics'. Some women complained that men did not want to have their hair cut regularly. 'It adds years to his age and gives him an ungroomed appearance, in spite of his very well-cut clothes. By the time his hair brushes the edge of his coat collar at the back, I feel absolutely frantic.'

Women, on the other hand, were copying men's 'discarded' styles, and had started to use their husband's tailors. Naturally the tailors were encouraging this trend—'the new masculine woman is good for trade, as she wants man-made tailored suits.' The latest items of masculine attire adopted by women were gaiters. Women were wearing them right up and over the knees, for golf, a ride in the car or a tramp in the country.

The Reverend J. Hardwick, a disciple of Bernard Shaw's views, said, 'The chief object of apparel is sex-appeal. Clothes were meant to attract the opposite sex. Man now loves decorative clothes as much as women. Perhaps women nowadays are forced to adopt male attire in order to attract a man: men have stolen women's methods of attraction. In due course of time it will perhaps happen that the female will become the dominant sex, and openly select its partner. Then women will go about in shabby black while men wear pink and magenta.' In 1929, however, man tended to assume his brightest plumes when women meant least to him: on the hunting field, on the golf course, at rugger or football matches, or whenever he had the occasion to don a blazer.

Man's evening dress was the final piece of his wardrobe to be attacked by the reformer. Dr Jordan suggested that a more suitable outfit for dancing could be composed of a pair of satin knee-breeches, silk stockings and buckled shoes; an artificial silk or satin blouse with either a loose open neck or perhaps a loose tie under a soft collar; and over this a short-sleeved or sleeveless jacket. Warnings were given of the consequences that might occur to those wearing such a garb in public places. Only last year, it was pointed out, two avant-garde New Zealanders wearing belted trousers and silk shirts with a collar and tie were refused food in a London restaurant. 'It must be remembered', said the manager, 'that this is the West End and not the seaside.'

To replace the rather formal evening dress overcoat, some young men in 1929 were doing their best to revive the good old days of 1829 by affecting cloaks in velvet or corduroy. They insisted that the cloak was more graceful and convenient than an overcoat, and that more people ought to wear it. Other young men had taken to wearing spats with their dinner clothes and even more were asking for backless waistcoats. The majority just seemed to want change, for if there were no change at all, how could there be any progress or excitement in clothes? Backless waistcoats could be obtained for the morning dress outfit, and the area of starched front on the dress shirt was reduced so much

that the remaining stiffness was only just sufficient to cover the vee-shaped opening on the front of the waistcoat. Perhaps the most remarkable reform of 1929 in the way of comfort for formal dress was shown, once again, by the Prince of Wales. He presented the prizes at the Boy's Club Boxing Championships wearing a gray pullover, a soft shirt and a double collar—with his dinner jacket.

In America, Mr Henry Ford, known as one of the best-dressed men, needed no advice in clothing matters. President Hoover, on the other hand—whose standard outfit for many years had been an almost patternless double-breasted blue serge suit, black or blue tie and a 'choker' collar—certainly needed to be reformed. After acquiring Boris, his valet, everything was changed. Boris perfected a system whereby, armed with exact measurements, he frequently ordered deliveries of clothing for approval. Now Mr Hoover 'accepts the new-fangled cuts without a struggle'.

For tennis, a one-piece garment comprising shirt and trunk drawers was invented, so that now, when the player indulged in strenuous exercise, there was no 'rucking up'. Mr Braeme Hillyard, the veteran international, made a breakthrough this year by appearing at a tournament wearing shorts and short socks with his white cap and shirt. Shorts were adopted, too, by the army. The discovery that shorts allowed greater freedom of movement and looked much neater than ordinary slacks had come at last. The shorts were cut so as to allow four inches to overlap the top of the puttee, and when one was sitting down they did not get baggy at the knees in the way that the trousers used to do.

From the continent the craze for the sport called 'sunbathing' became all the rage, although so far in England there were still clothes attached. The tendency had long been towards dull attire for bathing and swimming, with a regulation uniform of navy blue. Now there were marvellous swimming suits barred with huge stripes and jazzy effects. There were one-piece suits with shoulder straps and two-piece suits with a belt, with the top part in flaming reds, oranges and blues, for the most part striped with white, the bottom part, below the waist, being plain or dark-colored. There were bath robes and beach gowns to wear over the costume which were no longer made simply of plain towelling but were elaborate in pattern design, or brilliant and dazzling in color.

At the seaside the plus-four rig which had been popular last year was superseded by tennis gear this year. Man stalked in white flannels, Byronic shirts and white pullovers ringed with color at the neck and hem. With a racket tucked under the arm, the young blood walked along the front or sauntered along the pier for hours, and maroon, royal blue and boldly-striped tennis blazers gave rich color to the scene.

Finally, tropical clothing was finding favor in England. It only required a hot summer like that of 1929 to render it popular. At the seaside in Brighton a dozen tussore suits were on view all at once.

U.2.

A Patterned —

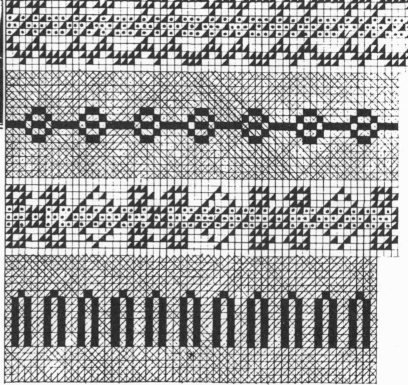

130 stitches, and work the first 6 rows in garter-stitch. Change the needles to No. 7, and work with the fawn wool in stocking-stitch for 5 rows, then the 1st pattern is started.

FIRST PATTERN

1st row: Plain row, 1 fawn, * 1 blue, 1 fawn, 1 blue, 2 fawn ; repeat from * to the end of the row, ending with 1 fawn.

2nd row : Purl row, 1 fawn, * 1 blue, 1 fawn, 1 blue, 2 fawn ; repeat from * to the end of the row, ending with 1 fawn.

3rd row : Plain row, same as the 1st row.

4th row : Purl row, same as the 2nd row.

5th row : Plain row, same as the 1st row.

6th row : Purl row, same as the 2nd row.

7th row : Plain row, same as the 1st row.

8th row: Purl row, 2 fawn, * 1 blue, 4 fawn ; repeat from * to the end of the row, ending with 2 fawn.

The next 5 rows are worked in the fawn wool in stocking-stitch, then the 2nd pattern starts.

SECOND PATTERN

1st row: Purl row, join on the green wool, and purl with this wool for the whole row.

2nd row : Plain row, * 3 flame, 3 green, 3 flame, 4 green, 1 flame, 4 green ; repeat from * to the end of the row, ending with 1 green.

3rd row: Purl row,* 2 flame, 1 green, 1 flame, 3 green, 1 flame, 1 green, 1 flame, 3 green, 1 flame, 1 green, 2 flame, 1 green ; repeat from * to the end of the row, ending with 1 flame.

4th row: Plain row, * 3 flame, 3 green, 3 flame, 2 green, 1 flame, 3 green, 1 flame, 2 green ; repeat from * to the end of the row, ending with 1 green.

5th row: Purl row, 1 flame, * 1 flame, 1 flame, 2 brown, 1 flame, 1 brown, 1 flame, 1 brown, 1 flame, 2 brown, 1 flame, 1 brown, 3 flame ; repeat from * to the end of the row, ending with 1 brown.

6th row: Plain row, * 3 brown, 1 flame, 1 brown, 1 flame, 3 brown, 1 flame, 3 brown, 1 flame, 3 brown, 1 flame ; repeat from * to the end of the row, ending with 1 flame.

MATERIALS

Six ounces of Baldwin & Walker's 4-ply Ladyship Scotch Fingering (fawn) were used to make the " pull-over " pictured on this page, 2 oz. of flame, 2 oz. of saxe-blue, 1 oz. of brown, 2 oz. of green, and a pair of No. 8 needles, also a set of No. 10 needles.

MEASUREMENTS

The " pull-over " measures from the shoulder to the lower edge 25 inches, the sleeves 21½ inches, width, at the lower edge, 41 inches.

TENSION

The stocking-stitch is worked at a tension to produce about 13½ stitches to 2 inches in width, and about 16 rows to 2 inches in depth. The whole of the " pull-over " is worked in stocking-stitch, with the exception of the first and last 6 rows (these are in garter-stitch) and the band for the V neck.

THE BACK

Commence at the lower edge of the back with the fawn wool and the No. 10 needles by casting on

■ · BLUE .   X · FAWN .   • • BROWN .   ▲ · FLAME .   ☐ · GREEN .

All-over Pull-Over

7th row: Purl row, same as the 5th row.

8th row: Plain row, same as the 4th row.

9th row: Purl row, same as the 3rd row.

10th row: Plain row, same as the 2nd row.

11th row: Purl row, same as the 1st row.

THIRD PATTERN

1st row : Plain row, join on the fawn wool, and knit for the whole row..

2nd row: Purl with the fawn wool for the whole row.

3rd row : Knit with the fawn wool for the whole row.

4th row: Purl with the fawn wool for the whole row.

5th row : Knit with the fawn wool for the whole row.

6th row: Purl row, join on the blue wool, 4 fawn, * 2 blue, 6 fawn ; repeat from * to the end of the row, ending with 4 fawn.

7th row : Plain row, 3 fawn, * 1 blue, 2 fawn, 1 blue, 4 fawn ; repeat from * to the end of the row, ending with 3 fawn.

8th row: Purl row, 3 blue, * 1 fawn, 2 blue, 1 fawn, 4 blue ; repeat from * to the end of the row, ending with 3 blue.

9th row : Plain row, same as the 7th row.

10th row : Purl row, same as the 6th row.

11th row : Plain row, same as the 5th row.

12th row : Purl row, same as the 4th row.

13th row : Plain row, same as the 3rd row.

14th row : Purl row, same as the 2nd row.

15th row : Plain row, same as the 1st row.

FOURTH PATTERN

1st row: Purl row, join on the green wool, and purl with this wool for the whole row.

2nd row: Plain row, 2 green, * 1 flame, 3 green, 3 flame, 3 green ; repeat from * to the end of the row, ending with 1 green.

3rd row : Purl row, * 5 flame, 1 green, 3 flame, 1 green ; repeat from * to the end of the row, ending with 1 green.

4th row : Plain row, 2 flame, * 1 green, 3 flame, 3 green, 3 flame ; repeat from * to the end of the row, ending with 1 flame.

5th row : Purl row, * 5 green, 1 flame, 3 green, 1 flame ; repeat from * to the end of the row, ending with 1 flame.

6th row : Plain row, * 1 brown, 1 flame, 1 brown, 1 flame, 1 brown, 1 flame, 3 brown, 1 flame ; repeat from * to the end of the row, ending with 1 flame.

7th row: Purl row, 1 brown, * 1 flame, 1 brown, 1 flame, 3 brown, 1 flame, 3 brown ; repeat from * to the end of the row, ending with 2 brown.

8th row: Plain row, same as the 6th row.

9th row : Purl row, same as the 5th row.

10th row: Plain row, same as the 4th row.

11th row: Purl row, same as the 3rd row.

12th row: Plain row, same as the 2nd row.

13th row: Purl row, same as the 1st row.

This completes the 4th pattern.

Now repeat the 3rd pattern, then the 2nd pattern, then the 3rd pattern, then the 4th pattern (only work to the centre of the 4th pattern, then work the armhole as the " pull-over " on pages 4 and 5), then the 3rd pattern, then the 2nd pattern, and lastly the 3rd pattern. Now the stitches will be cast off for the back of the neck ; this is worked in exactly the same way as the neck of the " pull-over " on pages 4 and 5. There will be 44 stitches either side, and 32 cast off in the centre. The patterns are carried on down the front, increasing 1 stitch at the neck edge of the work every fourth row, until the stitches number 60, but working the patterns all the time in the same order as the back. Repeat the 3rd pattern again, then the 2nd, then the 3rd, and don't forget to work your armhole increasings to correspond with the back of your work. Then

work the 4th pattern ; after this is done, leave that side and start to work the other side to correspond. When both sides of the V neck are worked to the same point, slip all the stitches on to the one needle, and work right across the 130 stitches. Now repeat the patterns to match the back of the " pull-over." When you have finished the 4th pattern for the last time the pockets are worked in exactly the same way as the " pull-over " on pages 4 and 5. Now continue to the end.

THE SLEEVES

Commence at the wrist, with the No. 10 needles, with the fawn wool by casting on 50 stitches. Work the sleeve in exactly the same manner as the sleeve on pages 4 and 5, but knitting the pattern all the time in the same order as on the main part of the work until the sleeve measures 21½ inches, or length required.

THE BAND FOR NECK

With the set of No. 10 needles pick up 124 stitches round the neck with the fawn wool, commencing in the centre of the V, and work round. Knit in ribs of 2 plain and 2 purl for 7 rows, but always taking the first and last 2 stitches together at the centre of the V. This will form a mitre.

Make up the " pull-over " in the same manner as the one mentioned before

A SUIT FOR THE SUN AND THE SEA

AN IDEAL GARMENT FOR HOLIDAY TIME
THAT PROVIDES FOR LAND AND WATER WEAR

This neat and practical suit is very original in style and a perfect garment for holiday wear, for besides being an excellent swimming costume it can be easily adjusted for sun bathing.

The upper part is made with a strap, which fastens between the legs and so prevents it slipping out at the waistline when worn in the water. By being made entirely separate from the knickers, the top part can be removed for sun bathing by just unbuttoning the strap and slipping it off over the head. A two-colour scheme of brown and orange has been chosen for this outfit, and a webbing belt is added at the waistline.

MAN'S SUN SUIT

MATERIALS

You will need 6 oz. of Baldwin & Walker's Ladyship Holiday Wool in brown and 5 oz. of the same make of wool in orange, two pairs of needles Nos. 10 and 13, also a bone button and a webbing belt.

MEASUREMENTS (after pressing)

The shorts measure from the waist to edge of ribbing 14½ inches, all round the waist 25 to 30 inches, all round widest part 40 inches. The top part all round the body (unstretched) 24 inches; length from shoulder to the lower edge 28½ inches. The stocking-stitch, worked on the No. 10 needles, produces about 13½ stitches to 2 inches in width and 9 rows to 1 inch in depth.

THE FRONT OF SHORTS

With the No. 10 needles and brown wool cast on 60 stitches and work in ribs of 1 plain and 1 purl for 10 rows, working the first row into the back of the stitches. Now work in stocking-stitch (1 row plain and 1 row purl) for 34 rows, ending with a purl row. Cut the wool and slip these stitches on to a spare needle while you work another piece exactly the same to match.

Next row : Knit across the work that you have just done, then across the first worked piece, making 120 stitches on one needle.

Next row : All purl.

Continue across all these stitches in stocking-stitch without shaping for 24 rows. Now commence shaping thus :

Next row : Slip 1, knit 1, slip 1, knit 1, pass the last slipstitch over the last knitted stitch. Knit to within 4 stitches from end of row, then knit 2 together, knit 2.

* The next 3 rows in stocking-stitch without shaping.

Next row : Decrease as in last decreasing row; repeat from * 8 times, thus reducing the stitches to 100. Now change to the No. 13 needles and work in ribs of 1 plain and 1 purl for 20 rows. Cast off loosely.

THE BACK OF SHORTS

These are worked exactly the same as for the front of shorts.

THE GUSSET

With the No. 10 needles and the brown wool cast on 1 stitch, knit 2 into it (1 in the back and 1 in the front of the stitches). Now knit 2 into each of these.

Next row : All purl.

Next row : Knit 2 into the first stitch, knit 1, knit 2 into the next, knit 1.

Next row : All purl.

Next row : Knit 2 into first stitch, knit until 2 remain, then increase in next, knit the last.

Next row : All purl. Repeat the last 2 rows until you have 40 stitches, ending with a purl row.

Next row : Slip 1, knit 1, slip 1, knit 1, pass the last slipstitch over the last knitted stitch, knit until 3 remain, then knit 2

together, knit 1. **Next row :** All purl. Repeat the last 2 rows until only 4 stitches remain, ending with a purl row.

Next row : Knit 2 together twice, and finish by knitting 2 together.

THE STRIPS FOR HOLDING BELT IN POSITION

With the No. 13 needles and the brown wool cast on 6 stitches and work in ribs of 1 plain and 1 purl for 20 rows ; cast off. Work 3 more strips exactly the same.

THE FRONT OF TOP PART

With the No. 10 needles and the orange wool cast on 2 stitches, knit 2 into each of these.

Next row : Knit plain, but increase 1 stitch in the first and last stitches. Repeat the last row until you have 20 stitches, then knit 1 more plain row. Now make a buttonhole as follows :

Next row : Knit 4, purl 6 ; turn.

Next row : Knit plain.

Repeat the last 2 rows twice.

Next row : Knit 4 plain, purl 6. Break off the wool, and with the purl side of the work (stocking-stitch part) towards you, rejoin at the buttonhole edge of the other 10 stitches and purl 6, knit 4.

Next row : 10 plain ; turn. Repeat the last 2 rows once.

Here is the suit with the belt slipped in position beneath the tabs at the waist.

Next row : Turn, purl 6, knit 4.

Next row : Knit right across 20 stitches.

Next row : Knit 4, purl 12, knit 4. Repeat the last 2 rows 9 times.

Next row : Knit 4, increase in the next stitch, knit until 6 remain, increase in the next stitch, knit 5.

Next row : Knit 4, purl until 4 stitches remain, then knit 4. Repeat the last 2 rows until you have 80 stitches. Now discontinue the edge stitches and work 76 rows of stocking-stitch without any shaping.

Next row : Knit 4, slip 1, knit 1, pass slipstitch over, knit until 6 remain, then knit 2 together, knit 4.

Next row : Knit 4, purl till 4 stitches remain, then knit 4. Repeat the last 2 rows 9 times (60 stitches).

Next row : Knit 4, decrease as before, knit until 6 remain, decrease, knit 4.

Next row : Knit 4, purl 21, knit 8, purl 21, knit 4. Repeat the last 2 rows 3 more times, keeping the 8 plain stitches over each other in the *centre* of every purl row. The decreasings will, of course, reduce by 1 the purl stitches on either side of these 8 plain stitches.

Next row : Knit 22, cast off 8, knit 22.

Next row : Knit 4, purl 14, knit 4 ; turn.

Next row : Knit 4, decrease, knit remainder.

Next row : Knit 4, purl until 4 remain, then knit 4. Repeat the last 2 rows 9 times. Now on the remaining 12 stitches work thus :

Next row : Knit plain.

Next row : Knit 4, purl 4, knit 4. Repeat these 2 rows for 20 times (40 rows in all), then cast off. Rejoin the wool to the neck edge (with the wrong side of the work towards you), and work this side of the neck to correspond with the one just finished.

THE BACK OF TOP PART

With the No. 10 needles and the orange wool cast on 20 stitches and knit 8 rows in garter-stitch, working the first row into the back of the stitches.

Next row : Knit plain.

Next row : Knit 4, purl 12, knit 4. Repeat the last 2 rows 13 times. Now work and shape as directed for the front until you have knitted 69 rows of stocking-stitch, ending with a plain row.

Next row : Purl 36, knit 8, purl 36.

Next row : Knit plain. Repeat the last 2 rows twice more.

Next row : Purl 36, knit 8, purl 36.

Next row : Begin the armholes and divide for the neck thus : Knit 4, decrease, knit 30, cast off 8, knit 30, decrease, knit 4. Now work up one side of the neck at a time.

Next row : Knit 4, purl until 4 remain, knit 4 ; turn.

Next row : Knit until 6 remain, decrease, knit 4.

Next row : Knit 4, purl until 4 remain, knit 4.

Next row : Knit 4, decrease, knit until 6 remain, decrease, knit 4. Repeat the last 4 rows until 9 stitches have been decreased at the neck (1 in every 4th row). While the armhole decreasings should be discontinued after 14 have been worked (1 in every other row), the 4 plain edge stitches should, however, be continued. You will now have 12 stitches. Work 50 rows, keeping the 4 edge stitches plain on either side of the 4 centre stitches in stocking-stitch ; cast off. Rejoin the wool to the neck edge of the other side, with the wrong side of the work towards you, and work to correspond with the side of neck just completed.

Hubby's swim suit follows a style very popular with men. The top can be made detachable if desired.

TO MAKE UP

Well pin out face down, and normally stretch the contracted edges of each part to good shape and correct size. Press well with a hot iron over a damp cloth, but avoid the ribbing. After sewing up all the seams, press them well on the inside. Work the buttonhole and sew the button into position. Finally, use a hot iron over a dry cloth and press the suit on the right side.

The 30s

The thirties girl preferred her boyfriend broad-shouldered, tall and with a soldiery carriage. He should look like Gary Cooper or Robert Taylor, dress with the flair and style of Jack Buchanan, and have the charm and old-fashioned manners of Leslie Howard or Cary Grant.

Virility was admired and effeminacy was scorned, but it was virility within civilized limits, not grubbiness, untidiness or smell. Girls preferred clean men with clean shirts, collars 'beyond criticism' and shoes well-shined. 'Perspiration control', fresh-smelling after-shave lotions and talcum powder to suppress the shine were approved of, provided the latter was skin-toned and did not show when rubbed in. Women did not like their men to have girlish hairstyles of any length, with partings in the middle. They preferred hair that was short and neatly trimmed, especially at the nape of the neck, with the parting on the left-hand side,

with hair cream or Brilliantine to keep all in place. The best-loved face was a clean-shaven one; a man should not be too hairy, and although he might be allowed a neatly trimmed moustache, if he had a hairy chest he would be obliged on the beach to wear a bathing suit to cover it.

The thirties man preferred his girlfriend to be feminine, soft and sexy. No longer was the tomboy of the twenties admired, with her straight-down silhouette, short cropped hair and short skirts. The girl of the twenties had gone, to be replaced by someone altogether more cuddly and feminine. She could learn from Mae West or Katherine Hepburn how to combine glamor and sexiness with the amusing or scathing comment (remember Mae West's: 'It's not the men in my life that count, it's the life in my men!). Some men liked and were amused by this and were able to give as good as they got, but this was by no

means universal, and many were frightened off by the girl with too witty a tongue. They felt that wit had reached such a degree of sophistication and artificiality that it was difficult to penetrate the web of mystery and complexity that women wove around themselves. 'The whole trouble', wrote F. E. I. Bailey, 'with such quasi sophistication is that no woman has the ability to proceed in a straight line. She shuns direction and simplicity like the plague.'

It was pointed out that if women were so devious and artificial in their behavior, then it would take twice as long to get to know them, and since men only had so many hours and minutes in their lives they must inevitably meet only half the number of women that they otherwise would have met, and that would be a great pity. But, countered the women, how could they be straightforward when men varied so much in the strength of their passion and came equipped with so many prejudices and preconceptions?

Hollywood got the blame for artificiality, for it was the filmstars whose 'looks, behavior, clothes, mannerisms, speech and tastes dictated the public's every fashion'. This influence may have been bad for women, but many men, especially those of a conservative nature, were much improved by it, learning confidence and poise and to shed some inhibitions. A 'nice' man of the previous decade would pride himself on knowing nothing whatever about women, and women knew that when such a man was in love he became dreadfully defenceless '. . . as defenceless as a little boy arriving at his boarding school for the first time', and that was how it should be. The love affair of the twenties had been a sentimental thing between a boy and girl; now the boy and girl had grown up and in the romance between man and woman there was less room for sentiment. They were not so much disillusioned about their lives as unillusioned.

Henry GARAT

The Frenchman who is to be Janet Gaynor's new partner.

Philip Slessor conducts a frank discussion
with Jack Buchanan, about—

Jack Buchanan and Tho

Margot Grahame

JACK BUCHANAN was once a chorus-
dancer. He came from Glasgow; he has
thick black hair, a kindly, humorous
smile, and long, loose limbs that are so
uncannily cunning in the dance. And he has
risen from the chorus to the front rank of world
comedians; he has produced his own stage and
screen productions, his own plays and films, and
gained a reputation wherever happy comedy
brings laughter to the world.

He works in an office above the Prince of
Wales Theatre, in London. It is a peculiar
office, in that it is round. Round all round, with
no corners for the dust to get into, and this
causes a strange and pleasing echo, of which you
will hear something later.

I called at the round office to see Mr. Buchanan.
A very lovely blonde passed me on the stairs.
She had been having an audition. . . . We
would, I thought, talk of blondes. I was shown
in to Mr. Buchanan. We drank tea.

" Talking of blondes, Mr. Buchanan," said I.

" We weren't," said Mr. Buchanan.

" No, but I got an Idea as I came in. Passed
the Idea, in fact. She was walking downstairs."

" I see," said Mr. Buchanan. " H'm. Yes. A
very pretty girl. You were saying? "

" I was going to say, ' Please tell me something
about Jeanette MacDonald.' "

" Well, in the first place, she isn't what you

Film Pictorial, May 13, 1933

66

Blondes

Jeanette MacDonald

Anna Neagle

call a blonde. That's to say, she hasn't got ordinary fair hair. She has——" Mr. Buchanan thought for a few moments, his blue eyes considering the round ceiling—" she has the most marvellous flaming red-gold hair you ever saw in your life. She's a wonderful girl. I loved working with her." Jack, you will doubtless remember, starred with Jeanette in *Monte Carlo*.

"Paramount sent for me to go to Hollywood specially to play with Jeanette," said Jack. "The script had been written up for the two of us and we thoroughly enjoyed making the picture! I'd love to make another one with Jeanette. Hope to, one day, if we can get the right story. Rather a different type of plot from my usual work, but great fun to do."

"And, talking some more about blondes, what about Anna Neagle?"

"A wonderful girl," said Mr. Buchanan. "She came up here for a chorus job in *Stand Up and Sing*. Just a chorus job. But when she came into the room, I thought to myself, 'She has that certain something.' I remembered her from the chorus in New York, too. I don't suppose I'd ever said more than 'Good afternoon' to her during that show, but I remembered when I came to think of it, that she had done her work joyously and well, and so I asked her would she care to give me an audition for a bigger part. Anna said, 'Oh, Mr. Buchanan,' or something like that. She turned out wonderfully, both in *Stand Up and Sing* and *Goodnight Vienna*. And the best of it all is that she's

completely unspoiled. Why, she—she just doesn't believe it!"

At this juncture, I discovered that by standing in a certain position in Mr. Buchanan's round office the wall echoed everything I said in an odd and mirth-provoking manner. I pointed this out to Jack and we spent some minutes taking it in turns to stand "on the spot" and shout "Oi" and "Ha!" and "Hallo!" When we settled down to work again, the talk had switched to Margot Grahame. Blondes again!

"Notice how she does her hair nowadays?" said Jack, with pride. "I had something to do with that. When I'd tested her and chosen her to play with Elsie Randolph and myself in *Yes, Mr. Brown*, I noticed that her hair was done over her ears. I had a peep underneath and found a very lovely line of neck and a very charming little pair of ears. 'Let's give the filmgoers a break, shall we, Margot?' I said. So we had her coiffure altered so that it revealed that lovely neckline and those two ears. We talked of Elsie Randolph, the supremely

clever little artiste who, Jack can claim, is his own discovery. He took her out of the chorus of a show and gave her a part in *Toni*. His confidence in her has been fully justified. "For," says Jack, "Elsie simply can't do a wrong thing once she gets on the stage or the set."

Then quietly Jack told me that he had discovered a girl out of whom he believes that one day he will be able to make a star. This was interesting. I was all alert. News, indeed! And, very cautiously, I said, "It would, I suppose, be indiscreet to ask her name?"

"It would. Frightfully," came the reply. I cast my eye eagerly round the photographs on the wall. "To darling Jack." "All the luck in the world to you, Jack dear." And so on. Mr. Buchanan laughed indulgently. "No use. She isn't there. She's the daughter of two very old friends of mine. I've known her ever since she was so high"—indicating with the flat of his hand a point some twelve inches from the floor. "She's only a kid, even now. A darling little brunette, with the most extraordinary face.

"I mean, she does not conform to any standard of classical beauty; yet I dare swear that, were I to slip one single momentary close-up of that face on the screen, no one in the audience would easily forget the thrill of that picture.

"She's very nervous, at present. I had the deuce of a job to get her to take a test. She was so very frightened!"

Well, there you have it. The Dark Unknown is to have a small part in a Jack Buchanan film as soon as possible. Then . . . who knows? An unknown little girl may suddenly find herself famous.

LONG, LEAN

A Chat about Courage as Portrayed by Gary Cooper and Leslie Howard

Above, is a charming photo of Gary Cooper—as himself. On the right, you see him as Lieutenant William McGregor, of the 41st Regiment of Bengal Lancers

Don't miss seeing Gary with Anna Sten in "The Wedding Night." If you admire these two stars, you'll simply love this film

WOMEN despise cowardice. Conversely, courage, among all masculine characteristics, gains most admiration and applause from the female of the human species, even though she suffer agonies of apprehension when her menfolk display that deliberate disregard of personal danger which we call courage.

Proof abounds that courage, more than anything else, is certain to arouse a sudden flush of emotion and excitement. Frequently this fervid admiration is impulsive applause, superficial and illogical; for it is just as intense when the courage is acted, when the danger is non-existent.

Two of the most popular performances on the screen this year are perfect portrayals of intensely courageous men. They are men who value life as nothing when conscience and duty make their call; men whose every action thrills and stirs the deepest emotions of the heart: Lieutenant William McGregor, of the 41st Regiment of Bengal Lancers, in *The Lives of a Bengal Lancer* and Sir Percy Blakeney, baronet, of London's clubland, in *The Scarlet Pimpernel.*

Both men's performances make you leave the theatre tingling with excitement and pleasure. Both fill you with a fervour of admiration for men who can so conquer the innate urge of self-preservation. And in both cases, though you may not realize it, the man who has mainly stirred your emotions and extracted your applause is the scenario writer. He has simply been supported by excellent acting.

Leslie Howard and Gary Cooper are both excellent actors, and both are very suitable to portray courageous men. Only in few other points are they alike. They both love horses. They both have been to English public schools. Both have married only once. Both are long, lean, and lovable.

Leslie is the more subtle actor, polished to a degree; Gary is more forthright, with an essentially human quality in his work. Leslie looks precisely right in his exquisite lace and ruffles, whereas Gary looks as if he would be quite at home sitting with your family round the dinner table. Gary would look as out of place in the dandy's finery of *The Scarlet Pimpernel* as Leslie did a year or two ago in the Westerner's check shirt and chaps of *Secrets.*

Gary is typical of the finest type of young American. Leslie is as little like an average American as anyone could

and LOVABLE

be, with his fascinating dreamy eyes; his lazy, whimsical manner; and his quiet, musical voice, perfectly modulated.

The two men's careers have been almost as different as their natural make-ups. Courage, mental, moral, and physical, has figured prominently in both.

Leslie Howard's blond locks first enchanted the ladies on April 3rd, 1893. He may be considered a "born actor," but he certainly was not born into acting. His father was a stockbroker, and Master Howard spent his nursery days among toy bulls and teddy bears, like any other kid. He was a completely normal youngster, and at Dulwich College proved himself an all-round sportsman. When maiden aunts asked him what he was ambitious to become when he left school, he invariably suggested a Surrey and England cricketer and a great writer.

He did neither. Instead he became a bank clerk, with Cox's Bank. He doesn't know why, except that his parents thought it a good idea. And it gave him the leisure to amuse himself with an amateur dramatic society and with horse-riding. They had been his keenest hobbies for years.

Then the War came, and Leslie went. He joined the cavalry and was attached to the 10th Hussars, with whom he served until, late in 1917, he was discharged as unfit for further service.

On returning to civilian life, the prospect of more banking seemed deadly dull, so, although it meant throwing up a safe and pensionable job, Leslie determined to try his luck as an actor.

Eventually, to keep him off the doorstep, a theatrical agent gave him the part of Jerry in a *Peg O' My Heart* touring company, at a salary of £5 a week. One or two other tours followed, but he

A romantic scene between Leslie Howard and Merle Oberon in "The Scarlet Pimpernel"

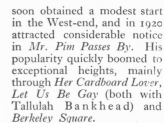

Photos from London Film Productions

You'd hardly believe these two photos are of the same one man, would you? Yet they are. Leslie Howard is a master of make-up

soon obtained a modest start in the West-end, and in 1920 attracted considerable notice in *Mr. Pim Passes By*. His popularity quickly boomed to exceptional heights, mainly through *Her Cardboard Lover*, *Let Us Be Gay* (both with Tallulah Bankhead) and *Berkeley Square*.

He dashed to and fro between London and Broadway, and built up huge followings in both places. Film offers that came his way were regularly refused, until at last he was tempted by the rôle of Tom Prior in *Outward Bound*, which he had played on the stage

This, though, was not his film début, although you will find it so described in the reference books. Soon after the War he had played the juvenile lead in a British silent film, *The Happy Warrior*, made at Croydon studio. It may explain why he refused Hollywood's bait for so long; he showed a similar distaste for films after making two or three of Hollywood's most mediocre talkies.

Continued on page 71

Gary Cooper

When one of the biggest studios offered him a long-term contract, at quite an attractive salary, he told them bluntly that they would have to guarantee to give him stories of which he approved. The deal fell through, and that studio barred him all round Hollywood on the grounds of his so-called obstinacy. No one would give him a job, so he told them some more home truths and packed his bags for England.

Here he was immediately signed on for *Service for Ladies* at £500 a week, the first time such a salary had been paid in British films.

Howard went back to New York to produce *The Animal Kingdom* on the stage there. It was an immediate success, so much so that every film company tried to buy the rights. But here Leslie had the whip hand, and he declined to sell the rights unless the buyer would also engage him as the star. He won, and made the picture with Ann Harding.

When the film was shown the producers swarmed round him like flies, all offering good contracts. But Howard had the courage to stick out for his own terms, which were that he had the final say about stories. Again he won. Leslie Howard's pre-eminent position to-day is due almost entirely to his wisdom and courage in refusing to sign the contracts offered to him. If he had accepted one of them he would to-day have been just another movie actor.

It is probably no exaggeration to say that that courage will have added £150,000 to his earnings by 1945 !

Gary was born on a ranch, belonging to his father, high on the Bitter Root Mountains near Helena, Montana. Dad was a Judge, and father and mother were both of English descent. The baby (they named him Frederick) was tiny—so tiny you'd never have thought he would grow to 6 ft. 2½ ins. And he was delicate.

Because of his frailty, Gary was kept on the ranch until he was twelve, when he was sent to England for education at Dunstable Grammar School.

He stayed four years at Dunstable, and then went home to sample American methods at Grinnell College, Iowa.

He was still terribly thin and delicate, and a motor accident damaged his constitution so much that the doctors said he would be an invalid for life. Imagine a youth of sixteen or seventeen having an ultimatum like that ! Gary determined to conquer his weakness.

For two whole years he lived and worked with the cowpunchers on his father's ranch, learning to ride, and shoot, and rope steers. His shoulders broadened, and his slenderness developed into lean, wiry strength, a triumph for his courage and conscientious application.

After Grinnell, Gary got a job as a cartoonist on the Helena *Independent*. On his own confession, his cartoons were not wonderful, and soon he was looking for another job. He became an advertising salesman, but three months later the agency failed. Eventually he was reduced to going from door to door as a photographer's canvasser.

When he was down to his last dime he applied for work as a movie extra. His height made him stand out, and, by drifting from one studio to another, he just managed to earn enough to keep alive. Finally he got a part in a flickering Western two-reeler.

Then, on June 13th, 1926, he answered a call for young men at the Samuel Goldwyn office, and with a hundred others paraded before the great producer. Goldwyn picked Gary because he thought he could develop something in the boy's personality, and despite the fact that " he looked the dumbest of the lot." Gary was hired at £8 a week.

He was sufficiently successful to be offered a long contract by another producer. When Goldwyn agreed to release him because he was bettering himself, Gary volunteered to return to make a picture for Sam when the contract expired. The contract lasted for eight years, but Gary remembered and kept his promise. The day it expired he presented himself in Goldwyn's office : the result is his co-starring with Anna Sten in *The Wedding Night*. Goldwyn paid him £2,000 a week, which is 250 times what he had paid him eight years earlier !

In those eight years Gary had climbed to the top rung of the movie ladder, and had to his credit such resounding successes as *Wings*, *Legion of the Condemned*, *Beau Sabreur*, *Shop-Worn Angel* (a poignant portrayal in this), *Lilac Time*, *The Virginian*, *Morocco*, *City Streets*, *The Devil and the Deep*, *Design for Living*, *Farewell to Arms*, *Now and For Ever*, and *The Lives of a Bengal Lancer*. And he had again heard the doctors say " An invalid for life."

It happened after making *His Woman*, with Claudette Colbert. He collapsed on the set when the film was finished and was carried to hospital. Then a retake was necessary, and, although his temperature was 103 degrees, Gary got up from his bed and worked on the shooting for sixteen hours.

The specialists decided that a long sea trip and a complete rest from films for twelve months might save him from permanent nervous trouble. Twelve months ! Just think what that means to a popular screen actor, who may be superseded by a score of new favourites in twelve months. But Gary realized it was his only hope of new health, and he resolved that when he did return to Hollywood he would win back his lapsed popularity (assuming it had lapsed in his absence) by acting as he had never acted before. He came to Europe, had a complete breakdown in Italy, went big-game hunting in Africa, and gradually won back his strength and his zest for living.

Even then he had not fought his last fight for fitness. After making *A Farewell to Arms* he fell and injured his knee, which failed to yield to treatment, and made him walk with a pronounced limp. It meant that his picture days were over if the knee could not be cured. He had surgeons from New York, and after some weeks' anxious treatment they triumphed.

What Gary's next bad luck will be goodness knows. But now, with a wife to look after him, and his glorious ranch " El Ranchilo " to keep him in the open air, the chances are his health will not let him down again. He will go on charming us with his rugged handsomeness, his honest blue eyes, and his economy of gesture.

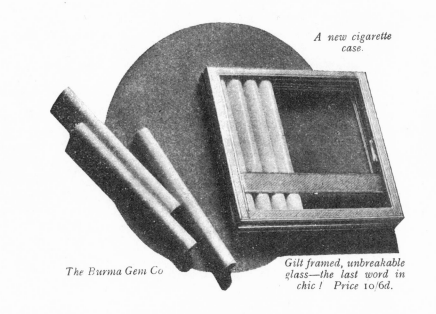

THE FREEDOM OF MODERN YOUTH

To-day parents are realising that engaged couples should be given every opportunity of getting to know each other before marriage. Long walks or cycling expeditions into the country afford such opportunities.

COURTSHIP

'It is very pleasant to see some men turn round, pleasant as a sudden rush of warm air in winter or the flash of firelight in the chill dusk.' *George Eliot*

It was advisable for a young man to be conversant with rules of etiquette if he wished to be successful with the opposite sex. Good manners were rare indeed, but could be learned, and should be learned so well that they became part of the man's very being, not something to be put on and off at the dictate of caprice. It was admitted that natural good breeding could not be expected of everyone. There was, for example, a way of gracefully holding the hat that every well-bred man understood but which was 'incapable of explanation', but many ordinary rules of behavior only needed a little thought, such as removing the right hand glove in readiness if a man saw a lady approaching with whom he wished to shake hands.

After a girl had made the acquaintance of a young man, it was quite possible that she might then ask him home to meet her mother. For such an occasion he should have a card (stouter than a lady's card; never more than 3 inches long by $1\frac{1}{4}$ inches in height, with town address in the left-hand corner and country address in the right), and two of these should be left by a bachelor if the lady was out. This elegant practice was rapidly in decline due largely to the regrettable use of the telephone, and the gentlemanly hats, sticks, gloves and calling cards that arrived in the hall were fast disappearing into limbo. If he had the luck to find the lady in, the young man should on no account look cautiously about him as if taking an inventory of the furniture, and in the course of any conversation that might take place he must, of course, steer well clear of any subject (such as religion or politics) likely to give rise to a heated argument. Finally, if as a result of all this exemplary behavior he became intimate with the young lady, he must never smoke a pipe in her presence unless he first ask her permission, nor ever presume to address her father as 'Guv'nor', 'old thing' or 'old bean', since however friendly and equal this might sound, it was inevitably bad form.

ASKING THEIR CONSENT

When asking the girl's parents for their consent to an engagement, is it necessary to say anything about marrying, or will it be necessary to ask them again when fixing the wedding day?—D. E. B.

WHEN you ask a girl's parents for their consent to become engaged to their daughter, it implies that you intend to marry as soon as possible, and therefore you will not have to ask their consent to marry her, when you are fixing the wedding day.

If they consent to the engagement, they obviously approve of you as a husband for their daughter, and unless they make some condition that you are not to marry until you are earning a certain income, or have reached a certain age, you need not formally ask their consent again.

You should, of course, consult them before actually fixing the wedding day. This is only the courteous and right thing to do.

HIS TROUBLE

I am a young man who suffers rather badly from blushing. Whenever I meet a member of the opposite sex or am brought into the limelight for any reason, I invariably blush. Could you please tell me a cure for this embarrassing complaint?—SELF-CONSCIOUS.

FRESH air, good plain food, plenty of sleep, in a well-aired room, and regular exercise should help you get over this trouble. Blushing is caused by nerves, and fresh air is the best cure.

You should also join a club and mix with other people. If you do this you will find that you soon get over being self-conscious when meeting girls or taking part in anything.

SOME ETIQUETTE QUESTIONS

May I pester you with a few etiquette queries? Is it necessary for a man to rise when others of his sex approach—when there are no ladies present, I mean? Is it correct to remove the lemon served with Russian tea, putting it on the side of one's plate? Are sandwiches ever eaten with a fork? Do men remove their gloves to shake hands with other men—and if not do they apologise?—A MERE MAN.

YOU do not "pester" me at all! I am very pleased to answer a mere man as well as my women readers. There is no need for a man to rise when other men approach; but, of course, he should always rise when a woman approaches.

No; it is correct to leave the lemon in the cup.

Sandwiches are sometimes eaten with a knife and fork, but it is more usual to use the fingers.

A man should *always* remove his right hand glove (not both gloves) when he shakes hands with anyone—man or woman.

A YOUNG MAN'S SIGNET RING

I should be most grateful if you would inform me on which finger it is correct for a young unmarried man to wear either a signet ring or any other ring. Also on which hand?—EDWARD.

HE should wear the ring on the little finger. It is generally worn on the left hand, but there is no special rule about this. He can wear it on the right hand if he likes to do so.

A YOUNG MAN'S QUESTION

I am twenty, working away from home, and for the last two or three weeks have been going with a young lady of eighteen who seems very much attached to me.

She speaks and dresses well—if a trifle flashily. When I leave her at night she does not allow me to escort her home, but says good-night elsewhere.

Not wishing to embarrass her I have not pressed for an explanation; but I believe she lives in rather humble surroundings.

Is it wise to continue the friendship? I come of good parentage and do not wish to be drawn into any questionable association.—PUZZLED PERCY.

I THINK you will do well to go warily. A girl who cannot take a boy—or who will not do so—to meet her parents does not seem a desirable acquaintance on the face of it. Especially as she is a girl who dresses "flashily."

Godfrey Winn SAYS

I Don't Believe in Long Engagements

GODFREY WINN— Young and Very Modern says —Get Married at Once . . .

THERE is a famous proverb —"Marry in haste, repent at leisure"—which has done more harm in the past than all the other proverbs put together! It has put all kinds of doubts into young peoples' heads that wouldn't have otherwise existed, it has made them go against their natural instinct and curb their natural desire—both being young, both being in love—to mate soon.

It has made them hesitate and wonder, and set traps to prove each other's love, and the traps haven't worked, or rather they have worked too well, and what might have been a very happy, successful marriage has in the end never taken place at all.

For if you marry at leisure . . . so often you never marry at all.

That, I know, is supposed to be the final proof of the supposed truth contained in the "marry in haste" proverb, but personally I think that, if it proves anything at all, it proves exactly the opposite. It proves that long engagements are a menace to marriage; that love that is made to wait too long turns sour; that the nerve strain attached to an engagement that is compelled to drag itself out over a period of years is usually too much for the average young couple.

After all, love is a very delicate thing, far more delicate than the bloom on a butterfly's wings. Those who for one reason or another advocate the need for long engagements seem to imagine that you can regulate love like a water supply ; that it can be turned off and on at will ; that it possesses unbounded reserves ; and that interrupting the stream by an

Your engagement is a public affair, and your love-making must take place in public

The fact of sharing a home will bring two people closer together in tolerance and understanding

enforced damming—as is what happens to an engaged couple when every meeting has to end in renewed separation, and, moreover, owing to the exigencies of time and space and work, even their meetings are often few and of short duration—does no permanent harm to the freshness of the flow or to its eagerness and strength.

And, of course, it does do incalculable harm. The freshness fades, the eagerness is turned into indifference, the power and the strength and the glory are frittered away in futile squabbles and misunderstandings that are not in their turn the result of any deep or dangerous differences in outlook towards life that would preclude a happy marriage, but merely caused by what the

Many a Miss Modern becomes a mass of nerves, after waiting for years outside the gates of paradise, . . . and breaks the engagement

modern school of psychologists call "nerve storms."

Inevitably, too long engagements breed "nerve storms," one of the main causes being the lack of privacy from which most engaged couples suffer, and which so often proves fatal to love. Once you are married you can close your own front door in the face of the world and what goes on behind that door is nobody's business except your own. True, that door may only lead to a garret, but for you that garret is paradise and the relief of being safely inside, away from everyone's gaping eyes, so enormous that nothing else matters. You are alone at last.

Engaged people are never alone. Never ? Well, hardly ever. Either you have to meet surrounded by each others' families or else by strangers. It is not only that your love-making has to take place in public, but also that your engagement is a public affair. Everyone thinks that they possess the right to give you advice, to warn you about this or that, to make you feel what a dangerous and hazardous adventure you are embarking upon in the near future. Still, that does not matter so much as long as it *is* the near future, but when you have to wait and wait and the chances of the consummation of your love seem to retreat farther and farther into the distance, it is not surprising if you begin to suffer from "nerve storms."

Cont'd on page 76

However much he professed to ignore the conventions of etiquette as taught to him by his parents, a man knew that he would create a favorable impression on his girlfriend if he observed at least some of them. The proposal, for example, although it would sound ludicrous if expressed in the high-flown terms and with the impassioned emotion that had previously been expected, should at least sound sincere and earnest.

If his proposal was successful, the well-bred young man would immediately seek the girl's parents and acquaint them with the news, hoping that they would approve of him as a son-in-law, and if he had not already done so, would reveal his financial status and prospects. He would of course make himself ready to answer any question her parents might ask.

The 'right age' for a man to consider marriage was twenty-five, when he could be expected to be in a suitable financial position, and the effect of the Depression was to lengthen engagements. Despite Godfrey Winn, writing 'Surely it is better to marry in the first great flush of love, even if it does mean love in a garret . . .', general female opinion was that a marriage was much more likely to succeed if it began in 'a nicely furnished little place with constant hot water and a labor-saving kitchen, and furniture which is all paid for.'

The restraints on behavior of the engaged couple were now largely self-imposed. Gone was the chaperone of former times, and 'mixing' was the order of the day, especially during sport and leisure activities. Mixed hiking trips were now acceptable, under influence from Germany; how could this be unhealthy

if it was taking place in the open air and everyone was dressed in 'unoppressive' clothing like shorts and pullovers ? The usual thing was to arrange a foursome of two engaged couples who during the day could be relatively free, though at night rules must be observed. A woman must never receive a man in her hotel room; it would 'place both in a false position and was a serious blunder to hotel etiquette'. However, such rules were not always strictly observed. At some of the new holiday camps there were rumours of 'goings on', and the worst of these could be blamed squarely on the now widespread knowledge of the means of preventing conception. Young men were increasingly unwilling to burden themselves with a family while they were able to enjoy themselves outside marriage. The young were bombarded with 'free love' literature from all sides, and told that marriage killed love, and that the knowledge of contraception gave women command over their bodies and equality with men. For the large majority of women it did nothing of the sort, of course, for they were still financially dependent on ultimately finding a good husband, and girls were

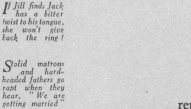

Being engaged is such fun, what with dances and jaunts to the seaside

If Jill finds Jack has a bitter twist to his tongue, she won't give back the ring !

Stolid matrons and hard-headed fathers go rapt when they hear, "We are getting married"

repeatedly warned that any man proposing an illicit relationship 'already had it in his head to leave her when wearied of her, and had no intention of being faithful to her.'

Older people were alarmed at the high number of broken engagements, for in their day only a ruthless cad would do such a thing, but now engagements were more of a trial period than the formal announcement of intended marriage. If everything went well and the wedding day was fixed, the man should prepare in detail for the event. He must learn his part well: he must know that at Church the clergyman would expect a guinea, the clerk ten shillings (50p), the beadle and the pew opener half a crown (12½p) each.

I Don't Believe in Long Engagements, by Godfrey Winn —— *Continued from page 74*

Time and again it happens that a Miss Modern who prides herself on not possessing a nerve in her body, becomes such a mass of nerves after waiting, say, for two years outside the gates of paradise that she simply can't stand the strain of waiting any longer. In a mood of black despair she decides to break off her engagement, and her family proceed to congratulate her on her " escape."

But how wrong they are ! For usually it isn't an escape at all, but a dreadful tragedy that could so easily have been avoided had the parents concerned allowed the young people to get married at the end of the six months.

That, in my opinion, is the ideal length for an engagement. There is plenty of time for the girl to get her trousseau with the maximum of success and the minimum of expense, and this applies also to the finding of a future home and its furnishing. On the other hand it doesn't allow time for doubts and reactions that are caused by too prolonged emotional frustration.

And when I get engaged—as one day I sincerely hope I shall—I mean to say to the lucky (?) girl—" Don't let's wait until I can keep you in the comfort to which you have not been accustomed—for comfort is so terribly unimportant compared with the miracle of our love—or until you have had time to find out all my bad faults and to forget my good ones —such as they are—but do let's get married at once while I can still see the miracle mirrored in your eyes. . . ."

The Husband

Bachelorhood, it was felt, 'could now be looked upon as sheer futility beside the happiness which could accompany a marriage where both worked to keep it going successfully.'

If the roseate glow had faded, and marriage had turned a leaden gray, advice columnists of the thirties tried to patch up the match. Godfrey Winn counselled that the development of a sense of humor would help: 'thousands of marriages are wrecked because one or the other party never laughed at the other's jokes.' It had to be the right kind of humor, though, not the 'warped' kind that some wives were inclined to use, making 'scathing remarks about their husbands before all and sundry, and dwelling on their weak points'. As far as he himself was concerned, Godfrey Winn had rather obtuse views of his own.

(Paul Tanqueray.)

GODFREY WINN

—Author of "Squirrel's Cage" and "The Unequal Conflict" gives you his Modern Views on Marriage.

I Won't Share A Home With My Wife

I WON'T share a home with my wife—for the simple reason that when I marry it is my intention,

if I can possibly afford it, to take two flats in the same building, next door to each other but entirely separate, and my wife will occupy one and myself the other. And I shall do this not from any silly idea of being different from other people, more "modern" or advanced, but because I honestly and sincerely believe that this arrangement gives a young couple the best chance of keeping each their own individuality and private life as inviolable and untouched as they were in their unattached days.

For why should two people, just because they are married, automatically cease to have any personality, any initiative, any existence, apart from each other? Why should they be expected to share their amusements, their friends, and even their thoughts, as if they were no longer two people but only one? Why should convention force them to spend every evening, every week-end, every holiday together?

Marriage under such conditions becomes, instead of the playground it ought to be—a playground large enough and open enough for the free exercise and development of mind and body and soul—a prison house, guarded by old-fashioned taboos and regulated by a time-table as unchangeable as the Law of the Medes and Persians. And it will continue to be a prison just as long as husbands and wives will persist in believing, even in this age of so-called enlightenment, that the first time their better half spends an evening—or, worse still, a week-end—out of their company and sight, the first step has been taken towards the breaking up of their married happiness. Automatically they suspect infidelity, mental or otherwise, instead of accepting these absences as reasonable and necessary, and encouraging them accordingly.

My marriage will never go "stale," since I shall take elaborate precautions to prevent it being restricted either by

I shall encourage my wife to fill her own flat with her own friends.

monotony, too-close proximity, or the fixed time-table of breakfast at eight, supper at seven, bed at ten-thirty, day after day, year after year, a time-table which is written not in ink, but in the heart's blood of so many husbands and wives. To prevent even the likelihood of this time-table ever coming into existence, I shall encourage my wife to fill her own flat at all times with her own friends, to dine out and spend a week-end away whenever she feels inclined and without questions being asked as to her company or destination, my only stipulation being that she will allow me equal freedom. And I hasten to remind those of my readers who feel that such a line of conduct is courting disaster, of the old and very true axiom that if you leave a cage door open all the time a bird soon loses its desire to fly out.

Again, my wife and I will never find ourselves suffering from "suppressed nerves" caused by the state of the too-close proximity, in which the majority of husbands and wives live their married existence. They are always near each other, day in and day out, until little mannerisms are exaggerated into monstrous faults. Tiny grievances are magnified into grounds for divorce, displays of temper and temperament becoming monotonously frequent. And so it goes on—to the terrible heartbreaking sensation of being shut up in a small airless cell, and they feel that they must escape from that cell and from each other, or else they will lose their reason. And, of course, in the end, they do escape, one or other of them, into somebody else's arms.

In the marriage I am planning, that crisis can never occur. At the first sign that either of us is getting on the other's nerves, we can retreat into the privacy of our own flats and shut the door and not re-emerge until the mood is past, *and we really want to see each other again*. Moreover, and this is a very important point, I feel we need never under any circumstances see each other *except at our best*. In that way the beauty of our courting days should be prolonged indefinitely. Ordinary couples have to face each other in the cold, plain-making dawn, and later across the breakfast-table force themselves to exchange polite platitudes about the weather and the news, but my wife will never encounter me unshaved, or at my conversational worst, while I shall never have my illusions about her looks destroyed by seeing her face powderless and, worse still, with cold cream smeared all over it.

Nor will I have to make myself polite to her friends, nor to my mother-in-law, nor she to mine. And when either of us has a cold we shall keep it to ourselves. And, finally, our children will live in her flat, cry in her flat, make a mess of her flat. They will only come and see their Darling Daddy when they are clean, smiling, and on their best behaviour!

One of the attractive new houses now available at Kenton

Where Shall We Live?

WITH the coming of spring many young couples are turning their attention to the all-important question of choosing a home.

At one time this choice did not offer many possibilities—it probably only amounted to the selection of one out of a long row of drab little houses in a smoky town—each house just like its neighbour in size, shape and character.

The hope of anything more attractive was ruled out from the start. The man with a living to earn must be within reach of his job. Therefore, being in those days without the travelling facilities of the present time, the average young husband was tied to the town.

There was no provision then for the family who, while not wanting to be " buried " in the depths of the country, still longed for room to breathe—for healthy, rural surroundings when the day's job was done.

The New Estates

BUT to-day all that is changed. On the outskirts of every big town there are growing up well-planned estates of detached and semi-detached houses and bungalows. These are delightfully designed and built on labour-saving lines, while, in many cases, each has its little plot of garden, and space for the addition of a garage.

Life on these estates involves none of the discomforts which are usually associated with the " ideal " country cottage ; nor are the house-owners cut off from the nearest town by a long, wearisome journey. Half-an-hour, or at the most, an hour in the train or ' bus is enough to take the working members of the family up to their place of business every morning. And cheap day tickets make shopping jaunts to town easy for the lady of the house.

And yet these delightful homes offer all the advantages of a country life—fresh air to breathe, sunshine, cleaner food and cleaner houses ; to say nothing of the joys of days in the open on the tennis courts and golf courses which are within easy distance of many of the estates.

They are, indeed, houses worth owning ! And ownership is within the means of most couples these days—thanks to the developments of the hire-purchase system.

Nowadays there is no need to pay out rent each week for a house that will never be yours. A small deposit and a weekly payment amounting to very little more, and, in some cases, less than you would ordinarily pay in rent, will ensure that at the end of a period of years the house becomes your own property.

The system can, of course, be carried out in several ways, but probably the most usual is by arrangement with a Building Society or Insurance Company.

Once the house is decided upon, the purchasers can set to work to choose, within certain limits, the decorations and interior fittings for the home that will one day be their very own.

No wonder that there is an added thrill in home-making when it can be done along these lines.

For those who want their homes to be on the outskirts of London, there are particularly attractive possibilities.

THE HOME

Home building in the 1930s was one of the decade's most important features. The period witnessed the birth of some great domestic architecture and many monsters. As an issue, private and public housing was a matter of urgent need and constant debate. The British government boasted of four million homes built between 1919 and 1939—a third of them council homes. The unprecedented development of the building society system came to the aid of the private house buyers by arranging for monthly repayments of loans for house purchase.

The theme behind the interior design and decor of 'modern' houses was 'beauty as an offspring of science'. Glass and metal were used extensively, with strong lines and bright colors in the furniture. The result was a common unified style, instantly recognizable.

"The day is not far distant when the majority of English people will be the owners of their own houses. The rapidly extending financial facilities for the purchase of such property have been among the outstanding benefits of this generation. Ownership, however, usually involves choice, with the result that the new order of things has created an immense public interest in house design. It is in our own interests to investigate the claims of the modern architect. He is our counsel and guide in this matter of house design, and just as we have come to appreciate the benefits of progress in medicine and engineering, so we are to expect comparable benefits from the training and research of competent architects. It is, indeed, necessary that the public should appreciate that modern design is not merely superficial embellishment, but the outcome of a knowledge of present day requirements, and the use of up-to-date materials in relation to these requirements. It is equally important that the public should realise that the best in housing, built under architectural supervision, is available to them without prohibitive cost."

Should any of our readers, during this winter, arrive at a determination to build a new house for themselves, they will find the process well set-out in an excellent booklet, *The Adventure of Building,* published for 6*d.* by the Architectural Press, 9 Queen Anne's Gate, S.W.1.

On the other hand, there are many people who are unable to build a new house because of their circumstances, the necessity to live in some particular locality where there are no building sites available—or where such are too far away from their place of business, schools, etc. (factors which, by the way, must be taken into account at the start in deciding whether to build a new house); or who may prefer to live in a real "town" house, an old "country" house, or one having an old, fully-matured garden; or again, those who are unable to wait so long for a new house to be completed. In this case, a search and choice of existing properties must be made, and when the choice has narrowed down to, say, two alternatives, the first thing to consider is that of neighbourhood. Is it likely to go "up" or "down" in value

House near Bristol, designed by **A. E. Powell, A.R.I.B.A.,** for the Electrical Association for Women and costing £1,000, including certain electrical equipment. The long room, which serves as dining-room and living-room, can be divided by curtains. The walls are of brick, rendered with cement and then distempered

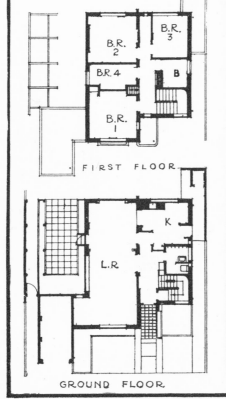

79

A modern bathroom designed by the architect of
Messrs. Pilkington's. It is in Wedgwood
vitrolite and pink silvered vitroflex, with
pink glass tiles

*H*ere is the exterior of the
modern house built and
decorated by Raymond
Nicholas. Note the unusual
treatment of the windows, and
the front door in frosted glass
and metal.

A House with Light, Space and Air
built in the modern style for £2,500

The house faces due south and is set in the garden by a terrace of ample proportions. This view shows the admirable balance of the design

DAWSON-THOMSON

It's *love* *at* *first* sight with these Tens

Things of grace, these Morris Tens with their care-free lines, and lithe low build (but an abundance of head room, nevertheless). Perfectly proportioned cars, all of them, immaculate, well bred, debonair. Amazing performance too ; a genuine 58 m.p.h., effortless acceleration, ardent hill climbing wherever wheels cán hold. And because these looks and performance originated at Cowley, you know for sure they'll last.

MORRIS TEN 4 models from £165
Lockheed Hydraulic brakes, Triplex glass throughout, and Dunlop tyres standard.
MORRIS MOTORS LIMITED, COWLEY, OXFORD

MORRIS

The CAR

Sir Percival Perry announcing the New Ford "Ten" at the London Casino. A minute later the curtain was raised to reveal the car, which was received with enthusiasm, by Dealers and Pressmen alike

The M.G. 1½-litre is a 4-cylinder (12 h.p. Tax £9). Overhead valves with high lift camshaft. Twin down-draught carburettors. Rigid box section chassis; semi-elliptic springs front and back. Wheelbase 9 ft., track 4 ft. 2 ins. Lockheed Hydraulic brakes. Four speed remote control gearbox with constant mesh (synchro-mesh top, third and second). Dunlops. Triplex. Prices (ex works): Saloon £325, Tourer £280.

Buy a car made in the United Kingdom.

The inter-war years were the period of *haute couture* in motor car design, with beautiful Mercedes, Daimlers and Bentleys vying for aristocratic patronage. Although the coming of the thirties meant the end of the vintage in car design, it also saw the elegant final flowering of the Hispano-Suiza, Delage and Bugatti, and the sporting significance of a new crop of initials such as ERA, HRG, MG and SS. This decade also saw, with the adoption of American mass-production methods, the true emergence of the People's Car, with Volkswagen in Germany, the *Traction Avant* Citroen in France and Austin in England.

All the sacrifice involved in saving up for a car was supposed to be well repaid in the improvement of bodily and mental health that ensued from being able to 'get away from it all' on rides to the country.

More people every year took to driving to work in London by car, and this was increased as more people moved into the suburbs, so that the traffic into and out of the city grew steadily worse. It was not helped by the recently adopted eight-hour day, which compacted the traffic into two rush hours, nor by the narrow winding streets which had never been designed for the car.

The New Ford "Ten" Tourer

Motoring Fashions of 1936

THERE is no doubt that 1936 will set new styles in cars. Streamlining, which was such a debatable topic a couple of years ago, will be found to have settled down to a rather more sedate dame than the flighty young thing which caused a furore at the Motor Show before last. The public decided then that it would not accept the designers' dreams of a radiator made in one with the car. Possibly the insurance companies had a hand in this, for even a minor accident with this type of construction involved so much cost in repair that insurance premiums were raised to compensate for the extra risks involved.

In spite of this, there was no doubt that the line of our cars had got to be made more "slinky," and the tendency could not be resisted of smoothing out angles and presenting a more flowing contour. When I visited Holland some two years ago, people there told me that the chief thing they had against the British car was the fact

The Hillman Minx for 1936 is an excellent example of the modern car—streamlining throughout and seating for all passengers within the wheelbase

that it was so square-looking and "boxy." They had been impressed by the graceful lines of the American cars they had seen on the screen; and undoubtedly, from the picture point of view, the streamlined car leaves little to be desired.

There were problems to be solved, however, such as the provision of adequate headroom in the rear seats, which could not be dealt with in an instant. It may seem a simple matter to build a body which looks pretty, but when you have to consider the comfort of the passengers, the task is not quite so easy. To cut down the back of a car and give a flowing line means the lowering of the seats, and, unless at the same time the comfort of the people who sit on them is forfeited, this entails a major operation.

Nevertheless, designs for 1936 reveal that a very satisfactory compromise has been reached. When Olympia opens its doors next month, one will look in vain for more than an odd one or two vertical radiators. More pronounced slope at the front, coupled with a boldly outswept tail, will be almost universal. The front of the car will be practically confined to a view of wings and radiator. All parts which collect mud, such as axle, brake

drums, etc., will be completely concealed.

To seat all four passengers within the wheelbase, or, to put it more practically, to seat your rear passengers in front of the back axle, has long been regarded as a desirable thing, but one difficult to accomplish, except on a car of considerable length. This, again, will be a feature of many 1936 models. It has been accomplished—on small cars especially—by placing the engine further forward in the chassis and so extending the body space. It is hard to understand why this should not have been done before.

Seating within the wheelbase gives a wonderful freedom from "pitching" in the rear seats. I can best liken it to the difference between a berth amidships on a liner and one that is at the front or rear end of the boat. You know how the motion is intensified the farther you get away from the centre. Many people who get a "seasick feeling" in the back seats of an ordinary car, find that they are quite free from it on a car with this new type of seating, which I regard as a feature of major importance.

I have stressed the appearance and comfort of the 1936 models, as I frankly regard them as being the leading points of the new cars. After all, we have little to grumble about so far as reliability and performance are concerned. Cars are to-day regarded more and more as means of conveyance and not as pets to be pampered and tinkered with. Most of us are content to leave the questions of oiling-up, brake adjustments and decarbonising to garages.

To return, for a moment, to this question of performance, we shall find the 1936 cars rather more "peppy" than their predecessors,

and here is the reason. Petrols from the best-known of the producers have improved in their anti-knocking properties so considerably, that manufacturers have been able to take advantage of this to increase the compression of their engines. As you know, the compression ratio of a motor engine is the degree to which the mixture sucked in from the carburetter is compressed before the electric spark at the points of the sparking-plug ignites it and causes the explosion inside the cylinder which actually produces the force to drive the piston.

Formerly a compression ratio of 5 to 1 —that is, the mixture drawn into the cylinder was compressed into a space of one-fifth its original volume before being fired by the sparking-plug—was regarded as being quite high enough for a touring engine, but there will be a pronounced jump up in many cases during next season, and 6 to 1, 7 to 1 and even 8 to 1 will not be unknown. If suitable petrols are used, however, such as those containing ethyl, or benzole mixtures, you will not be aware of anything save the fact that your car has more "life" and speed than your previous one. Economy in consumption may also be a feature, although in these days of reasonably-priced spirit one hardly pays a lot of attention to this.

You will have gathered from all this that the new cars are going to be a decided improvement on anything that has gone before, and their new, flowing lines are, I am sure, going to make us feel a little ashamed of our old models. Verily, the motor trade is as cunning as the dressmakers'.

Since its inception a few years ago, the sloping radiator has been adopted by most of the manufacturers. In the case of this De Luxe Ford, streamlining is got by a pronounced front slope

MORRIS BIG SIXES

SIXTEEN H.P.	TWENTY-ONE H.P.
TAX £12	TAX £15·15
EIGHTEEN H.P.	TWENTY-FIVE H.P.
TAX £13·10	TAX £18·15
FROM	FROM
£250	£265

EX WORKS

FATHERHOOD

Only in old-fashioned houses were domestic concerns still regarded as 'mysterious feminine rites from which man must be rigorously excluded'. The modern father 'rather fancied himself about the house', and to a man working all day in the factory or office a spell of cooking in the kitchen was a welcome change, and it was even a pleasure to lend a hand with the washing up. Sharing was the essential part of the comradeship that existed between husband and wife, and in true team spirit they brought up the family together, considering it their duty to educate their children as much in the home as at school. Women were surprised to discover that their husbands could be as gentle as any mother in handling even the smallest child, and that many were actually 'gifted' in this way. But after all, they reasoned, a chap who was always doing things with his wireless set got far more fun out of it than the one who never touched it, and this was just the same with baby. So the father took an active part in bringing up baby right from the beginning, and classes in father-craft had been instituted where Daddy could have instructive lessons and where there was a large doll to practise on. In special carpentry lessons he could learn to make a baby's cot 'from curtain rods and broom handles' or construct 'a serviceable little cradle' from empty orange crates.

By having a smaller family young couples could maintain a higher standard of living, and many were content with doing the best for the child they had, knowing that they could not give the same advantages to the second child. Some couples simply could not afford to rush into parenthood a second time. There were couples, of course, who preferred to spend their money on buying a car or other luxuries than on a second child.

During the decade the government became 'exceedingly anxious' over the falling population. The fundamental reason for this was not apparent but fewer marriages, later marriages, smaller families and emigration of young couples, combined with the increasing expectation of a long life due to advances in medical knowledge, all contributed to producing a population with more and more old people supported by fewer and fewer working young. Articles in the magazines encouraged couples to give their child a brother or sister. Great controversy raged around the question of birth control. It was no longer a matter of whether contraception as such was at any time moral, but to what extent it was right to use it, and what effect it would have on the shape of the family in the future. People now did not want to have as many children, and they knew how not to. There appeared for the first time the vision of a world with a static population. The birth rate dropped sharply as many wondered if the world was a fit place to produce children, with such an uncertain future ahead.

During the thirties fathers and mothers had found that with a little practice they could cope with the home and the child without the help of a nanny, maid or gardener. They enjoyed bringing up baby together as much as they enjoyed dancing or playing tennis together, and 'there was a much bigger adventure and excitement in it than in any of those things'. The family unit was a very strong and binding power during the thirties, and was made even more so by the Depression. The economic stress only bound the family closer together as it coped with the situation. Father made or mended their possessions while his wife knitted or sewed his or the children's clothes and preserved her own fruit and made jams.

I BELIEVE that in every man's head is the pleasant conceit that he is something very near the perfect parent, at any rate an infinitely better one than the man next door.

I am sure, too, that every man fancies himself as a father—not excepting the most hardened bachelor. I admit, that although I am not yet twenty-five, with a life full of work and interests and excitements and friends, yet quite often I reflect upon the kind of father I wish to be. For parentage seems to me a subject to which far too little attention is given.

We young men fall in love, accumulate sufficient money to marry and have children, before we have given half the time to the responsibilities of fatherhood that we devote to learning golf, or tennis or driving a car.

Because the potential father tends to hope for a son, rather than a daughter, I shall refer to "my son" throughout—though we are realizing more and more to-day that a girl can be quite as exciting as a boy.

possessive or jealous of the widening interests he will share with others of his own age, otherwise I shall be a failure and he will grow to dislike my company and resent my "friendliness."

Another thing I know. I must be ready to make allowances for the inarticulate stage through which every child passes, when he seems dull and uninteresting and has nothing to say at home. Whereas by treating him as a man when he is at the stage when a boy likes to be considered one, he will be given valuable confidence in himself.

I shall make a vow, too, never to laugh at my son's mistakes, never to comment on his *gaucheries*, moments when he falls, as it were, between the stools of adolescence and maturity, for to laugh then would be surely the cruellest and most fatal thing a father could possibly do. Yet how often is it done—even if unthinkingly.

Again, rather than force him into an uncongenial occupation to

The Kind of Father I Hope to Be

by KEITH BRIANT

Aged 24—educated Oxford—
Editor—Author, Journalist—
now writes of the most human
Career in all the World

I hope that I shall never fall into the fatal error of insisting on making a companion of my son. What I would like to do is to succeed in creating such a relationship between us that *he* made a companion of *me* when he felt he needed me.

The ideal—as I see it—is to create that intangible current which, when it exists between two people, gives the serene confidence that in an emergency each can call upon the other and know that he will never be let down.

Loyalty, each for the other, and security born of perfect understanding, that is the feeling I would like to foster between me and my son.

I am prepared—and I think every father must be—to resign myself to the fact that for the first two years of his life my son is bound to regard his mother as the be-all and end-all of his existence. But I shall endeavour to get an early foothold in his affections by taking an intelligently practical interest in the care of my son. Nightly baths and episodes with safety-pins will amuse me. I, too, will wrestle with them, and enjoy every minute of it, though I may be more successful at bed-time stories. I wonder!

I believe the vital years are up to seven, and that whoever has the influencing and training of a child until that age moulds him, to a large extent, for the rest of his life.

During that period my son's character will be forming, and, nurtured by the united love and affection of his mother and me, he will be more in contact with us than

at any other time in his life.

When my son starts to talk, then will a critical period begin. At this stage I know even now that I must gain his confidence or run the risk of a breach being formed which may never be bridged later. And that would be a tragedy. I realize that I shall have to try to answer sensibly and honestly the "million hows, two million wheres and seven million whys."

For instance, I do not believe in evading questions about sex. Whereas I do believe that frank, tactful, sympathetic answers to his natural curiosity will help to forge a lasting bond between us. Too many parents prate in tones of self-pity that their children "grow away from them" without having the sense or the honesty to see that—let us be frank about it—they have no one to blame but themselves.

Seeing myself as a parent, I know that during the years of adolescence my son will naturally gravitate towards me (naturally, too, my daughter towards her mother) for the solution of his physical and psychological problems. This I feel sure is going to be the time when all my capacity for parenthood will be strenuously required to avoid permanently warping my child's nature. Above all, I must not be clumsy in my handling of him.

Later, once my son goes to school, he will become an individual, an independent entity and then—compared with his earlier years—will, and, I believe, *should* grow away from me and his mother. I hope, too, that I shall not become

make him "stand on his own feet"—provided I believe he is sincere and not an idler—I shall try to subsidize him over the "difficult years" inevitable in certain occupations.

To my mind, when he becomes really "grown up," the chief danger to guard against will be failure to admit that he is. And still another common parental vice I shall do all I can to avoid, is laying down the law on the lines of "When you are my age. . . ." "I have seen so much more of the world . . ." Thus and thus.

Then, isn't it the most natural thing in the world to hope that one's children will share one's ideals? But all one can do is to offer advice, well-timed and sympathetic, and above all to avoid that pernicious bullying which consists in the parent playing on the child's love and gratitude.

Never will I try to mould my son's life or religion on my own pattern. Such handling is bound to foster a rebellious spirit and, who knows, lead to an inevitably sad estrangement between us, or result in a vague nonentity devoid of any individuality.

Finally, I hope that towards my children I shall always be true to what I consider to be the greatest human maxim : "Live and let live." Then perhaps I can hope to earn their devotion and enjoy a life-long, infinitely precious friendship, which I know I can earn in no other way.

HIS LEISURE

The jazzy frenzy of the twenties dance floor was replaced in the thirties by the music of Jack Hylton and his band, the dancers hoping, perhaps, that they looked like Fred Astaire and Ginger Rogers in the latest film at the Odeon, for the second great cinema boom was afoot. Super cinemas, showing super productions, were springing up in new sites on the edge of town or in new suburban developments, with their own cafes or restaurants to provide the means for a complete night out. A major influence in man's leisure was Oscar Deutsch, the founder of the Odeon chain. He wrote of his cinemas in 1937 (when he owned three hundred of them): 'It was always my ambition to have buildings which were individual and striking, but which were always objects of architectural beauty.... We endeavor to make our buildings express the fact that they are specially erected as the homes of the latest, most progressive entertainment in the world today.' Mrs Deutsch influenced many of the interior designs, gauging the atmosphere and social conditions of a particular locality and planning her decorations accordingly. Spacious, gold-colored interiors 'in impeccable taste' were considered appropriate at Hampstead, Haverstock Hill and Chester, while at the 'old and historic' towns such as Faversham the walls were decorated in half-timbered style. These cinemas were successful because they offered an escape from ordinary life, and could cheaply transport everyman to a luxury world.

By the thirties there was a wireless in almost every home, and as well as broadening people's outlook on topical events and politics it was creating a wider and wider audience for mass-consumption entertainment. There were those who voiced the view that the wireless and the phonograph were destroying home life, because people could no longer entertain themselves and relied instead on external distractions. Leisure in the past, for those lucky enough to have any, had been an escape into oneself, now it was an escape from oneself. By the end of the decade television had arrived as well, and there was 'hardly a sight or sound in the world that cannot be switched on and off at will'. It was feared that everyone's tastes were being standardized, and individuality lost.

In spite of uncertain economic conditions, ideas for filling leisure time and holidays of all kinds were available. Car owners went picnicking or took the children to holiday in a boarding house by the sea. Those without cars could hire a railway camping coach. These, for three or four pounds sterling, could be hitched on to a train on Saturday, taken to a siding near a beauty spot for the weekend, picked up again on Monday and taken to another siding, left there for the night and taken on again in the morning, and so on for a week. Cycling holidays were popular too. Father and mother could ride on a tandem, taking baby as well, either on the back or in a small side-car.

At home and in the garden the family man could pursue many hobbies—making and growing things for the benefit of the family. He built radio sets and garden sheds, or perhaps tried to create in miniature the kind of glorious garden that Beverley Nichols had made and described. Men were able to 'express their imagination through machinery'—by constructing a 'Flying Flea', the small aeroplane that could be built behind a suburban house. It was imagined that the sky over Britain would soon be 'swarming with these machines'.

Air and leisure sea travel were developing apace. Imperial Airways could now get you to the other end of the continent in only ten hours, and at the time the *Queen Mary* was launched in 1934, luxury cruises on modern liners cost about seven pounds a week. Some of the romance of the sea had disappeared however, for 'picturesque portholes are gone, and plate glass windows try to deceive people.' Many now travelled abroad who were completely ignorant of the rudiments of foreign travel. The traveller had to be cautioned in the popular press that it was 'in the height of bad taste to refer to victories obtained by troops of his own country over those of the country he is visiting', and that 'when in Iceland and eating raw fish, one should never tell the Icelanders that roast beef is much better, whatever one might think.'

There are a few important points to remember : (1) The tango is always danced on the ball of the foot, with the heel just off the floor, but under no circumstances should the tango be danced on the toes. (2) The knees are always slightly bent and flexible. (3) You should transfer your weight gradually from one leg to the other without jerking. (4) The rhythm of the dance is of a staccato nature and, this being so, you should step definitely and deliberately.

In this article I am describing the four fundamental steps of the tango, and if you can do these properly you have mastered the tango. The ladies' steps are exactly the reverse to those of the man. Exceptions to this will be pointed out during the description.

The Start

To start the tango properly, especially when learning, it is advisable to step forward with your right foot, and the lady, of course, back with her left, repeating this a few times, without moving your feet off the ground, and see that you are quite satisfied that you are swaying to the time of the music. From this position, when your weight is on your left foot, you start doing this with your right foot.

The Walk

By taking ordinary steps, each of them taking up two beats of the music, the same as in the balance of the start, you can walk as long as you like. From this you do

The Turn

This step starts with the left foot and takes up eight beats of the music, and when you have finished it you are sideways and in line of dance. The lady's steps are exactly the same as the man's, with the exception of the third step. The lady brings her feet together, when the man crosses his left foot in front of his right. From the walk, as the left foot is about to come forward :

(1) Step forward with the right foot, turning slightly to the right, bring your weight on to it, this step taking two beats.

(2) Continue turning to the left, take a short step backwards and in line of dance, with your right foot, bringing your weight on to it, this taking up one beat.

(3) Step back with your right foot, crossing it in front of your left, bringing the weight on to it, taking up one beat.

(4) Feet remain in same position, pausing for one beat.

(5) Continue turning to the left, step back with your right foot, your toe pointing inwards, bringing your weight on to it, this taking up two beats.

(6) Take a short step sideways and in line of dance with the left foot, bring your weight on to it ; one beat.

(7) Close right to your left, bring your weight on to your right, taking up one beat.

(8) Feet remain in same position, pause for one beat.

From this position, with the left foot, which is disengaged, sideways, and in line of dance, you do the next step, which is

The Promenade

(1) Step sideways and in line of dance with the left foot, bring your weight on to it, taking up two beats.

(2) Step with the right foot sideways and in line of dance, stepping over the left foot, bring your weight on to it ; one beat.

(3) Take a short step sideways and in line of dance with the left foot, bring your weight on to it, taking up one beat.

(4) Close your right to your left, bring your weight on to it ; one beat.

(5) Feet remain in the same position, just pause for one beat, and so completing the promenade.

From this position you may repeat the same step again with the left foot, sideways and in line of dance, or otherwise. You do the next step, which is the

Link Step

By the aid of this step it enables the couple to change the position from sideways and in line of dance into the original walking position. It takes up the same number of beats and it is done in practically the same way as the promenade, with the exception of, instead of doing it sideways and in line of dance, you turn gradually forward and in line of dance as you do the step like this :

(1) Step sideways and in line of dance with the left foot, bring your weight on to it ; two beats.

(2) Turning slightly to the left, take a short step forward with the right foot, crossing over the left and in line of dance, one beat, bringing your weight on to it.

(3) Step with your left foot to the side and parallel with your right, bringing your weight on to it ; one beat.

(4) Close your right to your left, bring your weight on to it ; one beat.

(5) Feet remain in the same position, pausing for one beat, weight still on right foot, and so completing the link step. From this position you continue with the walk, starting with the left foot.

The steps described may be done *ad lib.*, with the exception of the turn and the link step, which is only done once at a time.

For beginners it is advisable when learning the tango to follow this routine : A little balance, three walks, starting with the right foot, one turn, two promenades, one link step, and then repeat this sequence again and again until you feel absolutely certain of your steps, and then you can break them up and do them as you like.

Copyright by Santos Casani.

BEHIND the Screens at HOLLYWOOD

by Cecil Beaton

IT is an Elysium to visit for a holiday. The sun sparkles, the grass is lush, flowers bloom with amazing profligacy. It is all very gay, troubles do not exist, there is no mental strain or effort, and the childish exuberancy goes to your head the minute you arrive. Life is one big joke and, oh, the thrill of being in midwinter in this ever-summer climate. You can smell the orange blossom a mile away, food is paradisial : the avacado pears are the size of pumpkins ; drink is nectar and ambrosia ; the hotels are luxurious and cheap ; homes in the Beverly hills make you pine for love and domesticity. You feel incessantly as though you have just finished a champagne cocktail.

We arrive. Reporters ask, " Who are the six most beautiful women in Hollywood ? " In a town that contains Greta Garbo, Marlene Dietrich, Norma Shearer, Ina Claire, Joan Crawford, Lupe Velez, and Lilyan Tashman, how can a boy tell ?

A telegram arrives : " Will you dine with me. Please telephone my secretary, Granite 5111.—Mary Pickford." Oh, this is life ! We are escorted to the studios. For the ordinary human being it is as difficult to enter a film studio as it is to crash Buckingham Palace, but, thank heavens above, an official from the publicity department is taking this trouble for us, realising that if we are to take photographs of some of the stars it is he who is proudly responsible for the coup. Thanks to the official, we are not searched at the gateway ; we drive majestically past the doorman and soon it is as though we were undergoing the strangest, most pleasant nightmare. For one minute we are driving down a deserted street in China, with highly coloured stalls each side of the road, then, on turning a corner, we find ourselves in a war-stricken French village. Every pane of window is broken, trees are leafless and splintered, nothing much remains of the café except its painted sign. We drive along and unexpectedly come upon medieval England : huge castles, fortresses, turrets, towers, circular staircases, banners. On, on, round the corner is Russia in its hey-day. Our next crane from the car windows shows us a Texas village street, with wooden huts, the saloon bar where the well-known shootings take place. A few hundred yards within each other are Iceland, the Austrian Tyrol, India, Morocco, and Egypt.

91

Miss Anita Loos (Left), Mr. Wm. Randolph Hearst and Miss Marion Davies

Hollywood is one long eye-opener. Beauties abound everywhere. The clerks, soda fountain assistants, and shoe shiners are all unsuccessful Apollos. The waitresses and typists are Venuses without their coveted job. And when suddenly you meet the star whom you expect to find most beautiful of all, you may be shocked and amazed to find her extremely disappointing. She has a large jaw and a bad skin but the answer is that she photographs well and, in pictures, the waitress is, unfortunately, disappointing. It is her misfortune and tragedy, and on account of this she must continue serving chicken tamales, for she has not the railway fare back to her home where, in the old days, her aunt assured her she has a film face, that she was " made for pictures."

Most of the film stars are photogenique rather than beautiful. But there are exceptions. There is Lilyan Tashman, yet to have her deserved success on the screen who, though she is the outstanding personality, more beautiful, more witty, more hilarious, more sophisticated than any, has yet to establish the position outside Hollywood that she possesses in the film colony. But she will do it, for she is intelligent, determined, and each year improves in looks. Marion Davies, Hollywood's leading hostess, photographs " as is," without any of the camouflaging of make-up that is used to disguise the defects of so many of the stars. You are surprised to discover that the enormous faces that you know so well from close-ups belong to humans who are almost dwarflike in stature ; that Miss Gloria Swanson, Miss Norma Shearer, Mr. Ramon Navarro, and Miss Mary Pickford are all less than five feet in height. In this place Mr. Gary Cooper, a good six feet three, seems like a super being.

On, on. We watch films being made. A bell rings ; now silence, " Boys, all keep still " ; the cameras burr like moths'

wings. The heroine looks pained ; the hero ardent. The scene is repeated an endless number of times. Untold patience is necessary, and after a time we feel that however colossal their salary, the film stars cannot be overpaid. While they are making pictures they rise at 6 a.m. and, if through their day's work, retire at 6 p.m. But there are inevitable hold ups, and in order to finish the picture at the scheduled time there are days when work is not through by midnight. And now on to parties.

Miss Marion Davies orders a special train to conduct her seventy week-end guests up to the ranch at the St. Louis Obispo. A ranch it is called, but it is in reality a Gothic cathedral, an Italian renaissance palace, a baroque castle, and movie set, of the most utter extravagance, all in one. There is no describing the luxury and grandiosity. Guests can telephone through to the stables for a horse, to the instructors for tennis lessons, for golf lessons. After tea there is the thrill of seeing the animals fed in the huge private zoo. There are several bathing pools from which to choose, and a private cinema, where films not yet released are shown, and in Hollywood elaborate parties are always being given for some visiting celebrity. Miss Lilyan Tashman is certain to be present, brandishing her cheese-straw thin arms, claiming that everything is " done by mirrors " ; Miss Nancy Carroll will be very freckled and Miss Gloria Swanson, in black, will be eyeing furtively Miss Constance Bennett, who is supposed to be engaged to her former husband. Mr. William Powell, a very English American, is, of course, with Miss Carole Lombard. John Gilbert finishes a whisky and soda, and William Haines' wisecracks are received with thunderous applause. Gary Cooper looks pained and restless.

The days slip by too quickly. It is time to leave.

Now one cannot pick up a movie magazine without feeling homesick for Hollywood, where the sun shines so brilliantly, where every day there is every chance of suddenly coming upon Greta Garbo, Marlene Dietrich, Gary Cooper, Ina Claire, Joan Crawford, Lupe Velez, or Lilyan Tashman.

Ramon Navarro

FILM PICTORIAL

ALLIS HOUSE
ALLIS STREET
LONDON, E.C.4

Vol. III. No. 64.
May 13, 1933

Edited by CLARENCE WINCHESTER

One of the chief heart throbs of the year. Has been described as a "Second Valentino," but you needn't believe that. He has a distinctive personality, sleek black hair and a suggestion of smouldering passion behind those dark eyes. Has a drawling Bowery accent, but this doesn't jar. A rather curious type, in a way; an actor who sweeps you into excited enthusiasm or leaves you cold, wondering what all the fuss is about.

In "Night After Night" he plays the part of a gangster and it was this type of part that brought him to the top of the tree in "Scarface." Is an excellent dancer and has tripped the light fantastic in London; was engaged at a famous London club, where he met the Prince of Wales and taught him many new steps.

Born in New York's "Hell's Kitchen," one of the toughest districts. Was in Hollywood several years waiting for success to come his way. He's 33 and although a man of strange contradictions he seems destined to go on being successful, for he's just one of those natural actors who simply cannot help getting to the top.

Ida LUPINO

Stanley's daughter whose film debut you may see in "Her First Affaire" next week.

" MUSIC IS MAGIC "

Peggy Harper	Alice Faye
Jack Lambert ..	Ray Walker
Diane de Valle ..	Bebe Daniels
Peanuts Harper ..	Frank Mitchell
Eddie Harper	Jack Durant
Shirley de Valle ..	Rosina Lawrence
Tony Bennett	Thomas Beck
Producer Ben Pomeroy	Andrew Tombes
Señor Castellano ..	Luis Alberni
Amanda	Hattie McDaniels
Jim Waters	Hal K. Dawson
Theatre Manager ..	Charles C. Wilson
Director	Niles Welch
Mickey	Ed Gargan

A Fox Picture.

SURELY it is wiser for a famous film star to retire, leaving people saying " Why has she ? " instead of carrying on until they say, " Why *hasn't* she ? "

Diane de Valle, waning film star, cannot realise this, and carries on in a touring revue, causing it to " flop " and putting a young dancer and singer, and her sweetheart out of a job.

They decide to " crash " the film capital and their struggles to do so give quite a convincing peep into Hollywood life.

" CAPTAIN JANUARY "

Star	Shirley Temple
Captain January ..	Guy Kibbee
Captain Nazro ..	Slim Summerville
Mary Marshall ..	June Lang
Paul Roberts	Buddy Ebsen
Agatha Morgan ..	Sara Haden
Eliza Croft	Jane Darwell
Cyril Morgan ..	Jerry Tucker
Mrs. John Mason ..	Nella Walker
John Mason	George Irving
Deputy Sheriff ..	James Farley
Old Sailor	Si Jenks
East Indian	John Carradine

"TOUGH " old Captain January, lighthouse keeper with a tender heart, rescues a little girl from the sea, and spends most of the rest of his life saving the tiny mite from unhappiness.

The little girl in question is dimpled, be-curled Shirley Temple, who can dance and sing and mimic as well as most grown-ups ; rotund and jovial Guy Kibbee is the " Captain," and most of the picture has a background of sea and shore and the lighthouse.

You will find Shirley Temple quite enchanting in her sou'wester and her oilskins !

" FOLLOW THE FLEET "

" Bake " ..	.. Fred Astaire
Sherry ..	.. Ginger Rogers
Bilge ..	.. Randolph Scott
Connie ..	.. Harriet Hilliard
Iris	.. Astrid Allwyn
Dopey ..	.. Ray Mayer
Capt. Hickey.	.. Harry Beresford
Lieut. Williams ..	Addison Randall
Nolan ..	.. Russell Hicks
Sullivan ..	.. Brooks Benedict
Kitty .	.. Lucille Ball

A Radio Picture.

FOLLOWING the Fleet, and the appropriately fleet-footed Fred Astaire and Ginger Rogers through this light-hearted song-and-dance film is great fun.

The story doesn't really matter ; it is just a good excuse for giving us Fred and Ginger again, and Harriet Hilliard, a new-comer to the screen for whom you'll wish a big film future.

With songs by Irving Berlin, dance numbers more joyously exhilarating than ever by Fred and Ginger, and with spectacular scenes " afloat," you'll just sit back in your seat and laugh and be happy !

" THE PETRIFIED FOREST "

Alan Squier	Leslie Howard
Gabrille Maple ..	Bette Davis
Mrs. Chisholm ..	Genevieve Tobin
Boze Hertzlinger..	Dick Foran
Duke Mantee ..	Humphrey Bogart
Jackie	Joseph Sawyer
Jason Maple ..	Porter Hall
Gramp Maple ..	Charley Grapewin
Mr. Chisholm ..	Paul Hervey

A YOUNG girl longing for love, a disillusioned novelist who is trying to live deeply and truly—in the heart of the arid Arizona desert, romance and happiness come hand in hand with tragedy across the sands. . . . Yes, a " strong " film.

GOING TO THE PICTURES

" MODERN TIMES "

A Tramp..	Charles Chaplin
A Gamin..	Paulette Goddard
A Café Proprietor ..	Henry Bergman
A Mechanic	Chester Conklin
The Burglars	Stanley Sandford / Hank Mann / Louis Natheux
President of a Steel Corporation.. ..	Allen Garcia

THIS world of 1936—so full of mechanical devices, huge plants of machinery, and with happiness and tragedy personified by employment and unemployment—is brought to the screen in all its humour and its pathos by that genius, Charles Chaplin.

Mixing tears with smiles—sometimes broad humour—is the way this little comedian has always had of winning our hearts, and that he *does* win most hearts is certain.

Go and see this film. It will make you laugh ; but it will make you sigh as well— for the little man who sought a simple happiness, and for the dark-eyed girl waif who sought for it with him.

Although Charlie Chaplin still " refuses to talk," the musical accompaniment to this picture is so brilliant that you will hardly notice that it is, practically, a " silent."

" WIFE v. SECRETARY "

Van	Clark Gable
Whitey	Jean Harlow
Linda	Myrna Loy
Mimi	May Robson
Underwood ..	George Barbier
Dave	James Stewart
Joe	Hobart Cavanagh
Mr. Jenkins ..	John Qualen
Finney	Tom Dugan
Simpson	Gilbert Emery

HERE'S the eternal triangle again— but an extra exciting one, for we have Myrna Loy, of the tip-tilted nose ; strong, silent Clark Gable and vivacious Jean Harlow. Just a little misunderstanding between three delightful people !

" THINGS TO COME "

John Cabal ..	Raymond Massey
Oswald Cabal ..	
Pipper Passworthy..	Edward Chapman
Raymond Passworthy	
The Boss	Ralph Richardson
Roxana	Margaretta Scott
Rowena ..	
Theotocopulos ..	Cedric Hardwicke
Dr. Harding ..	Maurice Braddell
Mrs. Cabal	Sophie Stewart
Richard Gordon ..	Derrick de Marney
Mary Gordon ..	Ann Todd
Katherine Cabal ..	Pearl Argyle
Maurice Passworthy	Kenneth Villiers
Modern Mitani ..	Ivan Brandt

FOR colossal screen spectacle, for Mr. H. G. Wells' gigantic conception of the next century's living, and for superb acting and screen settings, you cannot afford to miss this film.

" THE MILKY WAY "

Burleigh Sullivan ..	Harold Lloyd
Gabby Sloan ..	Adolphe Menjou
Ann Westley ..	Verree Teasdale
Mae Sulliran ..	Helen Mack
Speed McFarland ..	William Gargan
Wilbur Austin ..	George Barbier
Polly Pringle ..	Dorothy Wilson
Spider Schultz ..	Lionel Stander

A Paramount Picture.

HERE'S the bespectacled Harold, innocent and wistful as ever, as a milkman with all his love given to " Agnes," the mare who pulls the rattling milk bottles through the streets in the early hours o' the morning. How he changes his milk round for another sort of round—ten cf them in the boxing ring—will make you laugh.

You will like Adolphe Menjou as the boxing manager, and Lionel Stander, who knows how to be " tough " and amusing at one and the same time.

Dorothy Wilson and Helen Mack provide the " heart appeal "—or, rather, part of it. " Agnes," the mare, provides the most, and gives quite the best acting performance. Must be very difficult to faint, with four legs to tuck under you. Yes, there are plenty of laughs.

" WHEN KNIGHTS WERE BOLD "

Sir Guy de Vere ..	Jack Buchanan
Lady Rowena ..	Fay Wray
Brian Ballymote ..	Garry Marsh
Aunt Agatha ..	Kate Cutler
Aunt Esther ..	Martita Hunt
Cousin Bertie ..	Robert Horton
The Canon ..	Aubrey Mather
Barker	Aubrey Fitzgerald

JACK BUCHANAN is transplanted into the " good old days," when knights wore armour, in the screen version of this popular and rollicking play.

The author of "Down the Garden Path"

Mr. Nichols's cottage is in the little Huntingdonshire village of Glatton, disguised in his books as "Allways." On the left is the author at the door leading to his garden, three glimpses of which are shown

I WAS up early that day, because it was a real Wordsworth morning, with all the roofs glittering in the sunlight and the smoke hovering in pale plumes over a thousand chimneys. And as I always live in Westminster (when I have to be in London) I pulled on a shirt and trousers and ran out to Westminster Bridge . . just because it *was* a Wordsworth morning and it was from this bridge that he wrote the sonnet beginning:

" Earth has not anything to show more fair . "

Surely, when I got out there, it was fair enough, with the barges ploughing through a Thames miraculously gilded, and a grey mist trembling over the Houses of Parliament Oh yes, the city did " *like a garment wear the beauty of the morning,*" and any self-respecting literary person would have repeated the sonnet in its entirety, and then have gone home to breakfast. But I couldn't do that because suddenly, across the river, I noticed a faint band of yellow in the gardens that lie by the side of the House of Commons. A faint band of yellow! And the Westminster sonnet was forgotten, and another Wordsworth poem began singing through my head . . you remember it? It ends with the exquisitely naïve lines :

" And then my heart with pleasure fills
And dances with the daffodils."

The ships, the towers, the domes, the theatres and the temples were forgotten —the noise of the traffic faded—the daffodils seemed to grow nearer and nearer, until they were dancing at my feet. But not the daffodils of Westminster—the daffodils in my own fields. a hundred miles away.

I took a step forward, to gather one. There was a shrill scream from a motor horn, and a grinding of brakes. Gosh . . that had been a narrow one! I *must* control this strange feeling of trance that comes over me when I see flowers! It landed me in a ditch in Holland once, in tulip time, and there was also a scaring episode on a cliff in Switzerland, when the crocuses were just beginning to weave a purple hem to the shrinking winding-sheets of the winter snows. We had better hurry to my cottage, straight We shall be safe there, and happy.

I am 35 years old, my cottage is 373 years old, and my garden is at least 1,500 years old, for I have found Roman coins in it, when I was planting snowdrops at the foot of an old mulberry tree. Yet we make a perfect trio, which shows you what nonsense it is

A BACHELOR'S GARDEN

By BEVERLEY NICHOLS

Photos . Humphrey and Vera Joel

to talk about "disparity of ages" as a bar to marriage.

For "marriage" is not too strong a word with which to express the relationship which exists between me and my garden. It has given me every ecstasy that passion can give. No mortal kiss can ever be sweeter than the brush of a dew-laden lilac across a man's cheeks at dawn. Nor has my garden given me passion only. It has given me a companionship that I have vainly sought in human relationships. Companionship, you say? But flowers can't talk! You think not? Well, of course, you can't prove these things, but if you could walk with me down my "crazy pavements" on a May evening, when the air is heavy with the scent of wallflowers, and the forget-me-nots are whispering together, and a tall spray of japonica slashes the fading sky like a brilliant epigram, you would hear enough!

Ecstasy, companionship, and wisdom too. . It has taught me the Continued on next page things in life which really matter, this strange marriage. And the extraordinary thing about it all is that it began as a *mariage de convenance*. Like you, gentle reader, I lost a packet in the slump. I had only two thousand pounds left in the whole world. With it I bought this crazy old place, twenty miles from Cambridge, and two miles from the Great North Road. I bought it as an investment, because I was tired of buying paper that went up in smoke. I wasn't a gardener in those days —five years ago. I was merely attracted by the house. So will you come over the house with me, quickly, before we go into the garden, before I give myself utterly away?

It is a typical Tudor cottage. Dick Turpin may have ridden by it on frosty nights—I don't know or care. All I know is that it stands in the quietest lane in Huntingdonshire, that its thatch is golden brown, and that the old oak beams have long ago been twisted, by time, into fantastic shapes.

Have you ever slept on a sloping floor? I mean the kind of floor where you have to put one end of the bed on stilts in order to avoid falling out of it. As I write, I chuckle to myself as I think how funny my upstairs furniture would look if you took it out and set it on the lawn. Chairs, beds and tables would reel about the grass, in shameless intoxication, because, you see, their long-suffering legs have all had to be sawn about two inches every hundred years, so some of them are naturally getting a little tired of it.

If you step out through the front window you will see a tiny garden, only the size of a large room, crammed with flowers, and walled with very ancient hedges of clipped May. For a moment you may wonder at its smallness, but if you look through the arch at the end you will see another garden, and then another— until, at the very end, you see green fields and sheep grazing.

For my garden is really a whole collection of tiny gardens, among which might be mentioned the Stolen Garden, and even the League of Nations Garden. These gardens may be separated only by a thin strip of box hedging, or the over-hanging bough of an old damson tree, so that they do not interfere with the general plan. But in their miniature confines I keep strictly to flowers of a certain character— and sometimes, I fear, flowers of a *bad* character!

For the Stolen Garden contains nothing but stolen goods. You see that row of hollyhocks, just beginning to rear their heads? They all came from Windsor Castle. I was walking in the garden at Windsor one day with a friend, and when he was not looking I nipped off a seed-pod. When the blossoms come they are a marvellous magenta that tries to be purple—as though they knew that they were royal, but illegitimate.

The Stolen Garden is next to the Woolworth Garden, which explains itself . . . and some of the sixpenny trees that I bought there, jostling piles of cheap handkerchiefs and Christmas baubles, are explaining themselves at such length that they will soon be disclaiming their humble parentage. The League of Nations Garden also explains itself, for it contains all the fruits of my travels . . . vines from Tunis, cyclamen from the hills of Rome (brought home in a sponge-bag), heather from the hills of Greece (the customs man thought the red roots were a form of Republican propaganda), the sweet bryony from Australia, and even a miniature ivy which I brought away from a fête at Long Island.

All these gardens have their different moods. Do you find that, too?

Come on, let's talk together! You can talk later, but you have to listen to me for the moment!

But seriously, haven't you noticed this change of mood, as you wander from place to place in your garden? The charm of a rock-garden, for example, is essentially *Lilliputian*. If you are not a good "shrinker," if you cannot cultivate the gift of shrivelling up, mentally, to a tiny little figure that can wander at will through groves of saxifrages and clamber up the stalk of a golden primrose to lie full-length on the glowing cloth of its petals—if you cannot do these things you will never know the full joys that a rock-garden has to offer. You will remain a huge clumsy mortal, bending down with an aching back, cursing the weeds, and wondering if it is worth while going back to the toolshed to get that thing which looks like a sardine opener in order to prod up the foul docks.

We are wandering from the point, as all good gardeners do, because a garden has no such dull things as "points." You go out to look at the lupins and you are enmeshed by the honeysuckle before you know where you are. And then you see there is a blight on the honeysuckle, and *that* takes you to the toolshed, and once you get in the toolshed you are lost, because no good gardener can find himself confronted by all those wonderful surgical instruments without wanting to use them.

Sometimes, in London, I have met people who seemed quite enchanting—women who, one thought, were witty and wise, besides having that faint tilt at the end of their noses which always gets a man down. Young men who seemed likely to develop into life-long friends—so gay were they, and so absorbing. Then eagerly I asked these people down to the cottage and they came. And somehow they did not fit. It was as though a woman whom one had thought lovely, at the other end of the restaurant, had suddenly moved into a different light, and one saw that there was a hard line about her mouth and discontented shadows under her eyes.

A garden, in fact, is a good character-reader. And the qualities I venerate in women are all to be found, in essence, in the gardener's craft. If a woman loves a man—a *real* woman—she will love him in sickness or in health—she won't mind dirtying her hands for him—she will do things that are physically revolting to her when he is stricken and unable to help himself—and always she will keep the pain and the disgust and the disillusionment to herself. A good gardener is like that. No good gardener's hands are ever quite clean—at least, I know mine aren't. And though a woman may feel sick at the sight of a slug, and have to clench her teeth when she sees all the awful wriggly black things which cluster round the roots of a Madonna lily, she deals with them! It is a queer thing, this, that we must be prepared to degrade ourselves if we are to be exalted. A very queer thing indeed, but in some ways a strangely beautiful one, so beautiful that it might tempt any writer to indulge in sentimental moralisations. Suffice it to say that the loveliest flowers have their roots in the dung—that the most exquisite and ivory of lilies is merely the fruit of manure. I think of the white and lofty bells that ring above it. All the same, at the moment of writing, my fingers are grimy with soot which I have been scattering round my lilies all day to keep off the slugs.

MR. BEVERLEY NICHOLS

H ERE'S a grand opportunity for me! Usually, I'm asked to write on some or other ridiculous subject of which I know little or nothing! But I *do* know a few things about myself! And myself "at home" suits me down to the ground—for that's where I always like to be!

I do not leave my country home unless I'm forced to do so. My one unfailing rule is to spend every week-end in it. I've only spent two week-ends away from the house in nine years—when I was abroad!

I refuse point blank to leave my comfortable house. When one has a nice home one's made oneself, it's only sense to stay in it. That's my idea of a real home— a place to *stay* in and be happy, not just a spot to park one's spare suit and the radiogram while one gallivants about here, there, and everywhere else in discomfort!

Though my mother has her own flat in Town, she always spends week-ends here with me. And we fill the house with guests. I get a lot of fun out of building on more rooms, so that I can have more people here. In the nine years I've had the house, it has increased from four bedrooms to twelve! In fact, they now sprawl about all over the garden—the bedrooms, I mean.

In the summer, I live in the country all the time. I love to see how much sun I can possibly get, It's gorgeous!

My chief hobby, apart from the theatre, is my gramophone. I have over four thousand records. Every kind — jazz, opera, symphony and all the rest of it—all carefully catalogued so that I can find any particular one in a second.

All my life I've been a keen autograph collector. I now have seven volumes of marvellous signatures, ranging from Michelangelo, Nelson, Lady Hamilton, William IV, and Queen Victoria down to Mae West and Shirley Temple!

At the moment, I'm renewing an interest in my stamp collection, commenced when I was a schoolboy. The world has changed so much in the last few years; it makes it most confusing to cope with stamps to-day!

If I could afford it, I should have a private aerodrome here at my own home, with gorgeous 'planes always ready to take off and carry me to lovely places all over the world, as the whim took me! Not that I'm keen on flying, as flying. It's rather boring! But it's grand to get to places so easily. I really hate travelling. I should like to be put to sleep and wake up

" It's a nightmare to me to have to carry parcels— though I like to receive them, naturally. ∴ . . ."

to find myself where I wanted to be!

I play bezique, six - pack bezique, a great deal. It looks very complicated when one is learning; but it's simple when you know how. We don't play for money, but keep a running score. At the end of the year, we all just even up, and no one has to pay anything!

In summer, of course, I play lots of tennis. It's grand playing in bathing costumes and then dashing off into the swimming pool afterwards.

All this sounds rather as if I were only a playboy. But I assure you, few people in the world work harder than I do! I work most when I'm actually preparing a show. I work then in really desperate spurts. And I think I do much better work this way. I have a workroom-studio built in the garden, right away from the house. I can shut myself up there and work in peace, even when the house is full of guests. I have a recording gramophone there, and work out all my music on it, making my

Myself at HOME by Ivor Novello

Being the frank confessions of a well-known Author, Actor and Playwright—who has also won fame as a Composer, Producer and expert Organizer!

records and playing them over and over till I'm satisfied with them.

I believe everyone needs a job to be happy. People, you'll have noticed, run to seed when they retire. That's why I shall never give up work, I hope!

I have little interest in food, but I am still very fond of ice cream. Make it myself now, so I can have lots of it without having to pay for cornets and wafers and the like!

Have I any special dislikes? Yes, rather! I hate carrying parcels! It's a nightmare to me to have to carry any— though, naturally, I like to receive them! I hate going to parties. Prefer to entertain people in my own home. I hate dial telephones. I loathe shaving. I hate getting up early in the morning, and I loathe hypocrisy in any shape or form.

I *like* reading, especially books of

memoirs. I like anything about Napoleon. I like the Albert Memorial, chiefly because most people dislike it! I love the theatre and the long rehearsals and all the muddle and work and glamour that is embodied in the stage. I adore animals, dogs and cats specially. My great favourites were two cats I once had, named "Fred" and "Adele," after the famous Astaires.

I like planning the redecoration and furnishing of my home—by myself. It is one of my chief hobbies, and I love moving the furniture around and putting it in the most unexpected places! In the decoration of my home, I love permanent things, such as panelling.

I love responsibility, both in my home and in my work. I love to feel that there are dozens of people whose well-being perhaps whose very existence, depends on me. It spurs me on to do my best work.

Flying Start

GARY CROFT,
the Flying Doctor.

I⊤ seems a pity to destroy one of the most popular and romantic of our modern myths : that the air-pilot must be someone of exceptional qualities. It is time that the man in the street took a closer and more analytical look at this very normal individual—the man or woman in the aeroplane.

The outward appearance of pilots in general is quite usual and ordinary. I can, of course, think of one air-liner captain who fulfils very admirably the popular conception of what an airman ought to be, and among the long-distance experts there is one who may be said to " look the part." These men, however, are exceptional. The tubby, phlegmatic, unimaginative type is far more common.

What is true of the men applies equally well to the women. Among women pilots one can think of several who are decidedly attractive. On the other hand, their appearance does nothing to suggest aviation as being their especial hobby They might equally well be exponents of tennis or swimming, or any other branch of activity. Indeed, one of the soundest woman pilots I can think of might well be a devotee of knitting—for all that any casual observer could guess to the contrary !

In other words, flying does not produce, or make its appeal to, any well-defined type of individual. The reason for this would be apparent enough, if once we could dismiss from our minds the traditional notion of aviation as a highly delicate and precarious business

From the Press and from the films we learn of only one sort of flying—that which is dangerous or spectacular Lacking personal knowledge, we are apt to assume that such flying is of normal, every-day occurrence, and to base our whole outlook on this most common of delusions.

In actual fact, the pilot of an ordinary aircraft, making a normal flight in ordinary weather, is a prosaic person, doing what is nowadays almost a prosaic job. So slight is the strain imposed upon him by the duties of control and navigation, that it is quite possible for him to suffer from a feeling of sleepiness, and to have difficulty in keeping his

faculties alert. The machine virtually " flies itself," and any slight deviation is corrected by control movements which become almost entirely automatic.

Here is an aspect of flying which, I am very sure, the general public never visualizes ; yet I am speaking now of what I myself have experienced. I have more than once been reduced to lowering my windscreen while in flight, so that the blast of air in my face should produce an enlivening effect !

Needless to say, such a peaceful picture tells only a part of the story of what actually goes on in the pilot's cockpit. There are times when the popular notion of " grappling with the elements " is not so very wide of the mark. To steer an accurate course when there is a strong cross-wind blowing, to make a neat landing in defiance of unexpected gusts, and to give correct allowance for those vertical air currents which lurk unseen over a mountainous country , all these things call for sound judgment and decisive action.

There is always, of course, plenty of scope for brilliance. Every landing, for instance, can be effected in either brilliant or mediocre style. The machine can be set down as lightly as a feather, sinking an imperceptible six inches as it makes contact with the ground, or again it may be dropped rather clumsily, albeit perfectly safely, from a considerably greater height. It may even be flown on to the ground at a slight angle, which will cause a bump and an excessive length of " run " before it comes, at last, to rest.

Compare these various landings with the various gear changes which can be made with cars of the non-fool-proof type. The gears can be meshed with perfect silence and exactitude, or again they can be engaged with a slight, but disagreeable, grating sound If the margin of error is small, no great harm will result.

Obviously, from every point of view, it is desirable in flying to give as " polished " a performance as possible It is pleasanter for the passengers, who are naturally impressed if they leave the earth and return to it again with perfect

smoothness. It is better for the machine, which consequently endures less wear and tear. It is infinitely more satisfactory to the pilot himself, who naturally takes a pride in carrying out every manoeuvre correctly.

Finally, once in every thousand flights, an emergency may arise in which the ability to exercise real skill may be of the first importance. Although it is improbable, an engine may suddenly give trouble, and the only field available for a forced landing may be quite unsuitable. In a ploughed field, for instance, the perfectly conducted landing would have a fair chance of being successful. The indifferent landing would almost certainly result in damage.

So rarely, however, does extreme skill become a vital factor, that mere dexterity is by no means the most common characteristic among civilian flyers. Their particular quality I should be inclined to describe as " soundness." It is the unsound, rather than the unskilled, pilot whose career is apt to be prematurely cut short.

All those who fly successfully must have a certain soundness of judgment, and solid common sense, and perhaps even a certain flair for knowing when to push on boldly, and when to remain prudently on the tarmac. Each pilot must know his own limitations, and learn to handle a machine accordingly. It is soundness that insists upon those vital margins—a margin of space, a margin of height, and at all times a margin of speed. It is soundness that foresees trouble, sometimes, in advance, and provides against it before it can materialize.

This quality of soundness is not especially rare. Many people possess it, and there is, therefore, no psychological reason why anyone, provided that she or he is free from any " jumpy " and erratic tendencies, should not make a perfectly adequate pilot. A certain amount of " nerve " is, of course, required ; but again, we must avoid giving an exaggerated value to this qualification.

The sort of " nerve " that is needed is a negative rather than a positive virtue. It is not the " iron nerve " of the legendary super-man ; it is rather the freedom, possessed by many unheroic men and women, from any liability to get " rattled " by an unfamiliar situation or an unexpected problem.

There are unfortunately still many real deterrents to keep back those whose ambition it is to get off the ground and to handle a machine in the air. The expense is very considerable ; it may cost the best part of £50 to obtain an " A " licence. Then, there is only one type of aircraft built to-day—the much discussed but little used Autogyro— which can operate successfully from any small meadow. Nearly all private flying is still done from public aerodromes, an obvious anomaly.

Do not, however, add to these drawbacks the imaginary need for special gifts of skill or courage on the pilot's part. The excuse, that " I should never be able to tackle it," will definitely not hold good when the problems of civilian flying are fairly and dispassionately examined.

By the EARL of CARDIGAN

When the Railway Companies Introduced Camp Coach Holidays, they Proved Such a Success that the Number of Coaches Available has now been doubled. You Would Be Surprised by the Comfort of These Homes on Wheels

THE coaches are completely equipped and designed on the lines of a modern bungalow, with sleeping compartments communicating direct with living-room and kitchen.

They provide accommodation for six, eight or ten persons, and may be hired from 50/- per week up to £5, according to the season chosen and accommodation required.

(Photo : G.W.R.)

A view of a living-room in a Great Western coach, with a glimpse of the kitchen beyond. Did you ever realise that the interior of a railway coach could be quite so homelike? On the left is a similar dining-room in an L.M.S. coach.

❧   ❧   ❧

Above: the new Mauretania
—all good luck go with her!

D. 11.

imply breadth and fullness in that region. Man still had a waist, but it had lost its prestige and served only to throw other parts of the trunk into relief. The waistline was set above its natural place, and buttons and pockets were moved up higher. The lapels were diminished in length and increased in width, helped visually by a double-breasted revere; and with a new soft roll they gave a swell to the front which was formerly flat. There were three buttons on the jacket, but only the middle one was fastened, as this gave a 'jaunty' look by causing the lapels to jut forward, making a flat-looking chest impossible. The shoulders were built up and the collar kept low and narrow so that it would not mar the squareness of the shoulders. If the sleeves, too, were narrowed as they reached the cuff, they would create the effect of a muscular upper arm. The cuffs were finished off with four buttons set close together, or 'kissing' in tailoring terms. The jacket fitted at the hips and was square-cut, defining the waist without fitting closely, the aim being to achieve ease with elegance, form without constriction.

For those who had the misfortune to be unathletic in figure, tailors were called upon to accomplish what nature had failed to do. Attention could be given to the building up of the shoulders by special manipulation of the canvas and shaping with the iron. The breast was worked out on the canvas with haircloth and shaped by means of seams and cuts; the back was eased and padding applied with considerable effect. All this was strictly against the wishes of the Dress Reformers, but it did mean that an ordinary 'undeveloped' figure could be made to assume at least an approximation to that of an athlete.

The trousers of the suit were nowadays cut to be close-fitting at the waist and to hang free and easy over the hips. Two generous pleats were fixed into the waistband of the new high waist to give extra ease, and the trouser leg was long enough to break slightly over the instep. A few smart men in the West End had their trousers with plain bottoms, but the majority had turn-ups with an average width of $17\frac{1}{2}$ inches, and it was thought that the habit of the turned-up bottom together with the sharp crease fore and aft had improved trousers no end, abolishing baggy knees and fringed hems.

City men were not enamored of the square shoulders and athletic look and made no change to their lounge styles, and business men were choosing to wear dark subdued colors again. 'The crusade against the drabness of suits and overcoats during the last few years had a powerful backing; webs of cloth dyed in vivid colors were put on the market and it seemed as if we were in for a gorgeous assertion of the male as peacock. Yet the color faded almost as the glow of sunset; man is almost as sombre as ever.' The prevailing conditions of business and the results of general depression were

In order to be fashionable in the thirties, every man tried to look like a strong and masculine athlete. He let his hair be bleached by the sun, and encouraged it to wave gently. His face was clean-shaven and had a healthy outdoor look; his chest was broad and well-built, his shoulders square and muscular, and his general appearance was bold and manly.

The lounge suit of the day was designed in a style that would enhance man's new image. It was generally thought that the long close-waisted lounge suit of the twenties, with its ample flare over the hips, gave too effeminate an aspect to many young men. Now the limelight was shifting upwards, for man had to have 'chest'—and many visual tricks were employed with cunning effect to help lift and expand the chest and

FASHION

held responsible. Quiet colors and neat patterns were chosen, particularly dark blue and black herringbones or small checks and pinheads on gray or brown. The only novel idea was to have tiny cluster designs of speckles, bird's eye and spot effects and even lines and dots used together. Streaks of color would at least give a hint of sparkle, and colored stripe effects would brighten the design, but they should not be too pronounced.

A new experimental suit launched by the Reformers had become quite a popular outfit in France and Germany. This garment was made of tweed and cut on the lines of an engineer's overalls. Instead of the usual jacket, waistcoat and trousers the new suit was all in one piece, with the jacket and trousers combined, with a belt around the waist and the top finished like an ordinary jacket with pockets and lapels. The usual shirt and collar were worn beneath it. It was a pity that this suit was not adopted more in England or America.

Those to whom the gods had given a striking personality wore daring clothes that needed carrying off 'with an air'. Mr Arnold Bennett, for example, could wear to the Royal Academy in 1930 a suit in a rich shade of brown 'with a hint of crushed strawberries in it'. But there were those famous people who abused their striking personalities by deliberately choosing what seemed to be an awkward attire. Mr Jacob Epstein passed through the Royal Academy galleries in a hat, suit and overcoat that had the 'heavy and massed effect of some of his sculptures', and Mr John Masefield, the new Poet Laureate, was 'not much of the poet' about his clothes. And other strange things appeared in 1930. The Prince of Wales, who epitomized 'good taste', very often wore brown suede shoes with almost everything but a brown suit. Although it was said that a black bowler hat should not be worn with light clothes, the Prince of Wales and many other of London's well-dressed men thought differently.

Many people had taken to wearing a black Homburg or even a black soft felt hat with the tuxedo or dinner jacket, in place of the topper or opera hat. They found it both 'artistic and dressy'. The dinner jacket was now very frequently taking the place of a dress coat for evening wear. As with the lounge coat, the square-shouldered effect was the outstanding feature of the present season's dinner jacket, and on many the lapels were faced with black silk. Men were choosing to wear a white waistcoat with the dinner jacket, but whether it was white or matched the coat it always had to be accompanied by a black bow tie. Jack Buchanan had introduced as a fashionable dress-wear accessory to London this year 'the walking stick cigarette lighter'.

If a man wore spats with his dinner jacket, he was 'putting his foot in it'. At the Derby this year, however, spats were creeping back into fashion, and some of the

S.6

smartest men were thus embellished. The close-fitting morning dress with stressed squareness of shoulder and fullness of chest had the coat more fitted at the waist than was so for other dress clothes. The starched collar, the top hat and the strung field glasses were 'sovereign remedy against slackness and enervation' in dress, and backsliders were reminded that in times like these 'full regalia should be looked upon as a tonic and not as tyranny'. Waistcoats were single or double-breasted, and if they were not in the same material as the coat they were white, gray, blue-gray, biscuit or buff. On their white shirts, the wing or double collar held a tie of a bow-knot or a wide cravat. Gloves were more in evidence than formerly, and were dressy and distinctive in colors of chamois, gray, putty white and fawn, some in reindeer skin. With the dinner jacket, the shirt collar had larger and bolder wings, but the show of white starched collars seen everywhere this year filled the Dress Reformers with great alarm, and they tried to popularize instead a silk printed foulard square that could be knotted into a tie and worn with a soft collar.

The increasing interest in neckwear caused all men this year to choose the neckline as a focal point. Upon his pale powder-blue shirt and sprouting from his double collar—which this year appeared with pointed fronts—a man would display his favorite school, college, club, university or regimental tie in prominent diagonal stripes and bright colors. A neat check or stripe followed in popularity and a new vogue was started for ties with large spots upon them. Spotted handkerchiefs were available to match the spotted ties, and special regimental cuff-links to match the regimental ties.

Many 'varsity men chose a scarf rather than a tie to festoon their necks. All the scarves were florid, gay and multi-colored, appearing in pink, red, pale green, dark and light blue. Some were knotted and bunched under the chin, while others hung down in stole-like fashion. With these scarves, and their other clothes, the undergraduates started a trend for what they termed 'studied untidiness'.

There was a big run on gray flannel trousers and jackets, especially popular among the 'varsity men. So admired was the gray flannel cloth that it was also adopted by the plus-four, and the smart young men who had affected this fashionable gray garment were fastidious as to its cut and fit. With plus-fours made much longer and wider again this year, it was imperative that they hung well, for nothing looked so unsightly as ugly folds forming at the back of the thigh. This year there were three pleats instead of two put into the waistband of the plus-four trousers and they were fitted with short side straps which buckled. For bona fide golf-players special fitting rooms had now been installed with a 'net' cleverly placed so that a man trying one of the plus-four suits could 'swing a club' to test the garments.

A Greek key-pattern cloth was a close runner-up to the gray flannel, and appeared in colors of fawn or navy. Sometimes the trousers would be heavily checked in small neat squares while the jacket was left plain. Like the lounge suit jacket, the plus-four jacket had acquired fullness in the breast, and the shoulders were made square.

The 'tubular' look of the twenties pullover, together with its baggy appearance, had departed forever, and a new style had replaced it. This pullover was much shorter and fitted quite closely at the waist. One of its attractions was that it could be tucked into the plus-fours or trousers, and this was 'quite the new thing'. A sleeveless pullover in this new style was popular for golf, and appeared this year in colors of fawn, blue or gray, and browns of various shades. Pattern designs were neat, inconspicuous Jacquard weaves, small

diamond checks and tiny speckled or flecked designs.

The cardigan (so named after Lord Cardigan of Crimea fame) had taken a fresh lease of life. The old-fashioned cardigan-jacket was a monstrosity. It was ugly, cumbersome, fitting everywhere yet fitting nowhere. Now a warm cardigan, preferably home-made, with pockets, and fashioned in the new waisted style, was an ideal gift for a man who loved the open air. The Fair-Isle pattern, too, had made a comeback, and was largely responsible for banishing the vogue for large checks and diamonds. Canary or hunting yellow invaded not only jumpers, waistcoats, sleeveless pullovers and cardigans, but scarves, gloves, braces, shirts and even woolly combinations!

Edward,
Prince of Wales.

Chapters of
ROYAL LIFE
by
Evelyn Graham

to Ambassadors' Court. That is a source of self-congratulation for His Royal Highness, for it is well sheltered from the noise and bustle of the traffic that flows outside, and once inside the rooms themselves one finds an air of quiet and repose that is very difficult to find anywhere in central London to-day.

Most of us have perforce to get accustomed to living in a perpetual hum of passing traffic, and so probably in time we become so accustomed to it that we are able to ignore it. But this the Prince after his residence in St. James's has never succeeded in doing, and it is a frequent joke of his with his brother, the Duke of York, that when he goes round to 145, Piccadilly " he cannot hear himself think." As a matter of fact, 145, Piccadilly is a singularly peaceful house considering its situation at one of the busiest corners of London's traffic ; but, in spite of that, the difference in noisiness between it and York House is most marked even to the not-very-sensitive ear.

It is this air of quiet that first impresses one on entering through the pleasant but quite unimposing glass door that leads from the porch into the entrance hall. The hall has an unostentatious dignity that is the heritage of houses built at its period, and the Prince has had the very excellent idea of decorating the white panelled surface of its walls with the trophies of his military service. There are brightly polished bugles of the Grenadier Guards, one of them in which the dent of a German bullet shows that the bugles were not meant for show. A beautifully chased sword that also hangs upon the wall is more interesting for the

MY first visit to St. James's Palace was in many ways memorable to me, for I got then an impression of the Prince of Wales' character that I had never obtained in half a dozen meetings with him in his public life.

The Prince's suite in St. James's Palace is far from being a luxurious or ceremonial abode. It is in York House, which is itself a part of the old Palace, and the entrance to it is under the glass porch that looks out on

The PRINCE of WALES in His Own Home

The Prince at work at his desk

The Prince of Wales is regarded as the best-dressed man in the world.

F. A. Swaine

intrinsic value of its workmanship than for any part that it was able to play in the recent war. But perhaps the crowning glory of the entrance hall is the very beautiful white panelled staircase that leads out of it up to the Prince's private apartments. It is a graceful staircase redolent of the days when the Palace of St. James echoed to the laughter of the gallants of the seventeenth century, and it seems almost sacrilege to walk up it in anything less romantic than peruke and a sword. But if you are going to have anything more than a mere formal interview with the Prince you will certainly have to walk up those stairs in your everyday dress, for the downstairs rooms—except the very charming panelled dining-room that is beyond a discreet door in the entrance hall—are devoted to the business part of the Prince's suite and are occupied chiefly by the secretarial staff. These rooms below are light and comfortable and efficient, but to describe them would be describing an office, not a palace.

It is upstairs that the Prince's personality has impressed itself upon his residence. There is a bachelor air about the rooms that makes you, or at least made me, immediately feel at home. Even in the two larger rooms which are in the nature of formal reception-rooms there was the feeling that they were intended to be lived in and the chairs (and this is a rare thing in reception-rooms) were made to be sat in.

But the most interesting room was that in which his Royal Highness received me. It is a quite small room, decorated in a quiet, restful green. The tall Georgian windows are draped with long, thick, green curtains; the two comfortable armchairs are upholstered in green, and upholstered in rather shabby green at that, for his Royal Highness has sufficient bachelor tastes to agree with most of us that no armchair is really worth sitting in until it is a little shabby. The rest of the furniture is of a graceful Chippendale design, except for the big, efficient-looking office desk that occupies one corner of the room. On this there is a monumental pile of papers and correspondence neatly arranged in heaps, answered on one side and unanswered on the other. But you would be making a great mistake if you thought that the Prince of Wales was responsible for the orderly character of his desk. As he once said to Sir Godfrey Thomas, his private secretary : " If it weren't for you, my desk would be buried in papers in less than no time."

And that is the impression that the Prince gives you from the very moment that he takes your hand in his firm grip. There is none of the grand seigneur about him when he meets you in that little office on the first floor at St. James's Palace. His ready smile as he greets you, the faint smell of tobacco smoke that lingers about the curtains, the half-smoked pipe lying on the mantelpiece, and the boxes of matches lying convenient to hand on every table and on every ledge, all tend to make you forget that you are meeting the heir to the Throne, and to remember that you are meeting a very pleasant and affable young bachelor with tastes somewhat similar to your own.

I must confess to being a little nervous the first time that we met, but that feeling was very swiftly dissipated by the Prince's personality. Characteristically like his father in these matters, he went straight to the object of my visit, and in a few minutes the whole matter was settled. It was only afterwards that I got a personal sidelight on the reason for his popularity. Almost before I knew it we were in the middle of an enthralling discussion of the prospects of the coming hunting season. How the subject was introduced to this day I shall never know, but within two minutes all feeling of restraint had vanished and I felt completely at home. It was not indeed until Sir Godfrey Thomas arrived in the room to warn the Prince that there was another caller due almost immediately that I realised that I was not talking with an ordinary friend in my own bachelor flat.

THAT air of simplicity which the Prince shows in his dealings with his subjects is well borne out in the arrangement and the habits of his home. There is not a room in York House that could be considered luxurious. His bedroom is of the simplest, an ordinary rather narrow wooden bed, two chairs, and a very beautiful but simple old chest of drawers comprise the sole furniture. Two doors lead off from it. One to his bathroom, white-tiled and cheerful, but less luxurious than many an ordinary bathroom in an American hotel. The other door leads to his wardrobe.

Here certainly there is not the simplicity that is such a feature of the rest of the suite. Naturally the Prince

of Wales has to possess a very large number of uniforms for use upon official occasions, but that does not by any means account for the whole of his Royal Highness's wardrobe. For he takes a very real and careful interest in clothes as such. Greatly exaggerated stories have been circulated as to the number of lounge suits that his Royal Highness possesses. I myself have seen figures in the Press putting the number at several hundred. That, of course, is untrue. The Prince would never have time to select several hundred lounge suits, considering the time he takes over selecting even one. But the number of his suits for ordinary wear certainly easily surpasses the twenty mark, and each of them has been carefully chosen and criticised by his Royal Highness in person. And as a reward for this purely altruistic pride and interest in clothes, I suppose it is not unfair to say that the Prince of Wales is generally looked upon as the best-dressed young man in the world, and this reputation has not been without its commercial value to London tailors as a whole !

This spartan simplicity about everything in the Prince's suite, except his wardrobe, is fully borne out in the routine of his daily life when he is in London. His meals are always of the simplest description when he is at home, and even at public banquets it is very noticeable how he avoids any food that is starchy or rich, and restricts himself to small helpings of the simpler dishes of the menu.

In his home life this care over his dietary is even more conspicuous. Breakfast generally consists of nothing more than cereals and toast, though often if he has been for an early morning run round the gardens of Buckingham Palace he will make a hearty breakfast of bacon and compensate for it by having a very light luncheon. At other meals there is one feature that is very noticeable No meal that is served to the Prince of Wales when he is dining alone contains any dish consisting of pastry, or any food that is fattening. In spite of 'seizing every opportunity to get in a game of squash rackets with a member of his staff during the morning, and in spite of his frequent morning runs round the gardens of Buckingham Palace, his Royal Highness finds it extremely difficult to get what he considers an adequate amount of exercise while he is in London, and now that he had foresworn hunting since the illness of H.M. the

Foulsham & Banfield

A delightful portrait of H.R.H. the Prince of Wales

King increased his son's official duties, he is more and more careful of his physical fitness.

BEFORE turning to various incidents in the less official and much misunderstood private life of the Prince, there is one side of his character that I must touch upon. I mentioned elsewhere that when he was a small boy he made several attempts at authorship, some of which are still preserved by his mother. Again when he was at Osborne his gifts as a raconteur stood him in good stead, and after he had been persuaded to tell his first story, very shortly after he arrived at the College, he was in constant request after lights-out to exercise his gifts. His popularity in the dormitory was greatly increased in this way. But it is not so generally known that far later in life the Prince of Wales carried his interest in authorship and at one time he had serious thoughts of bursting into print.

It was while he was at Oxford that the Prince first conceived the idea of writing a novel. It is a common ambition for many undergraduates to entertain, and while it is true that on the whole the Prince of Wales mixed chiefly with the hunting and sporting set while he was at the University, he had a very large circle of acquaintances among the more intellectual members of the University, and it was with the encouragement of these that he started off on his only literary work. That novel still lies hidden away in a drawer of his desk at St. James's Palace. It has not got very far in the plot, for the War came to interrupt his University career, and after the War was over he was much too busy to publish anything of the kind.

Most young novelists when they start their first book attempt to write about a side of life of which they know nothing, and at first the Prince of Wales was going to write this novel on the same plan. But fortunately a friend of mine who was up at Oxford with him and was in his confidence about his literary ambitions, persuaded him to do otherwise. "I told him," my friend informed me, "that he was probably the only writer in the world who knew exactly what it felt like to be a prince, and that he would be committing a literary crime if he did not use his opportunity in his writing."

Eventually the Prince of Wales took my friend's advice and started his novel about a prince. As I said before, the War came and effectually stopped all thought of its ever being finished—but what a book it would have made! No lover of literature or life can contemplate that unfinished manuscript lying dusty and forgotten in the drawer at St. James's without a sigh of regret at the opportunity that has been missed.

PERSONALLY what I could wish for even more than for the publication of that novel would be that the Prince of Wales should write his autobiography. It would be—for remember he has a gift for writing—the most interesting human document in the world. There can be few people who have crammed so much experience into a brief thirty-five years as has H.R.H. the Prince of Wales. There can be no one, as I know full well myself, who would have so many amusing incidents to recount. There can be very few who have met, and met on terms of familiarity, so many different types and classes of men in so many different countries and climes. But what would be most interesting of all would be to see exactly what the Prince thinks of his job and of the people he meets.

It is of course possible to get some light upon his views from conversation with him and from the reports of friends, but nowhere is it possible, quite naturally in view of his position, to get a complete exposition of his feelings. And that never will be possible until he writes his autobiography, which again will never be. Until then we must be content with accounts like this present series can give, at the best partial glimpses of his character and of his tastes.

a fair-isle pullover

MATERIALS

Paton's Real Shetland Wool, 2-ply, in the following colours: 5 ozs. drab, shade 648; 3 ozs. natural, shade 633; 2 ozs. dark brown, shade 671; 2 ozs. green, shade 672; 2 ozs. rust, shade 649. A pair of No. 8 knitting pins; a pair of No. 12 knitting pins.

MEASUREMENTS

Round the chest—40 ins. Length from shoulder to lower edge—24 ins. Sleeve, from shoulder seam to edge of cuff—26 ins. Sleeve under-arm seam to edge of cuff—22 ins.

TENSION

After pressing the Fair Isle fabric, 6 sts. make 1 inch in width, and 7 rows make 1 inch in depth.

COLOUR ABBREVIATIONS

D., drab; n., natural; b., brown; g., green; r., rust.

COMMENCE at the lower edge of the back by casting 110 sts. with d. wool on No. 12 needles. Work in a rib of k. 1, p. 1 for 3½ ins., which is about 40 rows. Cast on 1 st. at the end of the last row.

Now change to No. 8 needles and st.-st.

1st row: * 2 g., 2 b., repeat from * to the end of the row.

2nd row: P. each st. in the same colour as in 1st row.

3rd row: * 2 n., 2 g., repeat from * to the end of the row.

4th row: P. each st. in the same colour as in the 3rd row.

5th–8th rows: As the 1st–4th.

9th row: * 2 r., 3 d., 1 r., 3 d., 1 r., repeat from * to the end of the row, and work the last st. of *every row* the same as the first st.

10th row: * 1 r., 4 d., repeat from *.

11th row: * 4 d., 3 r., 3 d., repeat from *.

12th row: P. each st. in the same colour as in the 11th row.

13th row: * 3 n., 2 r., 1 n., 2 r., 2 n., repeat from *.

14th row: * 3 n., 1 r., 3 n., 1 r., 2 n., repeat from *.

15th row: * 2 n., 2 r., 3 n., 2 r., 1 n., repeat from *.

16th row: * 2 n., 1 b., 5 n., 1 b., 1 n., repeat from *.

17th row: * 1 n., 2 b., 5 n., 2 b. repeat from *.

18th–25th rows: As the 16th–9th rows, inclusive, worked in their reverse order. This completes the pattern once.

Work the 25 pattern rows 3 times, then work the first 13 rows. When the pattern is repeated for the 2nd, 4th or the 6th time, the k. rows become p. rows, and the p. rows become k. rows. If a longer pull-over be required, work the extra rows here.

The Armhole.—At the beginning of the next 10 rows, cast off 4 sts.; 71 sts. now remain. Continue in the pattern until it has been repeated 5 times, then work the first 12 rows.

The Shoulder.—Work till 6 sts. remain,

turn. *Next row:* Work till 6 sts. remain, turn.

Next row: Work till 12 sts. remain, turn.

Continue in this way until 24 sts. remain unworked at either end. Place each set of shoulder sts. on a safety-pin. On the 23 middle sts. work 12 rows of ribbing with d. wool on No. 12 needles. Cast off. Cast off each set of shoulder sts. with d. wool.

The Front.—Cast 130 sts. on No. 12 needles with d. wool and continue as for the back (increasing the sts. to 131 at the end of the ribbing) until 84 rows have been worked in the pattern.

Next row: K 65 sts. in pattern for the left front. Place the remaining 66 sts. on a holder. Work 3 more rows on the 65 sts. Now shape the neck and armhole. Cast off 4 sts. at the beginning of the row for the armhole, then k. till 2 sts. remain; k. 2 tog. for the V neck. Cast off 4 sts. at the commencement of alternate rows 4 more times for the armhole. For the V neck, decrease at the end of every 4th row until 15 decreases have been made.

When the pattern has been repeated 5 times, and 18 rows of the next repetition have been worked, shape for the shoulder as follows:

Next row: P. till 6 sts. remain, turn.

Next row: S. 1, k. to the end.

Continue in this way, working 6 sts. fewer in alternate rows, until the row with 6 sts. has been completed. Cast off with d. wool.

Return to the 66 sts. for the right front. Commence with a k. row, and work the 2 first sts. tog., to make 65 sts. K. to the end Work 3 more rows.

Next row: S. 1, k. 1, p.s.s.o., k. to the end.

Next row: Cast off 4, p. to the end.

Make this side correspond with the left side by casting off 4 sts. at the commencement of alternate rows, 4 more times, and by decreasing at the commencement of every 4th row for the V neck 14 more times. When the shoulder is reached, commence the shaping with a k. row, as follows:

Next row: K. till 6 sts. remain, turn.

Next row: P. to the end.

In every k. row work 6 sts. less until only 6 sts. have been worked in the row. Turn and p. these sts., then cast off with d. wool.

The Neck Edge.—Along one side of the V neck pick up a st. for every row of knitting with d. wool on a No. 12 needle. There should be about 68 sts. Work 12 rows of ribbing, and decrease in every row at the point of the V by taking 2 sts. tog. Work a similar edge along the other side of the V.

The Sleeves.—Commence at the cuffs by casting 60 sts. with d. wool on No. 12 needles. Work in ribbing for

3½ ins. Change to No. 8 needles and proceed in st.-st.

Start with the 9th pattern row. In every 6th row m. 1 st. at either end until there are 20 increases on either side of the sleeve. When 126 rows have been worked in the pattern, begin the shaping for the top.

127th row: K. 1, s. 1, k. 1, p.s.s.o., k. till 3 sts. remain, k. 2 tog., k. 1.

128th row: P. in the pattern.

Repeat the last 2 rows 5 more times.

139th row: Decrease as in the 127th row. *140th row:* P. 1, p. 2 tog., p. in the pattern till 3 sts. remain, p. 2 tog., p. 1. Repeat the last 2 rows 4 more times.

Next row: Cast off 4 sts., work to the end. Repeat the last row 9 more times. Cast off and make the second sleeve.

TO MAKE UP

Press the parts, except the ribbing, under a damp cloth. Make the shoulder, side and sleeve seams, and join the parts of the neck edging. Press the seams. Sew the sleeves in the armholes, with the sleeve seam about 2 ins. in front of the side seam. Give the garment a final pressing.

1931

In 1931 a new breed of people were abroad, reviving walking—or 'hiking' as it had now been rechristened—as a cheap form of recreation during the Depression. 'These people are neither walkers or ramblers, but something in between. They are characterized by a willingness to carry their own sleeping quarters in the form of small tents, or to improvize lodgings in a barn or other wayside structure. They are of both sexes but are mostly young, and they represent a new spirit in the country which is refreshing to see.' Both the men and women dressed very much alike, for they had taken to wearing 'drill' or other shorts, and their 'tops' were either a light open-necked tennis shirt or a special kind of khaki shirt with an attached polo collar, a zip-fastened front and two rather large patch pockets. Extras were a leather belt, golf-stockings and 'absorbent' underwear. On their feet they often wore crepe-rubber soled shoes. A roomy haversack or rucksack was required for sandwiches, giving 'complete freedom of choice as to the time and place to eat, as well as a welcome change from knives and forks', and a hiking jacket made of Grenfell cloth (invented by Sir William Grenfell) and designed to withstand the severest Arctic conditions. This had a special cape that strapped under the arms and protected the shoulders and rucksack from the rain. On their heads, if they wore anything at all, was a newly-fashionable beret of the type that was worn in the Basque country.

This new hiking activity had started a demand for lightweight clothes, and there was soon a vogue for 'travel-light' articles of all kinds. There were lightweight hats and feather-weight macs which rolled up to be carried in the pocket and weighed only a few ounces; sleeveless gauze, net or artificial silk shirts, pajamas and underwear. In the interest of health and hygiene many cloths, such as the new Grenfell cloth, were 'scientifically constructed' so that air could penetrate the material, and many sweaters and pullovers were knitted in a basket-weave stitch which made the garments lighter and at the same time allowed air to circulate freely. Men were at last realizing that weight was not necessarily essential to warmth and, 'following the fair sex, were reducing the weight of their wearing apparel to a minimum'.

Traveling-coats of all kinds were shorter, lighter in weight and handsome in style. They protected without oppressing, and were made of materials that were pliable yet durable, light yet warm.

The plea from the Dress Reformers to ban pockets had no effect. Men insisted on being 'marsupial', for 'the very attraction of an overcoat for the thirties man is the extra room its pockets provide for carrying some of the toys dear to him—a pouch and pipe, a slim book or some small parcels.' Raglan-styled overcoats were the most popular, particularly those which were not too close-fitting to the waist. The lapels were faily bold, the pockets large and roomy and there had to be three buttons on the cuff. The chesterfield, too, had become easier in fit without becoming voluminous, and was straight-hanging. The lapels buttoned high, the cuffs turned back and the pockets were patch-pockets with flap fronts. Double-breasted greatcoats, as shown opposite, three-buttoning and with an all-round belt in fawn color, were popular—the Prince of Wales had one. Some wore a guard's overcoat with a center pleat and a half-belt. This year at the 'varsity match coats were cut to show at least four inches of baggy plus-fours beneath. With them were colorful scarves in black, white and red—but no hats. At Wembley the rain brought out a display of macs in fawn, brown, khaki, yellow, green, navy blue and a shiny black.

Leather was being used more and more in garments for motoring, flying, golfing and for other sports outfits, and suede in particular was employed for windjammers, jackets, waistcoats and even knicker-bockers. In many of these garments the zip-fastener replaced buttons as being infinitely smarter and neat in appearance. Elastic, too, was replacing belts and braces, and was used with great effect around cuffs, collars and hems. For the cyclist, a new cape which fastened with a zip-fastener to the neck had, in addition, two small tabs of elastic stitched to the front to hold the cape down to the handlebars when out in windy weather. For the skier, a one-piece woollen gaberdine suit in fawn or blue had a zip-fastener all the way down the front; and for the golfer a 'sportex' coat, which was a kind of cross between a jacket-blouse and windjammer, was made in tweed of the popular basket weave. With the waist held in by a wide band of elastic, it was zipped or buttoned up to the top of the collar.

Trying to keep up with the Prince of Wales and his fashions could sometimes be bewildering and expensive. At Walton Heath in July the golfing dress worn by the Prince was gray plus-fours, a pullover of dark blue silk, a blue short-sleeved shirt worn open at the neck with a knotted silk handkerchief instead of a tie, blue stockings, black and white shoes and a beret pulled well forwards over the forehead.

One of the strangest fashions this year was the appearance of black sweaters on young men in London who sought the spotlight: 'They hailed from Chelsea and Bloomsbury, and had artistic leanings.' Other smart men were wearing green suits with a matching green tie and soft-brimmed felt hats that could be 'moulded into any shape the wearer desired'. These were available in 'an entirely new shade of green'. There were even some green plus-fours.

Flannels were increasingly popular this summer, especially those in a pale gray or fawn. They had ample width in the leg and turned-up bottoms. The Prince of Wales and his brother George had taken to wearing their flannels fancy-striped, and these or a checked pattern were increasingly adopted by the smarter set, together with a matching jacket which had long wide lapels and three patch pockets. For cricket and tennis cream flannels were worn with a loose-knit cable sweater which had a polo or rolled collar. Rings of color decorated the neck and cuffs, and on cricket

sweaters the county arms were displayed on the breast. New 'gripu' tennis shoes had come to the aid of the tennis player. These were made with built-in canvas strapping that braced the instep. Shorts still raised eyebrows on the tennis courts, although they were used for cycling and hiking. The beret had been adopted by the cyclist too, and occasionally the motorist wore one with a tassel hanging down over one side.

In 1931 the correct dress at the seaside was without doubt the yachting rig: a smart pair of flannels worn with a navy-blue blazer which had gilt buttons on the

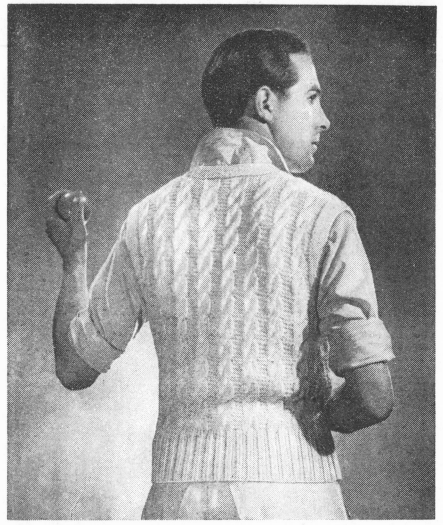

The THING HE NEEDS!

Every Smart Young Man Approves Of A Cable Stitch Design For His Sports Pull-over.

2ND ROW: K. 2, p. 6, * k. 4, p. 6; repeat from * until 2 remain, k. 2.

Repeat these 2 rows 3 times more.

9TH ROW: K. 2, twist the cable as described above, * k. 4, cable; repeat from * until 2 sts. remain, k. 2.

10TH ROW: As 2nd row.

Repeat these 10 rows 5 times more, when the armhole will be reached. To shape the armhole continue in pattern casting off 2 sts. at the beginning of each of the next 2 rows, then cast off 1 st. at the beginning of the next 16 rows.

There are now 80 sts., on which work 42 rows straight,

H E will find so many uses for this practical pullover! For tennis and cricket, punting, and holiday wear, particularly.

This pull-over is worked up in double knitting wool, so it is not tedious to make.

MATERIALS: 11 ounces of "Greenock" double knitting wool (obtainable only at one of the branches of the Scotch Wool & Hosiery Stores); two pairs of bone knitting needles, No. 7 and No. 9, and a short spare needle.

TENSION AND MEASUREMENTS: Worked at a tension of 10 sts. (one cable pattern) to 1¾ inches in width on the No. 7 needles, the measurements on the diagram are attained after light pressing.

ABBREVIATIONS: K., knit plain; p., purl; tog., together; sl., slip; st., stitch. Directions in brackets are worked the number of times stated after the brackets.

TO TWIST A CABLE

T RY this on an odd piece of knitting, with 20 sts. on the needle. K. 3, slip the next 3 sts. on a short spare needle and bring them to the front of the work. K. the next 3 sts., then slip the 3 sts. from the spare needle back to the left-hand needle, and k. them in the usual way. Thus reversing the position of the first and last 3 sts. on the k. 6 rib.

TO WORK

B EGIN at the lower edge of the back by casting on 100 sts. and work 32 rows in k. 2 and p. 2 rib. Now work in cable pattern with the No. 7 needles as follows:

1ST ROW: With the right side facing, k. plain.

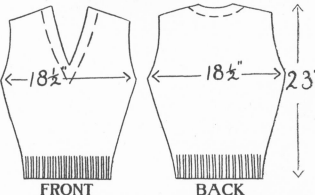

FRONT   BACK

These are the exact measurements of the pull-over.

when the shoulder line will be reached. To slope the shoulders cast off 6 sts. at the beginning of every row until 32 sts. remain.

Change to No. 9 needles and k. 3 rows.

Next row: With right side facing, k. 7, k. 2 tog., (k. 6, k. 2 tog.) twice, k. 7.

K. 6 rows more and cast off.

THE FRONT

W ORK as back until the 10 pattern rows have been worked 6 times to the armhole. Now divide the sts. equally, passing the last 50 on a spare needle for the right shoulder, leaving 50 for the left shoulder.

LEFT SHOULDER.—Continue in pattern, decreasing at both ends as follows : At the armhole cast off 2 sts. at the beginning of the next row, then cast off 1 st. at the beginning of every alternate row, at the same end, for 8 times, after which keep this end of the row straight. At the same time work 2 tog. at the neck end of every alternate right-side row (that is, every 4th row) until only 24 sts. remain. Work 7 rows more (8 rows more on the right front) then cast off 6 at the beginning of next row, and every alternate row at the arm-hole end, until all are worked off.

RIGHT SHOULDER.—Join to the neck end of the right front sts. and work as given for the left front.

FRONT NECK.—With right side facing and using No. 9 needles, pick up and k. 60 sts. from each side of the front neck (3 st. to 4 rows) 120 sts. on the same needle, k. 1 row.

1ST DECREASE ROW : K. 57, slip the next 2 sts. separately, k. 1, pass the sl.-sts. over, k. 3 tog., k. 57.

* K. 1 row, then repeat the decrease row with 2 sts. less, before and after the centre decreases, than on last decrease row.

Repeat from * 3 times more, and cast off rather loosely.

Sew the front and back shoulders together.

THE ARMHOLE BANDS

WITH the right side facing and using No. 9 needles, pick up and k. 93 sts. round the armhole K. 10 rows and cast off rather loosely.

Work the second armhole in the same manner.

TO MAKE UP

PRESS with a damp cloth over the wrong side of the work, taking care that the ribbing is not stretched. Sew up the side seams and press all joins.

front. For sunbathing and swimming a woollen one-piece suit with skirt attachment was the favorite costume, and it was accompanied by a vividly-striped beach wrap of the kind that now professed to be scientifically pre-shrunk and fast dyed. No longer could a man wear an old mac or top coat on the beach without seriously spoiling the holiday or wrecking a romance.

There was a rumour that plus-fours were beginning to go out of fashion, and that many young men were reverting to trousers. They found that odd trousers and jackets were more useful and also cost less. The truth was that more people were tending to order an extra pair of trousers, which with the plus-fours, jacket and waistcoat made a four-piece suit that could be used for business as well as sport, especially if it came in a versatile color and a subdued Glen Urquhart check.

Pullovers worn with a lounge suit instead of a waistcoat were beginning to be seen, and because of this tendency the latest designs of pullovers and cardigans were less loud and in quiet colors like old heather or fawn. But many thought that a pale brown woolly worn with a dark brown suit or a light pullover with a blue-gray suit looked too informal and out of place for work. The most jarring note of informality that occurred this year was when Prime Minister Ramsay MacDonald wore a bowler hat with a morning coat when he went to see the King in September.

The depressed conditions of industry were reflected in men's working suits, which tended to show little variety in style or extremes in color. Patterns were still small and neat: a few white lines, pinheads, herringbones or no pattern at all. This year it was New York

that stated optimistically that 'people in business should avoid pessimism and cultivate a cheerful outlook'. They suggested brighter clothing as a cure, 'in happy colors such as greens, grays, blues and browns, or black and white checks in times of business depression'.

The Men's Dress Reform Party still battled on in Britain with its reforms to men's business clothes and dress clothes, but many people took the Party as a good joke, or felt that 'the times were too serious for such frivolities under the guise of reform.' Dr Jordan complained that certain people, especially the women, who two years ago had bared their arms and left their necks open, had now defected and let the cause down.

Russia seemed to be the only country that was not lagging behind in an attempt to reform men's clothes. Russian men, it was declared, will all be dressed alike: 'Their trousers will be supported by a belt on which bags would hang to take the place of pockets. They will be full at the waist but tight below the knee, so that the Soviet citizens will be unable to spoil them by pulling them off over their boots. The waistcoat is to be abolished. Coats will be short, loose at the shoulder and without collars, and the shirts will be open at the neck.' This was thought by the English to be too like a uniform and therefore a negation of individual freedom ... although it was certainly very like the Dress Reformer's ideal outfit.

1932

'Once upon a time men put away their straw hats and flannels at the end of September; now there is no chronology in clothes and flannel bags flop over brown shoes as much in January as in June.'

The virtue of the gray flannel suit was that one could wear it on train journeys and on board ship, especially if it was worn with a shirt and collar in broad pink and gray stripes, with the gray stripes matching the gray of the trousers. Even the women were affected by the craze, and in Hyde Park in May husbands and wives appeared in sartorial harmony clad in gray flannel suits.

By the end of the year the Oxford men, bored by their own fashion, tried to stop the grayness and took to wearing black flannel trousers with a tweed jacket, long scarf, pullover and no hat. But it was too late; gray had already spread from trousers and had engulfed sports jackets, shirts, socks, pullovers and woollies. At Eton this year, though the boys had been banned from wearing fancy waistcoats, they had been allowed to replace the usual knickerbockers for football and other games with a pair of ordinary shorts . . . in a suitable gray.

Plain dark gray flannels for golf had been dealing the death blow to plus-four knickerbockers, and any plus-fours remaining were themselves in a plain gray cloth or gray basket weave, with only a few found in brown or an indistinct check. These modern plus-fours had the garters finished with crepe elastic instead of the usual buckle. Most people copied what the Prince wore for his golfing outfit, which was now a dark blue pullover or knitted sports vest with a small collar, a blue beret, blue waterproof jacket, and flannels. Some were influenced by the French golfers who wore bright orange, blue or maroon pullovers finished at the neck with large knitted bobbles.

To offset the grayness, pullovers in a bright all-over color, some with a pattern in a fancy stitch like cable stitch, were worn. Prince George was seen wearing a dark crimson pullover, the University men took to bright yellow pullovers, and in Hyde Park this spring several young men wore red and blue colored pullovers with turtle or roll-collared necks. A man who wanted to be different could wear a plain pullover which had the collar and cuffs in a contrasting color, accompanying this with fawn flannels.

The riders along Rotten Row normally wore the correct riding habit of a fashionable Glen checked jacket (now with slits at the sides and back), and jodhpurs and riding hat. In 1932 some were shocked to see instead 'many people of both sexes turning up in our wonderful Rotten Row in costumes that were not only a disgrace to our Royal Park, but to our country. Many were without hats, others in stockings and pullovers of every bright shade and variety.' Meanwhile, Sir Samuel Hoare, the Secretary for India, had thoroughly abused the archetypal riding garment when

18½" 21" FRONT

18½ 21 BACK

A SLEEVELESS PULL-OVER

Instructions On Opposite Page

in February he caused a mild sensation by appearing on the ice rink in jodhpurs.

It was increasingly evident that the motorist no longer needed to own a Sunday suit. 'Men have evolved into crustaceans, with motors forming their outer shells as handsome and polished coverings.' The young men all over England had become noticeably less smart in their dress. A ready-made sports jacket with an equally cheap ready-made pair of flannel trousers, together with a tarnished macintosh, summed up the outfit of many men in their twenties. Some liked to imagine that old clothes were the hallmark of ancient lineage, others that the cult of shabiness was the latest fashion. Although men's wear was never cheaper than at the present time, with many genuinely reduced prices—in some cases back to pre-war levels—the majority admitted that their untidiness was due to the financial depression, and only the nouveau riche were distinguished by their brand new suits. The poorer men were as anxious as ever to look smart; most wanted clothes that would prove cheap but serviceable, and demanded what they termed as a solid two-year suit in a material that would wear well, keep its shape and not shine. The tailors observed that there were 'three ages of man . . . that it was the younger man who was the smartest as he earned money only for himself and spent a lot of it on his personal appearance. Then there was the rather older man who, having met the girl of his choice, became shabbier as he tended to cut down on his tailoring bills and started to save up. Thirdly, it was the married man who was the untidiest of all as he only bought the clothes that were absolutely necessary.'

The wealthy young men still managed to dress fashionably. They adopted the special novelty cloth for their suits which, being made in a 'shot' effect turned either blue or brown according to how the light fell upon it. Or they followed the lead of Jack Buchanan by wearing a double-breasted gray flannel jacket with white trousers. They demanded a deeper waistcoat pocket for fountain pens, which now came with a pocket clip.

A SLEEVELESS PULL-OVER

THIS pull-over is made with deep armholes, so that there is no uncomfortable bulk under the arms.

MATERIALS: 5 ounces of "Greenock" 4-ply super-fingering from the Scotch Wool and Hosiery Stores (No. 466 is a marl mixture of nigger, fawn and white, suitable for men's wear), a pair of long bone knitting needles No. 8, and a spare needle, a pair of knitting needles No. 10.

TENSION AND MEASUREMENTS: Worked at a tension to produce 6 st. to the inch in width . the measurements on the diagram are attained after light pressing.

TO WORK: Begin at the back waistline, and with No. 10 needles, cast on 110 st. Work 34 rows of single rib. Increase 1 st. at end of last row, making 111 st., this finishes the waistband. Change to No. 8 needles and work in the following pattern.

1ST ROW: With the right side facing, k. plain.

2ND ROW: All purl.

Repeat these 2 rows twice more, making 6 rows in s.s.

7TH ROW: K. 3, p. 5, * k. 5, p. 5, repeat from *, finishing with k. 3.

8TH ROW: P. 3, k. 5, * p. 5, k. 5, repeat from *, finishing with p. 3.

Repeat these 2 rows twice more which gives 6 rows in 5 and 5 rib.

Work the 1st and 2nd row 3 times, giving 6 rows of s.s., then work the 8th and 7th row, in that order, 3 times. This gives another 6 rows in 5 and 5 rib, with the rib reversed over the last ribbed strip, giving the under and over effect of the reeds in basket work.

Repeat these 24 rows once more, then work 12 rows more in pattern (60 rows above the waist rib), when the armhole will be reached.

To shape the armhole, cast off 2 st. at the beginning of each of the next 8 rows, then work 2 tog. at the beginning of each of the following 10 rows. There are now 85 st., and on these work 46 rows straight. (Here note that the p. 3 and k. 3 at the beginning and end of pattern rows is omitted, as the pattern is now in line with the k. 5 or p. 5 as the case may be.)

To shape the back shoulders, continue in pattern, casting off 6 st at the beginning of each of the next 6 rows, then cast off 7 at the beginning of each of the next 2 rows. There are now 35 st., and with the No. 10 needles k. 11 rows. (Work 2 tog. at each end of the 5th and 9th of these rows.) Cast off rather loosely.

THE FRONT: Work as given for the back until 59 rows have been worked above the waist rib.

NEXT ROW: With wrong side facing, work 55 st. for the right shoulder and slip these on a spare needle, cast off 1 st., and work 55 st. for the left shoulder.

THE LEFT SHOULDER: Work in pattern with shaping at both ends of work as follows: Cast off 2 st. at the beginning of alternate rows (armhole end) 4 times, then work 2 tog. at the same end of alternate rows for 5 times, after which keep this edge straight. In the meantime, work 2 tog. at the neck end of every 4th row until there are only 25 st. left. Work 5 rows more (6 rows on the right shoulder) when the top shoulder-line will be reached.

To shape the shoulder cast off 6 st. at the beginning of every alternate row (armhole end), until all are worked off. Draw the wool through the last st. and fasten off.

THE RIGHT SHOULDER: Join the wool to the neck end of the right front st. and work as given for the left front.

THE FRONT NECK: With the No. 10 needles and the right side of work facing, pick up and k. 68 st. at each half of front neck, missing every 6th st. on the edge of the knitting, so that the work will not be fluted. There will be 136 st. on the same needle. ** K. 1 row with the wrong side facing.

DECREASE ROW: K. 65, slip the next 2 st., k. 1, pass the slipped st. over, k. 3 tog., k. 65.

Repeat the last 2 rows from ** until the 5th dec. row has been worked. (Note that each time the dec. row is worked there are 2 st. less at both ends than on previous dec. row.)

Cast off loosely Sew the front shoulders to the back shoulders.

THE ARMHOLES: With right side facing and with No. 10 needles, pick up and k. 112 st. round one armhole, in the same manner that they were picked up round the neck. K. 10 rows and cast off. Work the second armhole in the same manner.

TO MAKE UP: Press all except the waist rib with a damp cloth over the work; press the shoulder seams. Sew up the side seams, darn in all ends and press these seams.

To the Private View at Burlington House, the smart men wore the newest fashionable overcoats which were in a dark blue, navy, black or gray. Many of these were silk faced and had piping at the cuffs or velvet collars upon which rested a bunch of violets. Others wore carnations and a few affected orchids. Mr Richard Sickert was as unconventional in dress as in art, and came dressed in a white bowler hat with his check tweed suit. One brave man wore a shirt and collar in a tiny floral print. There was a tendency for both old and young to display much handkerchief. The older men's handkerchiefs 'foamed at the pocket mouth', but the latest idea for the young men was to wear monogram handkerchiefs which were so deftly folded that the corner neatly turned over the pocket mouth like a flap of an envelope, displaying the letters.

In February the Prince of Wales appeared publicly at the Academy wearing a scarf which had white spots on it, and immediately they became an inspiration: men and women everywhere breaking out into spots. Neckwear was the most infected, and ties made from a wool and silk mixture had spots of green, red or black; flannel-matching gray ties were embellished with red spots. White spots seemed the most contagious kind, and scarves, mufflers and all types of bow-tie and cravat, whether in red, yellow, blue or green, were spotted in white. Other garments soon caught the illness—woollen golf hose became spotted, dressing-gowns in pure silk became spotted and soon handkerchiefs, pullovers and bedroom slippers appeared in spots of varying dimensions. Many people became worried that the lounge would not be immune.

The wearing of a bright tie was a compensation for many men during the Depression. 'Today will see scores of men with rather shabby suits and unusually brilliant ties, with broad vivid stripes as associated with schools, clubs and regiments.' Bright red ties everywhere cheered up the ubiquitous gray suits. The Prince himself liked to wear a bright tie with his gray flannel trousers and blue beret, and nowadays he more often than not replaced the waistcoat with the newly fashionable slip-over. This was the latest type of pullover, and was sleeveless with both the neckline and armholes designed to be rounded and low. The pattern was often a neat Fair-Isle in two or more colors. Being such a versatile garment it very soon became the most popular type of pullover to wear for sports, and in the more subdued colors for replacing the waistcoat to wear with the lounge suit.

Sports shirts could be colorful and gay. The Dress Reform shirt had a polo collar and came in a great range of colors: scarlet, green, navy, black, white, slate gray and fawn. Today political significance in the color of the shirt was an increasing occurrence, and in February—in rivalry with the red shirts of the Communist International and the black shirts of Mussolini's *Fascisti*—The Green International, an organization of peace-loving people which included Einstein and Gandhi, urged its members to wear green shirts. In England, green was certainly becoming a popular color to wear, especially for sports and country wear, but for other than political reasons. The Prince of Wales, during his visit to Cannes whilst on holiday with Prince George, took the air in a red shirt, and only changed to a green one when he left for Biarritz. Both he and Prince George favored dark glasses against the sun. The Prince of Wales wore a pair of blue trousers such as Breton fishermen wear, an open neck shirt and a straw hat, and Prince George wore gray flannel shorts and a little dough-boy cap, after the fashion of American servicemen.

The Prince of Wales had given much variety to men's hats during the past few months by wearing first the beret, then a white felt hat underbrimmed with green for golfing, and for summer the straw hat or boater (see page 32). Once the popular Prince had worn it, the boater became fashionable, but 'neither the Prince nor Maurice Chevalier had been able to popularize the idea with the motorist, because it was none too comfortable and inclined to blow off.' Well-dressed men at Lords cricket ground this year wore Panamas or boaters which had multi-colored bands around the rims. These they wore with their gray flannel suits, spotted ties and slip-overs instead of waistcoats. In July a boater was seen in the House of Commons, and this caused a stir—it was probably the first ever to be seen there.

At the seaside the popular swimsuits had the back of the costume in a Y formation like a pair of braces. It was so hot this summer that white was adopted for many garments and tropical kit of white drill and tussore and pith helmets were the most cool and inviting things to wear. For cruising, tennis and the river the latest sporting jacket came in a creamy white with the collar, cuffs and waistband knitted and the pockets and front fitted with a zip-fastener.

In America the men had rebelled against wearing black dinner jackets with stiff white shirts in the hot summer, and had adopted instead a 'monkey jacket' made of cool white cotton drill and a cummerbund of black silk. In London some men arrived at the Savoy wearing short white coats of an almost naval cut over their boiled shirts. The majority of English people preferred the black dinner jacket, and nowadays favored it more than tails for formal evening wear. The best-dressed people, like Prince George and the Prince of Wales, wore their jackets double-breasted with the reveres slightly longer than formerly. There was now a vertical flower hole in the silk-faced lapel and the custom of wearing a black felt hat with D.J.s was generally accepted.

The stiff upper lip brigade railed against those who were so informal and slovenly as to dine out in the West End in day clothes. 'Such slackness in dress will in the long run make for slackness in behavior, and it is not so wild as it sounds to say that society will fall to pieces, and man will revert to a state of savagery. A man who, alone in the jungle, changes into his dinner jacket every evening, does so to convince himself that he is not a savage.'

Whatever the pleasure
PLAYER'S complete it

Had a good swim?..Fine! water beautifully warm this morning; better than yesterday... Smoking?... Thanks, I always "round off" with a "Player"... Unlike the weather, they're reliable.

PLAIN OR CORK-TIPPED

20 FOR 11½ᵈ

BE IN THE "SWIM"...SAY *Player's Please*

THE LEADING AUTHORITY ON STYLE AND CLOTHES

THE TAILOR & CUTTER
AND OUTFITTING NEWS

4D

1933

Some men in 1933 listened to the call for a return to formality, and were certainly encouraged by women to create an image of dark sombre elegance in order 'to act as foils to their glittering mates'. The up-to-date style of dress coat worn by slim young men achieved harmony, proportion, simplicity and restraint. The coat was short and straight in front across the waist and long in the skirt. The jacket lapels were broad and more often than not covered with black silk. The square shoulders depended as much on art as nature, for there was more than a suspicion of wadding at the shoulder. The trousers, with their row of double braiding, were on the wide side and the material for the outfit was a dull black barathea with a small herringbone pattern or neat fancy basket weave. A goodly expanse of white marcella waistcoat upon which jewelled buttons gleamed, and a glossy shirt front, were in sharp contrast to the raven coat with its black ivory buttons. The stiff collar with heavy wings and sharp angles was softened by a bow-tie 'as graceful as a flower'. Both the wings of the collar and the tie ends were longer and bolder, as this area was still the focal point of the outfit. A spice of cambric arose from the small breast pocket, and between the white gloved fingers rested a cigarette, often in a long ivory holder. Around the neck was hung an Inverness cloak or an opera cloak with a deep collar.

The Prince of Wales had favored fresh tendencies in dress waistcoats and he, and those who like him wore dress clothes constantly, could flirt with three or four different styles. To give maximum variety to a night out there were also a great number of dress shirts in piqué or marcella to choose from. The latest novelty shirts were either in black silk cord marcella or a black moiré silk with black moiré silk braces to match. There had been recent complaints that men's braces were too dull and drab, and in the West End braces could now be obtained on which all the clasps and buckles were old gold. Men were 'as vain and touchy about their clothes as women, and as anxious as to features of style and in terrible earnest over details.' A new note was the appearance of black suede shoes to wear with the dress coat, and these, being matt like the coat, looked very smart, but if black leather shoes were worn they should have no toecaps as these were only appropriate to wear with a dinner jacket. The cloak was considered glamorous by all men, for it added style to evening dress. Even the evening dress overcoats had become cloak-like, for there was a loose type of raglan designed with such extreme width and depth of arm-hole and such full sleeves that it fell like a cape.

It had become very popular to wear a midnight blue dress coat, and to match this a chesterfield evening dress overcoat in the same midnight blue. This year the morning dress coat arrived also in a midnight blue, in a shade slightly lighter than that of the evening dress coat, and this was given the lead by the well-known society figure, Mr Eddie Tatham.

City workers had already shown some innovations in their dress; they were tending to discard their waistcoats in favor of marl-colored knitted cross-over waistcoats ribbed at the bottom and fastened with two buttons set close together at the bottom front. Their black bowlers, like that of the Prince of Wales, were lower in the crown and had smaller brims to give a jaunty youthful appearance. Their soft hats, too, had smaller brims and the crowns were more square in shape than before. This was the result of an increasing need for a more independent-looking hat. 'These new hats are more rakish. They will have special appeal to the city man and will keep their place in any wind, will not get out of shape, and can be worn in any way.' There was also an increase in the number of umbrellas seen in the city and a corresponding decrease in the number of walking sticks, for the new umbrella with steel stick could be tightly folded and did for both.

For the West End worker, fashion still favored the sportsman-like figure, and there was a profusion of athletic shoulders in the streets. The draped effect achieved by the back of the lounge jacket falling straight from the shoulder gave 'soft shadows and an alertness and clean-cut quality as of modern houses where the ivy has been cut away and the moss removed'. Trouser widths were now 22 inches at the knee and 19 inches at the bottom for the older man, and a wider 20 inches at the bottom for the younger man. Materials for the lounge suit had patterns in the weave picked out with colored stripes, checks, or interwoven strands against a plain blue, blue-gray or gray background. Very often the West End man replaced his lounge waistcoat with a newly fashionable reversible slip-over which displayed a completely different pattern on each side—perhaps a

The Polo Sweater

'A "Free-and-Easy" Garment For Week-Ends And Holidays!

THE latest thing in men's wear!

A polo jumper is such a useful woolly for the man who likes to be busy about the house, and for the boy who is keen on sports.

MATERIALS: 12 ozs. of "Greenock" 4-ply Super Fingering (from the Scotch Wool and Hosiery Stores), (No. 341 to match the cardigan), a pair of long bone knitting needles No. 8, and a spare needle; a set of 4 knitting needles, No. 11 with double points.

TENSION AND MEASUREMENTS: Worked at a tension of 6 st. to the inch in width, the following measurements are attained after light pressing: round body 39 ins.; length from shoulder to hem, 26 ins.; underarm seam of sleeve, including cuff, 23 ins.

TO WORK: Begin at the lower edge of the back, and with the No. 8 needles cast on 114 st. Work 20 rows in single rib.

Now work in the following pattern:

1ST AND 2ND ROW: K. 6, * p. 6, k. 6, repeat from * to end.

3RD AND 4TH ROW: P. 6, * k. 6, p. 6, repeat from * to end.

Repeat these 4 rows 28 times more, when the armhole will be reached.

To shape the armhole, cast off 3 st. at the beginning of each of the next 2 rows, then work 2 tog. at the beginning of each of the following 18 rows. There are now 90 st., and on these work straight for 36 rows up to the top shoulder line.

To slope the shoulders, cast off 6 st. at the beginning of each of the next 10 rows. Now cut the wool and draw through

Something cosy to slip on after the game is over !

these remaining 30 st. until they are needed for the back of the collar.

THE POCKET LININGS: With No. 8 needles cast on 30 st. for pocket lining, and work the 4 pattern rows 10 times.

Cut the wool and slip the st. on a spare needle until needed. Work a second lining in the same manner.

THE FRONT: With No. 8 needles cast on 114 st. and work 20 rows in rib. Now repeat the 4 pattern rows 8 times.

NEXT 7 ROWS: Work 12 st. in pattern, rib 30 st. for pocket top, work 30 st. in pattern, rib 30 for the second pocket top, work remaining 12 st. in pattern.

NEXT ROW: Work 12 st. in pattern, cast off 30 st. and slip

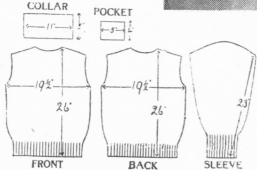

COLLAR — 11"

POCKET — 5"

FRONT 19½" 26"

BACK 19½" 26"

SLEEVE 23"

124

distinct check on one side and diamonds on the other. If a waistcoat was still worn it was *never* double-breasted.

Athletic underwear had arrived for the athletic man, and a new style of trunks, with elastic at the waistband which would not perish and would keep the garment in position with just the right amount of tension, came together with the 'athletic vest', a sleeveless, low-necked garment with elastic at the waist. A new age of elastic had swept away the use of buttons, braces and suspenders and there was a delight in having garments that seemed to be held up without any visible means of support. A self-supporting sock called Samson had the top part fitted with a narrow band of elastic called 'gentle grip', thus rendering garters and suspenders completely unnecessary. Woolly combinations for winter came without any buttons or fastenings, but were fitted instead with an elastic waistband. It was estimated that 90 per cent of the male population of the United States wore these woollen union or combination suits in the winter. Not only did they save time in dressing but were economical to wear and gave greater freedom of movement.

It was stated that 'one of the small revolutions of our time is the supercession of the night shirt by pajamas in striped effect. Most men prefer these to other kinds of pajamas.' Recently, however, an attempt to stage a comeback for the nightshirt had caused men to have to take a difficult decision as to what to wear at night. In summer most men had taken to wearing the new type of pajama which had short waisted pants held up by elastic and a jacket top that was sleeveless.

These were considered to be healthy and exciting to wear. Only a few years before it was considered un-hygienic to wear anything but white for underwear, but with the great improvement in the permanency of dyes this prejudice had been broken down, and although men's underwear was not yet as intriguing as women's, with the rise of artificial silk it was becoming increasingly varied. The previous year colors such as brown with darker brown edges and heliotrope with dark heliotrope were gaining favor, and this year 'if the truth be known man is taking to pink and blue underwear'. Silky under-garments also came in sky-blue, peach, lemon and other pastel shades. 'In 1933 . . . long legged pants for summer are quite a thing of the past, excepting with men of advanced years. The young modern man prefers knickers.'

THE POLO SWEATER (*Continued from previous page*)

the 30 st. from one pocket lining in place of these (the wool end of lining st. to be nearest the centre front of pullover) work 30 st. in pattern, cast off 30 and slip the second lining st. in place of these (the wool end of lining sts. to be nearest to the side seam of pullover) work remaining 12 st. in pattern.

Work the 4 pattern rows 19 times more to the armhole. Shape the armhole as given for the back and then work the 4 pattern rows 7 times on the 90 st. at chest.

Now shape the shoulders as follows :

THE LEFT SHOULDER : Beginning at the armhole end, work 38 st. in pattern, turn and work back to armhole end.

Work 36 st. in pattern, turn and work back.

Work 34 st. in pattern, turn and work back.

Work 32 st. in pattern, turn and work back.

Work 30 st. in pattern, turn, and on these last 30 st. work 9 rows more in pattern. Cast off 6 st. at the beginning of the next row and every alternate row (armhole end) until all are worked off. There will now be 60 st. on a needle for the front neck and right shoulder From neck end of these slip 22 st. to other working needle, join on the wool and work next 38 st. in pattern to armhole end.

THE RIGHT SHOULDER : Work exactly as given for left shoulder until the shoulder sts. are cast off. There are now 30 st. for the front of neck.

Sew the front shoulders to the back shoulders.

THE COLLAR

WITH No. 11 needles pick up and k. 1 round with 110 st., taking 30 st. from back of neck, 20 from the end of rows at each shoulder, and from the 30 front neck st. take 13 from the first 8 st., k. the centre 14 st., and take 13 from the last 8 st. (The latter can be done by knitting in the front and back of some of the st.). Divide these 110 st. on three needles and work 48 rounds in rib. Cast off loosely. (Here is a special method of casting off loosely, which in this case will allow the turn-over edge of the collar to expand to the thicker part of the neck, and is particularly useful for small openings that have to be drawn over the head : K. the first st., then pass it back on the left-hand needle, * k. 2 tog., then pass the resulting st. from the right-hand needle back on to the left, and repeat from * until all the st. are cast off.)

THE SLEEVES

BEGIN at the wrist, and with No. 11 needles cast on 66 st. Work 55 rows in rib. Change to No. 8 needles and work the 4 pattern rows 3 times. Continue in pattern, increasing 1 st. at each end of next row, and every following 10th row, until there are 90 st. on the needle. Work 9 rows more, when the full length of the underarm seam will be attained.

To shape the top of the sleeve, cast off 6 st. at the beginning of each of the next 2 rows, then cast off 2 at the beginning of every row until 26 st. remain. Cast off and work the second sleeve in the same manner.

TO MAKE UP

FIRST press all the pieces with a damp cloth over the work, taking care not to stretch the rib. Sew the pocket linings to the wrong side of the front. Stitch the sleeves into the armholes, and press the seam while the work is open. Sew up the side seams and press.

This fashionable gathering, on a *Viceroy of India* cruise,
1933, includes a number of men.

Women's suits were following male fashions. 'Her jackets and coats were cut on masculine lines with the severe square-shouldered effect in direct imitation of a man's. For her sportswear she had adopted plus-fours for motor-cycling and other sports. She bought her scarves and pullovers from men's shops and it was no uncommon sight to see girls and their boyfriends dressed exactly alike in style and material.'

Mary Pickford said that she did not care for the new Hollywood fashion of trousers for women, and that she did not even care for the trousers as garb for men. Like many other reformers she wanted instead the return to the flowing robes of the ancient Greeks. In America 'reformed' men were wearing lounge and evening suits entirely made of artificial silk. In England men were soon to have a dress salon of their own, twice a week in a fashionable part of the West End, with young men of leisure to act as mannequins. Peter Russell, a dress designer of Bruton Street, was to lead this latest crusade, starting with a show of dressing-gowns. 'I am making my dressing-gowns with cravats, for how many wives have finally decided on divorce after being confronted time after time at breakfast by a husband's bare throat above a dressing-gown?'

In country and casual wear an attack was mounted

against plus-fours. Mr Frank Swinnerton described them as 'monstrous deflated balloons.... Why men should wish their legs to resemble the legs of chickens I haven't a notion. Do not the wearers know how sloppy they look with skinny fragments of limb protruding from each leg?' Mr Dion Byngham called them 'the ugliest, stuffiest, silliest, baggiest bifurcations ever invented. But for them,' he said, 'we might have had shorts much sooner.'

Shorts in velvet cord of gray, fawn and navy were now worn for cycling, hiking, camping and holiday wear, and perhaps one day white cord shorts will be accepted for tennis. Although on the courts 'the girls were wearing just an ounce or two of flimsy material and a pair of shorts', the men still preferred to wear trousers, though now of white velvet cord. They still feared to show their legs. Some men with ugly knees had already lengthened their holiday shorts to just below the knee. Many thought that if only the Prince could be persuaded to wear shorts for sportswear then in a few months everyone else would be wearing them. But the Prince of Wales stuck to his plus-fours, especially those in a prominent check. 'I believe in bright checks for sportsmen. The louder they are the better I like them.'

Prince George and the Prince of Wales started yet another fashion for men—the use of the zip-fastener for their trouser flys, and their lead was followed by thousands in Britain and in the United States. Lord Louis Mountbatten is understood to have recommended the idea to the Princes, and as these three men were highly regarded in the United States as leaders of fashion the idea was quickly adopted. Tailors were undecided about the idea at first but they soon saw that the zips made trousers hang better and prevented much creasing.

1934

The old King still insisted on having a side crease in his trousers instead of one at the front like everyone else. His Majesty was teased many times by his sons on the matter, but the King stuck to his own taste and chose this year a new article for his wardrobe—a pair of boldly checked plus-fours which had creases at the sides. Only royalty can start a new fashion at events like the Chelsea Flower Show, and this year the King did so by wearing a blue lounge suit with a bowler hat instead of his morning dress or his usual frock coat. This meant that in future lounge suits would be worn

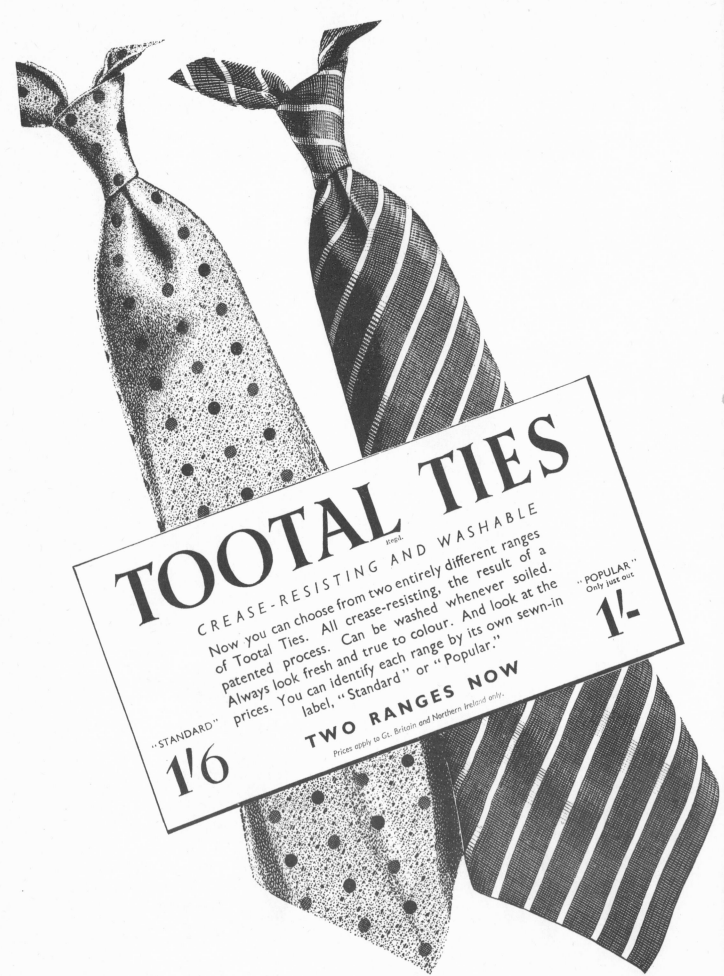

TOOTAL TIES
Regd.

CREASE-RESISTING AND WASHABLE

Now you can choose from two entirely different ranges of Tootal Ties. All crease-resisting, the result of a patented process. Can be washed whenever soiled. Always look fresh and true to colour. And look at the prices. You can identify each range by its own sewn-in label, "Standard" or "Popular."

"STANDARD"
1/6

"POPULAR"
Only just out
1/-

TWO RANGES NOW

Prices apply to Gt. Britain and Northern Ireland only.

by every man, and blue became the color of the year, with pale blue, royal blue or turquoise for ties, shirts and socks and Balmoral blue for plus-fours.

Returning prosperity was probably responsible for all the optimistic colors that were reappearing in men's clothes, and there was also more choice than before. New lounge suits were made of polychromatic worsteds with a design of two or more colors set against a plain background. These designs had no suggestion of gaudiness, but the effect was rich and the colors in perfect taste. The suits were now cut with two slits at each side of a longish jacket and horn buttons often replaced ordinary buttons, giving a special effect to the whole outfit. The shirt to wear with the suit showed variety in color and style rather than in pattern, and the latest trend was to dispense with the detested back collar stud and replace it with a narrow band which, being passed around the back of the neck of the shirt and slotting through the collar, held it in position without the need for a stud. An old idea revived was to buy a shirt supplied with two detachable cuffs as well as two detachable collars, one collar with long points, the other an ordinary double collar with short points. On the plain but brightly colored shirts, the kipper tie in diagonal stripes was frequently being replaced by the novel idea of a tie cut on the straight with straight sides. This, as well as allowing a man to have straight stripes, was economic because both ends of the tie could be used. Some ties were washable and uncreaseable, and knitted and silk ties in green, canary, scarlet and blue were the height of fashion. The strangest novelty was to wear a floral pattern tie with flannels.

Apparently the tie was the first thing a woman looked at, for a man, it seemed, could be summed up at a glance by his tie. The man who wore a plain tie could be trusted, for he was unostentatious and honest. Men who went in for big spots were boastful and terribly conceited. Men who wore ties with very tiny black and white checks were kindly and rather interesting and usually men of imagination, and as there were very few nice club or regimental ties which were neither loud nor went ill with a man's complexion, men who wore them were usually boring and had very little 'personality or imagination.' In spite of such alarming warnings most men seemed to prefer a club tie with a scarf to match—and a tobacco pouch covered in the same club colors.

Men, like women, were beginning to give thought to their waistlines. The women had lengthened their skirts in order to look tall and thin and had started a craze for slimming, and the men—needing to match these slim silhouettes—were doing likewise. Men wanted to look good on the beach or next to the pool. They wanted to be healthy and fit and aimed to reach the ideal in physical perfection. Women had changed their hair from straight to curly and they now admired a man who had similarly curly hair. Women who would have been called flappers in England, but in America were called 'young buds', had their hair permanently waved, and encouraged their boyfriends to do the same.

'The custom of cruising or going down to the sea in ships for holidays has spread like wildfire. It is now within the reach of all, even for a weekend.' White looked cool and correct for cruising and smart deck suits in heavy white linen trimmed with contrasting colors, with bell-bottomed trousers and a short sack jacket of cream flannel, were worn in the day for the promenade along the deck. For a more casual cruising outfit, smart flannels in blue, gray, white or green were worn with an open-necked sports shirt in a striped or plain-colored rayon that was both lock-knit and ladderproof. Over this, the really well-dressed man wore a smart blazer and cravat, and he sometimes indulged in the permanent wave. For evening the 'Tropica' white satin mess-jacket was worn, and with a slim silhouette essential the new backless waistcoat that combined waistcoat and braces in one was chosen by many men. Seaslips or 'trunks', as they were more often called, were worn at sea if one had a good chest. But with the shocking fact that some men and women had become members of nudist societies, law had enacted that various parts of the body both male and female were indecent and must not be disclosed to the public. Bathing rules for men were that 'the lower part of the body must be clothed in shorts or bathing trunks, but covering to the shoulder may be demanded in some places ... though not on a cruise or on the continent, where men are allowed to go naked to the waist.'

The average man no longer bought his dressing-gown merely for utilitarian purposes, and colorful robes for travelling, the seaside or a cruise had reached degrees of splendor never before obtained. A couple of nights in a hotel demanded an attractive dressing-gown made in foulard silk or brocaded and beautifully ornate in design. Pajamas had appeared that out-rivalled the gowns, and novelty pajamas

Cossack Pajamas

129

looked extremely smart in a fancy design of green with black edgings to the pockets, cuffs, turn-ups and waistband and a black stripe down the trouser leg. Pajamas of a Russian style with stand-up Cossack collar came in bright colors of red, scarlet and orange and other colors that were so vivid that 'they threatened to murder sleep'. Even Belisha pajamas had arrived to celebrate the invention this year by Mr Hore Belisha of the flashing striped Belisha beacon as a warning road sign. These came in black stripes graduating on a background of orange.

In the heatwave of 1934 Englishmen were gradually taking to light suits and accessories for the summer. Tropical suitings in silk, linen, fine wool and cotton were available and there were fewer men refusing to go to the office in a flannel suit—a garb in which they would have trembled to appear not so many years before. Waistcoats, too, were disappearing in the heat, and the Prince of Wales and Prince George left theirs off even with the morning coat suit. Shirt sleeves had been in evidence in some Government offices without giving offence. 'Thousands of women have taken to going about without stockings. One sees them walking about in shorts and flannel bags with no stockings, and sandals. We men are more properly garbed than many of the fair sex today, although admittedly some have been seen in blazers, shorts and baby socks.'

Doctor Jordan of The Dress Reform Party stated that 'We are now a healthier race than ever before, and for this we have to thank a victory over the tyranny of clothes that are unsuitable for an active life.' The latest type of clothing that healthy and athletic people of both sexes were taking advantage of was a new Aertex garment, as for underwear these were not only superbly comfortable but ensured free access of air to the body and afforded maximum protection against overheating. Aertex pajamas were especially healthy. A training suit for athletes called Olympic was invented in a woollen material. The jacket was blouse-shaped with a collar and zip-fastener front. The trousers had elastic at the waist and zip-fasteners at the ankles. It was hoped that this suit would become highly fashionable—it did, as the track-suit.

The women in 1934 had the following comments on the kind of man they liked. 'Well dressed certainly, but not extravagantly dressed. Let his suit be unobtrusive in color but well fitting, and not too much padding in the shoulders. No waistline, for that makes him look effeminate, and not too much 'hanky' showing from his breast pocket either, if he favors this style. He must be restrained in his shirts, hose and tie, for a man who is too glaring in his hose, shirt or tie is a bit of a 'Sammy'. Nor should he be over-decorated with jewellery either, in the way of a tie-pin or ring, and if he must wear a wristlet watch, then for goodness sake let it be as unobtrusive as possible. Perfume is suspect; a perfumed man makes one feel he is in need of soap and water.'

1935

King George celebrated his Silver Jubilee year with an eleven-week Jubilee Gala, and 'every night in London there are functions where men may be seen in symbolic, ritualistic and traditional garments. Men go to Italy and Greece to see the wonders of the past; they come to London to see the greatness of the present. Huge liners have crossed and are crossing the seas, laden with folk of all nations eager to view London in gala dress.'

The Jubilee color of silver-gray was chosen as being a clean, restrained color, light and gala-like. It could be adopted effortlessly by men for their clothes. Jubilee gray and wine for blazers and pullovers, Jubilee gray and red or blue for pajamas, and the 'flannel grayers' became available in a lighter shade of gray. The King was already faithful to the flower in his coat—orchids and gardenias as well as roses and carnations—but in Jubilee year the buttonhole habit brightened up everyone's appearance and gave a gay festive note.

During the season at royal Ascot, gray was the predominant color for the formal morning suit. This was made of a thinner material now to help to give an appearance of slimness, and a backless waistcoat was chosen for the same reason. A pale topper was worn in preference to the black or dark gray for Ascot, garden parties, weddings and similar functions, and having also received favor from the Prince of Wales and his brothers was given the seal of youth at the wedding of the Duke of Gloucester to Lady Alice Scott. The fashion for wearing gloves seemed to be on the decline and few men now considered it necessary to wear white leather gloves for dress wear. Smart men wore gray or fawn boots with suede uppers or plain black shoes. Spats were worn this year at the 'varsity match and morning coats were braided. Cravats with bold safety-pins or sapphire tie-pins added variety to the rigs and 'haughty monocles met one at every glance'.

Although a few distinctive dressers still favored upright collars with cravats in gray, black or small check, gray knotted ties were the latest vogue. The Prince of Wales and Prince George had their stiff double collars with the points cut away at an acute angle and liked to wear a large check tie with their morning dress. Regimental ties with their bold stripes were considered too vivid to wear with dress clothes, so Harrods had ties made with small shields upon them in which were depicted the appropriate colors.

The walking stick was becoming fashionable again instead of the tightly rolled umbrella, and was noted at weddings or in the hands of filmstars and statesmen such as Anthony Eden. The French admired the Eden silhouette and thought Captain Eden the best dressed Englishman. 'He creates a good impression everywhere he goes with his looks and attractive clothes, and believes in style rather than extreme measures . His black Homburg, sometimes called the Foreign Office hat, is worn on most occasions, slightly tilted to the left, and makes the crowning point on a shapely and well built edifice.'

131

Anthony Eden

You Ought to Know About
Noel COWARD

The Gold Fish, and shortly afterwards played in *Where the Rainbow Ends*.

An experienced actor, aged twelve, he toured in Charles Hawtrey's company, playing all kinds of parts. Before his seventeenth birthday he was leading man in *Charley's Aunt*.

When he was barely twenty-one, he had his first play, *I'll Leave It to You*, produced in London and acted in it himself. Not a great success; but the young playwright was not disheartened. A year later, he won instant recognition with *The Young Idea*, in which he played both in England and America. Fame arrived with *The Vortex* and then success followed success—*Private Lives*, *This Year of Grace*, *Bitter Sweet*, *Design For Living*, *Cavalcade*, *Conversation Piece*, to name a few of his latest. He acted in all of these with the exception of *Bitter Sweet* and *Cavalcade*, and supervised the screen versions of all his plays that have been filmed.

Tall, slight, and pale with keen blue eyes, Coward is one of the world's hardest workers. He rises very early, has the lightest possible breakfast after a few strenuous exercises to keep him fit, has half-an-hour's massage, and gets down to his day's work before nine o'clock. He works throughout the day with scarcely any break, until bedtime. And he still gives time to the study of the essentials of his craft—dancing, poise, rhythm, fencing, voice production, music, dramatic art, and the mechanics of lighting and other stage-craft.   D. O. B.

FAMOUS as playwright, musician, producer and stage actor, Noel Coward now makes his film début in *The Scoundrel*. A chance meeting in a New York restaurant with Ben Hecht and Charles MacArthur, who wrote the story and produced it, resulted in Coward agreeing to star on the screen at last.

Born in Teddington, Middlesex, on December 16, 1899, Noel Coward was educated at Croydon and at a West End school of dramatic art. Here he had as a classmate a little girl called Gertrude Lawrence, and, with her, appeared in many children's plays. At the age of eleven he made his professional début in

---

A bowler boom was said to be on the way, and a Bowler Hat League had been formed at Cambridge to promote the cause. The Prince of Wales liked to wear a small-brimmed bowler with his double-breasted chesterfield, and the King favored a gray bowler or brown bowler with a pronounced curly brim. Many young men preferred soft hats which had a tendency towards wider crowns, which allowed the sides to be neatly dented without the crown having a pinched and unsightly appearance. These came in colors of pearl-gray, fawn and rich brown. 'There is a holiday jauntiness in its curves and laxity in its individual moulding, whereas a bowler is a bit of modern armour against the hard times, and it can be raised easily.'

Coats, particularly the new travelling coats, were much longer and reached well down below the calf. Such a large overcoat made a man look bigger and more dressy and gave a sense of well-being and opulence. Mr Noel Coward favored a camel travelling coat with raglan sleeves, patch pockets with flaps, straps to the cuffs, an all-round belt and a tweedy scarf. The Prince of Wales wore his double-breasted chesterfield with a shaped waist, but cut longer than before, in gray herringbone pattern. In America the men were wearing colorful lounge suits and over them overcoats with blue velvet collars and blue Homburg hats. Shoulders were still wide, collars narrow and low, and lapels wide. In Germany these so-called 'American shoulders' were no longer employed as such, as not only did the shoulders devour an unnecessary amount of cotton and padding, but it was said that the German silhouette was sufficiently square to need no further emphasis.

When dining out in London on Sundays in a restau-

rant where tails were not the order of the night, the 'Stock Exchange rig' of a black jacket and waistcoat and striped trousers had become quite acceptable to wear as a semi-formal outfit. Really smart young men wore the champagne jacket from America which came in various pastel shades and had a shawl collar, or a colorful velvet dinner jacket that looked well in claret, burgundy and port—'a comfortable luxury but rather expensive'. But most men preferred to wear an ordinary dinner jacket in a thinner material to make the garment slim-looking. Color on the whole for evening dress clothes was ignored by the Englishman and it

was only for his smoking jacket or 'home-gowns' that a touch of color was appreciated. The smoking jacket in velvet, serge velvet or velveteen had 'a hint of the fancy-dress about it, a sultan-like magnificence, and a suspicion of playing the part'. The jacket was single-breasted and closely followed the figure, well defining the waist and with a medium length roll collar, two buttons and two jetted pockets. The collar and cuffs were both covered with silk and the front often trimmed with cord or frogging. Colors were brown, claret, black, navy, blue, wine purple, green and gray . . . and Mr Lloyd George was partial to one of a puce hue.

In October a thoroughly sensible change was made to the lounge by the Prince of Wales when he appeared in a lounge suit that was straighter-hanging than usual. The jacket was a two-buttoned double-breasted reefer with an exceptionally wide overlap that almost reached the side pockets. The lapels appeared to be on the narrow side and the side pockets were jetted, whilst the breast pocket had a welt. The trousers hung straight, with the waist less pulled in and they were much shorter in length. This change was considered 'interesting and agreeable'. To accompany his new suit the Prince also set a new hairstyle; his hair was drawn flat across the top of his head, and at the sides, which had been allowed to grow a little longer than usual, it was brushed well back.

—1936—

The death of King George V in January threw the whole court into full mourning for three months and into half-mourning for a further three. The public introduced into their clothes suitable touches of black. Nearly every man, whatever his degree, was wearing a black tie, and there was a corresponding increase in the demand for black hats and overcoats. The passing of King George saw to some extent the demise of conservatism. At the Chelsea Flower Show the new King Edward VIII wore a straw hat with a black band around it and a dark gray double-breasted suit with black tie, gray shirt and collar and no waistcoat.

King Edward's Coronation Day had been fixed for the following May, and already the military tailors had begun work preparing full dress for officers of the Army, Navy and Air Force. The whole empire became involved in making the costly multitude of court dresses and uniforms. Even an ordinary sized ermine cloak took over one hundred and fifty skins, and the peers' robes would cost about seventy guineas. Attempts to brighten up the police, taxi-drivers, postmen, and hopefully also the politician's outfit, in time for the Coronation were made—the postmen for example were to have more fashionable, lighter summer uniforms in blue serge, the shoulders of which were to be padded.

The general public was already buying ties and hosiery in Coronation stripes of red, white and blue. Pajamas were available in white with a portrait of the King woven into the chest. Scarcely a week passed without new designs and fresh ideas in the way of accessories for young men. It was thought that the reason for a young man's fancy being so varied and abundant was because these goods were much cheaper than formerly. Many, however, thought that the true reason was that 'the younger men of today were restless and discontent, which they expressed in whims and fancies. They turned to dress for stimulation; they tired more quickly of things than they used to and liked constant change and novelty.' The favorite novelty of the year was to be painted neckwear; upon heavy crepe or silk scarves and ties miniature patterns and designs and all kinds of stripes were painted by hand. A Tyrolean influence invaded neckwear, and upon Tyrolean ties were depicted fir trees, a cottage, a garland of hearts, squares or triangles in folk colors such as bottle green, blue and brown. One could buy, too, an interesting 'League of Nations' tie which had crossed twin blue and white stripes against a black background. Socks now arrived marbled in black, white and 'nigger', or blue, white and stone; and there were cashmere socks or knitted half-hose in a gay Jacquard design. Braces were no longer just braces, but as if in a fight for survival against elastic belts appeared in a special lightweight fabric and much narrower than before—some no more than one inch wide. Braces for

the occasion was now the rule with various styles for dress wear, braces with monograms embroidered on the left strap, gray and brown colored braces to wear with the lounge and braces from green watered silk to go with a lovat green suit, green tie and green handkerchief. The sporting man was provided with braces of a sporting nature with birds and dogs heads, horse shoes and animal motifs and a new and unusual design of 'a nymph in the state of undress'.

Art Deco or geometric designs, cubes, spots, crescent-shaped weaves and waved stripes were found on ties, and also spots, figure motifs or broken checks in neat arrangement. Sometimes the whole tie would be covered in a mosaic or Paisley effect, pheasant, pheasant eye or crescent-shaped weaves. Socks had the geometric patterns worked in colors that blended with the ground color, and slip-overs had small-scale patterns or relied upon variety in stitches to produce a neat pattern of bars, honeycombs, wavy lines or intricate fancy ribs. Some shirts had small quarter-inch spots, checks or figure motifs which floated on a background of white. From America a semi-stiffened or 'Trubenized' shirt arrived with a neat design of swastikas. In 1936 a shirt for dinner wear with a collar attached arrived from Vienna. Mr Izod, the Court Hosier, announced that this year all men in the West End would be wearing white collars and that the colored collar was finished except for country wear.

Each year saw a new variety of styles and shades in soft felt hats. The brims of the latest hats were decidedly smaller. Some had cut edges, others bound. The 'Camber' hat had a convex curve to its brim and the rain-proofed 'Rigitile' hat had a soft crown but a rigid brim which retained its shape even in the worst of weathers. Rich browns, dainty beiges, bright grays and dark blues were safe colors, though some young men preferred loud colors in their soft hats. Shoes were available in canary, green, black, brown and wine, and in antelope skin with perforations, from America.

For weekend wear, a Harris tweed suit was becoming more popular and appeared to have taken the place of the plus-four suit. In the shape of the jacket there was a marked return to the yoked back, with pleats and patch pockets. In America these sports-coat details were put into business clothes, for they believed in comfort whilst the Englishman sacrificed everything for convention. The result was that the Englishman was often profoundly uncomfortable.

Trousers in America were now higher at the waist, more closely defined over the trunk, had no turn-ups and no crease at all. In England, although there was a distinct call for such trousers by the smartest men, the majority of Englishmen thought that they had discounted two of the most notable improvements to trousers—the stopping of baggy knees and frayed

The new King

Winston Churchill

existence. We shall wear cloaks, too. Clothes will last a week and then be thrown away. The filmy underwear will last for three days.'

The fashion experts had devised the last word in men's underwear; this was made from artificial silk with the waist all tucks and pleats, and provided with an elastic waistband two inches wide. The legs were baggy or balloon shaped and they were called 'bloomers'. 'The point is will they take on? The very suggestion of bloomers for men will provide merriment and laughter.' They did not take on, for the Englishman decided to favor instead the new style cut-away pants and vest from Aertex, and it was the men's plus-fours

edges. They believed that 'the badly dressed business man reduced his commercial value by 50 per cent, and the moral effect of baggy knees was beyond computation.' On the lounge jacket the collar was a fraction shorter so that the points of the double-breasted lapels were higher up and the shoulders were square, in many cases without being padded.

H. G. Wells, who was always thinking about the future, said that 'today we wear thick suits padded a little to protect us, and with innumerable pockets to hold parcels and things, but in 1980 we shall have simpler and more beautiful clothes, wide at the sleeves and with gauntlets to hold the small impedimenta of

Continued from previous page

row.—P. 4, (k. 4, p. 8) 5 times. *34th row.*—P. 1, (k. 8, p. 4) 5 times, k. 3. *35th row.*—P. 2 tog., (k. 4, p. 8) 5 times, k. 2 tog. *36th row.*—(K. 8, p. 4) 5 times, k. 2. *37th row.*—P. 3, (k. 4, p. 8) 4 times, k. 4, p. 7. *38th row.*—K. 6, (p. 4, k. 8) 4 times, p. 4, k. 4. *39th row.*—P. 5, (k. 4, p. 8) 4 times, k. 4, p. 5. *40th row.*—K. 2 tog., k. 2, (p. 4, k. 8) 4 times, p. 4, k. 4, k. 2 tog. *41st row.*—P. 6, (k. 4, p. 8) 4 times, k. 4 p. 2. *42nd row.*—K. 1, (p. 4, k. 8) 4 times, p. 4, k. 7. *43rd row.*—P. 6, (k. 4, p. 8) 4 times, k. 4, p. 2. *44th row.*—K. 3, (p. 4, k. 8) 4 times, p. 4, k. 5. *45th row.*—P. 2 tog., p. 2 (k. 4, p. 8) 4 times, k. 4, p. 2, p. 2 tog. (58 sts.). *46th row.*—K. 4, (p. 4, k. 8) 4 times, p. 4, k. 2. *47th row.*—P. 1, (k. 4, p. 8) 4 times, k. 4, p. 5. *48th row.*—K. 6, (p. 4, k. 8) 4 times, p. 4. *49th row.*—K. 3,, (p. 8, k. 4) 4 times, p. 7. Cast off loosely.

Sew up shoulder seams matching pattern and press with a warm iron and a damp cloth.

ARMHOLE BANDS.

Pick up 88 sts. round armhole and k. 1, p. 1 for 6 rows. Cast off with No. 6 needles.

NECK BAND.

Commence to pick up at centre point and with right side facing pick up 44 sts. on each 3 needles.

1st round.—K. 1, p. 1 ribbing to end, turn. *2nd round.*—With wrong side facing, k. 2 tog., k. 1, p. 1 rib to last 2 sts., k. 2 tog. at end of round, turn. *3rd round.*—As 1st round. *4th round.*—As 2nd round. *5th round.*—As 1st round. *6th round.*—As 2nd round. *7th round.*—As 1st round. Cast off loosely with No. 6 needles.

TO MAKE UP.

Sew up small seam to form V of centre front. Sew up side seams. Re-press side seams. Re-press with a warm iron, taking care not to stretch garment.

THE "DAVID" PULLOVER

A Useful Sleeveless Garment for the Young or the Older Man

THIS serviceable pullover, knitted in a neat vandyked design, is suitable for the older man no less than for the younger. Made up in a fawn or grey shade of wool, it would be right for wearing during working hours; or, knitted in one of the lighter colourings, it would be useful for wearing at tennis or on other sports occasions.

MATERIALS REQUIRED.

11 ozs. Golden Eagle "Hastenit" 2-ply.
1 stitch-holder.
1 pair No. 6 Knitting Needles.
1 set No. 10 Knitting Needles (pointed at both ends).
Measurements: Chest 40 ins. to 42 ins.
Length from shoulder 22 ins.
Abbreviations: K. knit; p, purl; sts., stitches; tog., together; rep., repeat.
Tension: 4 sts. to 1 inch; 6 rows to 1 inch.

FRONT.

Cast on 84 sts., using No. 6 needles. Knit into back of cast on sts. Now knit in a rib of k. 1, p. 1 for 2½ ins. K. one row. Commence pattern with wrong side facing :—

1st row.—*K. 4, p. 8. Rep. from * to end of row. 2nd row.—K. 7, p. 4, * k. 8, p. 4. Rep. from * to last stitch, k. 1. 3rd row.—P. 2, k. 4, * p. 8, k. 4. Rep. from * to last 6 sts., p. 6. 4th row.—K. 5, * p. 4, k. 8. Rep. from * to last 7 sts., p. 4, k. 3. 5th row.—P. 4, * k. 4, p. 8. Rep. from * to last 8 sts., k. 4 p. 4. 6th row.—K. 3, * p. 4, k. 8. Rep. from * to last 9 sts., p. 4, k. 5. 7th row.—P. 6, * k. 4, p. 8. Rep. from * to last 6 sts., k. 4, p. 2. 8th row.—K. 1, * p. 4, k. 8. Rep. from * to last 11 sts., k. 4, p. 4, k. 7. 9th row.—P. 6, * k. 4, p. 8. Rep. from * to last 6 sts., k. 4, p. 2. 10th row.—K. 3, * p. 4, k. 8. Rep. from * to last 9 sts., p. 4, k. 5. 11th row.—P. 4, * k. 4, p. 8. Rep. from * to last 8 sts., k. 4, p. 4. 12th row.—K. 5, * p. 4, k. 8. Rep. from * to last 7 sts., p. 4, k. 3. 13th row.—P. 2, * k. 4, p. 8. Rep. from * to last 10 sts., k. 4, p. 6. 14th row.—K. 7, * p. 4, k. 8. Rep. from * to last 5 sts., p. 4, k. 1. 15th row.—*K. 4, p. 8. Rep. from * to end of row.

This completes the pattern.

Rep. from 2nd row to 15th row inclusive until 4½ patterns have been worked, finishing with 8th pattern row.

Now shape neck and armholes thus :—
1st row.—Cast off 4 sts., p. 1, (k. 4, p. 8) 3 times.

Put remaining 42 sts. on a stitch-holder and work on sts. left thus :—
2nd row.—P. 1, (k. 8, p. 4) 3 times, k. 1. 3rd row.—K. (4, p. 8) 3 times, k. 1. 4th row.—P. 2 tog., p. 1, (k. 8, p. 4) twice, k. 8, p. 1, p. 2 tog. 5th row.—K. 1, (p. 8, k.4) twice, p. 8, k. 3. 6th row.—(P. 4, k. 8) 3 times. 7th row.—P. 7, (k. 4, p. 8) twice, k. 4, p. 1. 8th row.—P. 2 tog., p. 2, (k. 8, p. 4) twice, k. 6, k. 2 tog. 9th row.—(P. 8, k. 4) twice, p. 8, k. 2. 10th row.—P. 1, (k. 8, p. 4) twice, k. 8, p. 1. 11th row.—K. 2, (p. 8, k. 4) twice, p. 8. 12th row.—K. 2 tog., k. 5, (p. 4, k. 8) twice, p. 1, p. 2 tog. 13th row.—K. 3, (p. 8, k. 4) twice, p. 5. 14th row.—K. 4, (p. 4, k. 8) twice, p. 4. 15th row.—K. 3, (p. 8, k. 4) twice, p. 5. 16th row.—K. 2 tog., k. 4, (p. 4, k. 8) twice, p. 2 tog. 17th row.—(P. 8, k. 4) twice, p. 6. 18th row.—

K. 7, p. 4, k. 8, p. 4, k. 7. 19th row.—P. 6, (k. 4, p. 8) twice. 20th row.—K. 2 tog., k. 7, p. 4, k. 8, p. 4, k. 3, k. 2 tog. 21st row.—P. 3, (k. 4, p. 8) twice, k. 1. 22nd row.—(K. 8, p. 4) twice, k. 4. 23rd row.—P. 5, k. 4, p. 8, k. 4, p. 7. 24th row.—K. 2 tog., k. 4, p. 4, k. 8, p. 4, k. 4, k. 2 tog. 25th row.—P. 6, k. 4, p. 8, k. 4, p. 4. 26th row.—K. 3, p. 4, k. 8, p. 4, k. 7. 27th row.—(P. 8, k. 4) twice, p. 2. 28th row.—P. 2 tog., p. 3, k. 8, p. 4, k. 7, k. 2 tog. 29th row.—P. 7, k. 4, p. 8, k. 4, p. 1. 30th row.—K. 2, p. 4, k. 8, p. 4, k. 6. 31st row.—P. 5, k. 4, p. 8, k. 4, p. 3. 32nd row.—K. 4, p. 4, k. 8, p. 4, k. 2, k. 2 tog. 33rd row.—P. 2, k. 4, p. 8, k. 4, p. 5. 34th row.—K. 6, p. 4, k. 8, p. 4, k. 4, p. 7. 36th row.—K6, p. 4, k. 8, p. 3, p. 2 tog. (22 sts.). 37th row.—P. 1, k. 4, p. 8, k. 4, p. 5. 38th row.—K. 4, p. 4, k. 8, p. 4, k. 4. 39th row.—P. 3, k. 4, p. 8, k. 4, p. 3. 40th row.—K. 2, p. 4, k. 8, p. 4, k. 4. 41st row.—P. 5, k. 4, p. 8, k. 4, p. 1. 42nd row.—P. 4, k. 8, p. 4, k. 6. 43rd row.—P. 5, k. 4, p. 8, k.4, p. 1. 44th row.—K. 2, p. 4, k. 8, p. 4, k. 4. 45th row.—P. 3, k. 4, p. 8, k. 4, p. 3. 46th row.—K. 4, p. 4, k. 8, p. 4, k. 2. 47th row.—P. 1, k. 4, p. 8, k. 4, p. 5. 48th row.—K. 6, p. 4, k. 8, p. 4. 49th row.—K. 3, p. 8, k. 4, p. 7. 50th row.—K. 6, p. 4, k. 8, p. 4. 51st row.—P. 1, k. 4, p. 8, k. 4, p. 5. 52nd row.—K. 4, p. 4, k. 8, p. 4, k. 2. 53rd row.—P. 3, k. 4, p. 8, k. 4, p. 3. 54th row.—K. 2, p. 4, k. 8, p. 4, k. 4. 55th row.—P. 5, p. 4, k. 8, p. 4, k. 1. 56th row.—P. 4, k. 8, p. 4, k. 6. Cast off loosely.

Put the other 42 sts. on to a needle and with wrong side facing work thus :—
1st row.—(K. 4, p. 8) 3 times, k. 2, cast off 4 sts. 2nd row.—Join on wool again and p. 3, (k. 8, p. 4) twice, k. 8, p. 3. 3rd row.—K. 2, (p. 8, k. 4) 3 times. 4th row.—P. 2 tog., p. 3, (k. 8, p. 4) twice, k. 7 k. 2 tog. 5th row.—P. 7, (k. 4, p. 8) twice, k. 4, p. 1. 6th row.—K. 2, (p. 4, k. 8) twice, p. 4, k. 6. 7th row.—P. 5, (k. 4, p. 8) twice, k. 4, p. 3. 8th row.—K. 4, (p. 4, k. 8) twice, p. 4, k. 4, k. 2 tog. 9th row.—P. 6, (k. 4, p. 8) twice, k. 4. 10th row.—P. 3, (k. 8, p.4) twice, k. 7. 11th

row.—(P. 8, k. 4) twice, p. 8, k. 2. 12th row.—K. 2 tog., k. 7, p. 4, k. 8, p. 4, k. 7, k. 2 tog. 13th row.—K. 1 (p. 8, k. 4) twice, p. 7. 14th row.—K. 6, (p. 4, k. 8) twice,, p. 2. 15th row.—K. 1, (p. 8, k. 4) twice, p. 7. 16th row.—K. 2 tog., k. 6, p. 4, k. 8, p. 4, k. 6, k. 2 tog. 17th row.—P. 6, (k. 4, p. 8) twice. 18th row.—P. 1, (k. 8, p. 4) twice, k. 5. 19th row.—P. 4, (k. 8, p. 4) twice, p. 7. 20th row.—P. 2 tog., p. 1, (k. 8, p. 4) twice, k. 1, k. 2, tog.—21st row.—P. 1, (k. 4, p. 8) twice, k. 3. 22nd row.—P. 2, (k. 8, p. 4) twice, k. 2. 23rd row.—P. 3, (k. 4, p. 8) twice, k. 1. 24th row.—K. 2 tog., k. 6, p. 4, k. 8, p. 4, k. 2, k. 2 tog. 25th row.—P. 4, k. 4, p. 8, k. 4, p. 6. 26th row.—K. 5, p. 4, k. 8, p. 4, k. 5. 27th row.—P. 6, k. 4, p. 8, k. 4. p. 4. 28th row.—K. 2 tog., k. 1, p. 4, k. 8, p. 4, k. 5, k. 2 tog. 29th row.—P. 5, k. 4, p. 8, k. 4, p. 3. 30th row.—K. 4, p. 4, k. 8, p. 4, k. 4. 31st row.—P. 3, k. 4, p. 8, k. 4, p. 5. 32nd row.—K. 2 tog., k. 4, p. 4, k. 8, p. 4, k. 2. 33rd row.—P. 1, k. 4, p. 8, k. 4, p. 6. 34th row.—K. 7, p. 4, k. 8, p. 4. 35th row.—K. 3, p. 8, k. 4, p. 8. 36th row.—K. 2 tog., k. 5, p. 4, k. 8, p. 4. 37th row.—P. 1, k. 4, p. 8, k. 4, p. 5. 38th row.—K. 4, p. 4, k. 8, p. 4, k. 2. 39th row.—P. 3, k. 4, p. 8, k. 4, p. 3. 40th row.—K. 2, p. 4, k. 8, p. 4, k. 4. 41st row.—P. 5, k. 4, p. 8, k. 4, p.1. 42nd row.—P. 4, k. 8, p. 4, k.6,. 43rd row.—P. 5, k. 4, p. 8, k. 4, p. 1. 44th row.—K. 2, p. 4,. k. 8, p. 4, k. 4. 45th row.—P. 3, k. 4, p. 8, k. 4, p. 3. 46th row.—K. 4, p. 4, k. 8, p. 4, k. 2. 47th row.—P. 1, k. 4, p. 8, k. 4, p. 4, k. 1. 48th row.—K. 6, p. 4, k. 8, p. 4,. 49th row.—K. 3, p. 8, k. 4, p. 7. 50th row.—K. 6, p. 4, k. 8, p. 4. 51st row.—P. 1, k. 4, p. 8, k. 4, p. 4, k. 1. 52nd row.—K. 4, p. 4, k. 8, p. 4, k. 2. 53rd row.—P. 3, k. 4, p. 8, k. 4, p. 3. 54th row.—K. 2, k. 4, p. 8, p. 4, k. 4. 55th row.—P. 5, k. 4, p. 8, k. 4, p. 1. 56th row.—P. 4, k. 8, p. 4, k. 6. Cast off loosely.

BACK.

Work exactly as for the front until 4½ patterns are again worked, finishing with 8th pattern row, then work for armholes thus :—

1st row.—Cast off 4 st., p. 1 (k. 4 p. 8) 6 times, k. 4, p. 2. 2nd row.—Cast off 4 sts., p. 2, (k. 8, p. 4) 6 times, k. 1. 3rd row.—(K. 4, p. 8) 6 times, k. 4. 4th row.—K. 1, (p. 4, k. 8) 6 times, p. 3. 5th row.—K. 2 tog., (p. 8, k. 4) 6 times, p. 2 tog. 6th row.—K. 2 (p . 4, k. 8) 6 times. 7th row.—P. 7, (k. 4, p. 8) 5 times, k. 4, p. 3. 8th row.—K. 2, (p. 4, k. 8) 6 times. 9th row.—K. 1, (p. 8, k. 4) 6 times, p. 1. 10th row.—P. 2 tog., p. 2 (k. 8, p. 4) 5 times, k. 8, p. 2 tog. 11th row.—K. 4, (p. 8, k. 4) 5 times, p. 8, k. 2. 12th row.—P. 1, (k. 8, p. 4) 5 times, k. 8, p. 3. 13th row.—(K. 4, k. 8) 6 times. 14th row.—K. 7, (p. 4, k. 8) 5 times, k. 4. 15th row.—K. 2 tog., k. 2 (p. 8, k. 4) 5 times, p. 6, k. 2 tog. 16th row.—(K. 8, p. 4) 5 times, k. 8, p. 2. 17th row.—K. 1, (p. 8, k. 4) 5 times, p. 8, k. 1. 18th row.—P. 2, (k. 8, p. 4) 5 times, k. 8. 19th row.—P. 7, (k. 4, p. 8) 5 times, k. 3. 20th row.—P. 2 tog., p. 2, (k. 8, p. 4) 5 times, k. 4, k. 2 tog. 21st row.—P. 4, (k. 4, p. 8) 5 times, k. 4. 22nd row.—(K. 8, p. 4) 5 times, k. 5. 23rd row.—P. 6, (k. 4, p. 8) 5 times, k. 2. 24th row.—P. 1, (k. 8, p. 4) 5 times, k. 7. 25th row.—P. 2 tog., p. 6, (k. 4, p. 8) 4 times, k. 4, p. 6, p. 2 tog. 26th row.—K. 6, (p. 4, k. 8) 5 times. 27th row.—K. 1 (p. 8, k. 4) 5 times, p. 5. 28th row.—K. 1, (p. 4, k. 8) 5 times, p. 2. 29th row.—K. 1, (p. 4, k. 8) 5 times, p. 5. 30th row.—K. 2 tog., k. 4, (p. 4, k. 8) 4 times, p. 4, k. 8, p. 2 tog. 31st row.—P. 6, (k. 4, p. 8) 4 times, k. 4, p. 6. 32nd row.—K. 7, (p. 4, k. 8) 4 times, p. 4, k. 4, p. 5. 33rd

instead which lengthened themselves right down to the ankles, and were commonly referred to as 'drooping drawers'. They did look very smart, being made from a softer material and in restrained patterns.

The golfer followed closely every move and change ordained by King Edward. For golf he wore plus-fours in the winter and spring, and in summer either changed into flannels or a fashionable pair of gaberdines. His cap, set fairly long, was patterned in black or brown, black and white, or in Glen checks of gray, brown or fawn. He wore white-and-tan golfing shoes with his wine color stockings or a beautiful plum shade of suede with his heather mixture tweeds. For a visit to Sandown, a pair of magpie shoes in brown, black or white was correct. His socks were an all-over ribbed style in plain fawn, brown and gray or sometimes the tops were checked in a quiet blending tone, and his pullover in diamond checks was worn with a scarf and gloves to match. The knitted sports shirt, which was so popular for golf, was worn by the King when hunting with the Quorn.

For winter the sports shirt with collar attached came in blue, green or brown cashmere. In summer the shirt with attached or unattached collar came with half-sleeves and two or three linked buttons for the neck, and was made in a light unshrinkable crepe wool in colors of delicate green and yellow or patterned with unusual horizontal stripes.

Over the sports shirt, garments that in some way incorporated the new zip-fastener were popular. Sleeveless coats in Grenfell cloth, or suede windjammers with collars, cuffs and waistband in knitted rib or elastic: both had a zip-fastener front; slip-overs had the zip down part of the front and woollen waistcoats and lumber-jackets with short roll collar and patch pockets had the whole front zipped. The King's dark red suede sports jacket had the pockets lined with leather 'for he liked to carry his pipe about with him'.

Corduroy, usually patronized by bohemians, had now been taken up for hiking, motor-cycling and mountaineering and was made even more popular by the King (cord-du-roi) when the previous year he had included it amongst other spectacular gear for a holiday in the Tyrol. 'The Prince wore a pair of black and yellow checked plus-fours, with a glowing yellow roll-necked woolly to go with them and a pair of high doeskin zip-fastened boots; and when ski-ing in the Tyrolese, a pair of buff corduroy trousers together with a high necked blue suede jacket with a belt at the waist and a zip-fastener down the front, or a narrow navy blue wind jacket and scarlet scarf; and he affected one of those amusing Tyrolese peasant hats . . . a green one with a long white feather pierced through it.'

But on 18 December of this year a sudden announcement interrupted the flow of social and fashion news, and stopped designers in their tracks. The King announced his abdication and on the following week a further announcement appeared in the tailoring trade press. 'Our King is gone, and with him a mixture of esteem and love.' *The Tailor and Cutter*

"Farewell Sire, and good fortune go with you."

"I do not think that styles and colours will be any the more sombre than before," he said. "The late Monarch was responsible for many innovations, notably the soft fronted dinner shirt and soft collar, as well as for cooler and more comfortable sports wear. The new King's tastes may be quieter, but it is likely that they will show a more original trend at a later date."

CLARK GABLE.

Clark Gable

METRO - GOLDWYN
MAYER.

The English tailors knew that the new King George VI's taste would be quieter to start with, but hoped that he would show a more original trend later. Mr Izod, Court Hosier, announced that 'His Majesty is the perfectly dressed Englishman. The fact that his dress is conservative will not hinder our trade, rather it will be helped, simply because the average man likes to be quietly attired. Because he is more correctly dressed he will be more help to us than was the Duke of Windsor, and one of the reasons why he is so well groomed is that he is neat and conservative against some more extravagant styles worn by the Duke of Windsor. He must now be regarded as England's best-dressed man.' Mr Izod knew his position, and wanted to keep it. It was soon obvious, however, that popular taste which once came from the upper classes of England now came first and foremost from America. The best dressed in Holywood were voted as, 'First: Clark Gable; second: Lewis Stone; third: William Powell; fourth: Robert Taylor; and tied fifth: Ronald Colman and Robert Montgomery.' Even Mr Roosevelt, the President, had been hailed as 'the only President in the last thirty years who could intelligently be termed a well dressed man'.

The English public, strangely silent about Edward, Duke of Windsor, turned their minds towards celebrating the new Coronation in May. They bought knitted slip-overs, sports shirts and sweaters in navy blue with red and white flecks or horizontal stripings on them. Even the suits came in a material which had red, white and blue silk decorations cleverly incorporated into the weave. Many men were shy of wearing the Coronation colors except on braces, belts and golf flashes, and preferred safe colors, but on underwear and slumberwear they felt more inclined to abandon themselves to celebration. Red, white and blue pajamas had the rampant lion of Scotland embroidered on the front, and there was a new range of white cossack pajamas with a portrait of George VI woven upon the breast.

The Coronation was adjudged a success, although all Councillor Y. Darling could say about it was that 'the Coronation was a garbing of men in women's clothes. When men want to be impressive, they dress up as women. His Majesty wore a robe, the archbishops, bishops and all the great officers of state and peers were also in habiliments of a more feminine than masculine cut.'

The Coronation created a substantial boom in court wear. King George stipulated that the black cloth breeches should now be made of the same material as the evening coat instead of black silk, but that the black silk stockings and pumps were to remain the same, and this improvement was noted later in the year at the ball at Buckingham Palace given in honor of Leopold, King of the Belgians.

At Ascot white toppers were seen, but no spats. Fancy waistcoats were apparent once more. On formal evening occasions the tails of the tail coat were both shorter and wider; the waistline was natural, with the old-fashioned waistline seam reinstated. The jacket was cut with fullness under the arms. There was no breast pocket, and the sleeves carried false cuffs. The latest waistcoat had neither lapels or points at the bottom and was made in a piqué material to match the shirt and tie. The shirt was a two-stud, open-fronted model with a high collar with the broad wings extending just a little beyond the ends of a semi-butterfly tie. At least one inch of shirt cuff had to show below the sleeves.

For less formal occasions the double-breasted dinner jacket had come to stay, with its wide shawl collar. Higher-waisted trousers necessitated a shorter waistcoat with cut-away points, and the new 'dress scarf', which had color incorporated into the scarf ends in the form of club, regimental or old school colors, completed the outfit.

Flannel trousers with fancy stripes that fitted the waist closely were fashionable, and the thing to wear at Le Touquet were chalk-stripped flannels in various shades of gray. Jackets matched or came in Glen Urquhart checks, and polo shirts matched in stripes or were worn plain. At the seaside 'people are bathing

John Gielgud

For the Man in the Family

A Knitted Sports Shirt in a Simple Stitch

TENSION
Seven-and-a-half sts. and 10 rows to 1 in.

THE *Back*.—Using fawn wool, cast on 150 sts. and work in st.-st. for 2 ins., working into the backs of the sts. on the first row and ending with a p. row. Turn the work up on the wrong side and k. through a st. on the needle tog. with the corresponding st. on the cast-on edge all across, thus forming a hem. P. 1 row.

Now continue in st.-st. and work in the following stripes : 6 rows fawn, * 2 rows brown, 4 rows natural, 8 rows brown, 4 rows natural, 2 rows brown, 12 rows fawn, (2 rows brown, 2 rows natural) twice, 2 rows brown, 12 rows fawn. Repeat from * for the length required.

When work measures 18 ins. from the beginning, shape the armholes by casting off 6 sts. at the beginning of the next 2 rows and then dec. at both ends of the following 4 rows. Continue straight in st.-st. in the stripes as before until work measures 25 ins. from the beginning. Shape the shoulders by casting off 11 sts. at the beginning of the next 8 rows. Place the remaining sts. on a holder.

The Front.—Work as for the back till work measures 17½ ins from the beginning, ending with a p. row. Leave this part of the work and start the plastron as follows : Using brown wool, cast on 1 st. and work 3 times into it, then work in k. 1, p. 1 rib and inc. at both ends of every row until there are 13 sts. on the pin.

Return to the main part and k. across 75 sts., then work in k. 1, p. 1 rib with brown wool across the 13 plastron sts., turn and place the remaining 75 sts. on a holder.

Continue in the sts. on the pin, working 75 sts. in the stripes as before and the 13 sts. of the plastron in brown wool, and always twisting the wools round each other when changing colour.

When work measures 18 ins. from the beginning shape the armhole by casting off 6 sts. at the beginning of the next k. row and dec. at the same edge of the following 4 rows. Continue straight

THE SUNSHINE

A selection of new woollies for holiday wear, specially designed for you by "Finella"

with the sts. arranged as before until work measure 19 ins. from the beginning, then work a buttonhole in the plastron as follows : K. 65, rib 5, cast off 4, rib to end. On the following row cast on 4 sts. to take the place of those cast off.

Work two more buttonholes in the same way at 2-inch intervals, and when ½ inch has been worked above the 3rd buttonhole, shape the neck as follows : Cast off 17 sts. at the beginning of the next row which starts at the centre front. Dec. at the same edge of the following 12 rows, and then dec. at the same edge of the following 5 alternate rows. Shape the shoulder by casting off 11 sts. at the beginning of the next 4 k. rows.

Return to the sts. on the holder, join the wool to the centre front and cast on 13 sts. Now work across all sts. in the stripe pattern. When work measures 18 ins. from the beginning shape the armhole by casting off 6 sts. at the beginning of the next p. row, and then dec. at the same edge of the following 4 rows. Continue straight till work measures 23½ ins. from the beginning.

Shape the neck by casting off 17 sts. at the beginning of the next k. row, then dec. at the same edge of the following 12 rows, and then at the same edge of the following 5 alternate rows. Shape the shoulder by casting off 11 sts. at the beginning of the next 4 p. rows.

The Sleeves.—Using fawn wool, cast on 98 sts. and work in st.-st. for 2 ins., working into the backs of the sts. on the first row and ending with a p. row. Turn up the work on the wrong side, and work a hem as for the back. Now continue in stripes as for the back from *, and inc. at both ends of every 6th row until there are 110 sts. on the pin. Continue in the stripes till work measures 7 ins. from the beginning, then shape the top by casting off 6 sts. at the beginning of the next 2 rows, and then dec. at both ends of every row until 64 sts. remain. Dec. at both ends of every alternate row until 30 sts. remain. Cast off.

The Collar.—Join the shoulder seams, then with brown wool pick up the sts. round the neck, working twice into every 4th st. (144 on original model.) Now work in k. 1, p. 1 rib with brown wool for 2½ ins., and inc. at both ends of every alternate row. Cast off.

To Make Up.—Press the st.-st. part of the work on the wrong and then on the right side with a hot iron over a damp cloth. Sew the sleeves into the armholes and join the side and sleeve seams. Catch down the bottom of the plastron and the under-flap, and sew on buttons to correspond with buttonholes. Press all seams.

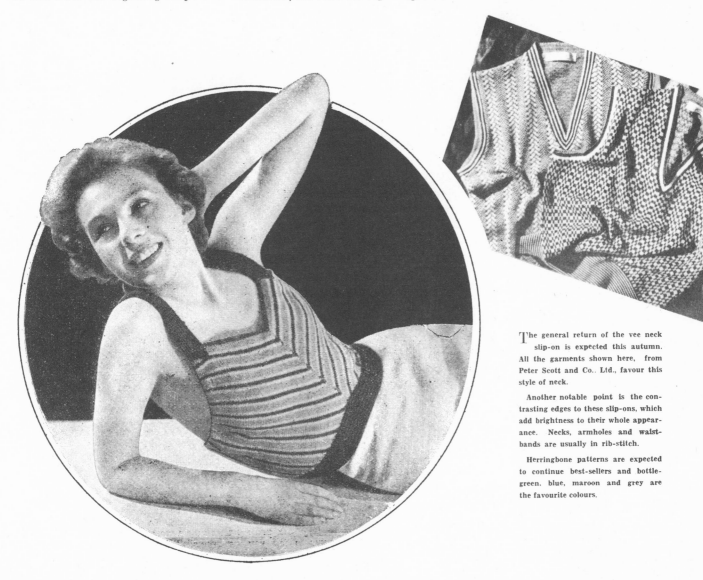

The general return of the vee neck slip-on is expected this autumn. All the garments shown here, from Peter Scott and Co., Ltd., favour this style of neck.

Another notable point is the contrasting edges to these slip-ons, which add brightness to their whole appearance. Necks, armholes and waistbands are usually in rib-stitch.

Herringbone patterns are expected to continue best-sellers and bottle-green, blue, maroon and grey are the favourite colours.

morn, noon and night and playing tennis the livelong day. Bathing especially is on the increase and holiday-makers often spend the whole day, or any rate up to afternoon tea, in their bathing huts.' The weather, the keep-fit campaign and the fact that more bathing pools had been opened all helped to make a boom in the sale of bathing 'trunks'. The young man, objecting to the patchy effect resulting from wearing a costume, was 'exposing the manly chest'. Many of the seaside resorts and public swimming pools which had objected to the wearing of bathing slips or trunks were lifting their restrictions this year, and suddenly over 75 per cent of swimwear sold was in the form of trunks. The only men buying costumes were men with 'unusually hairy chests', and even they were less afraid and less self-conscious than hitherto. For the promenade along the beach many men were forsaking their white trousers for shorts.

Although in 1934 Mr Bunny Austin had been 'content to wear shorts' as they gave him extra speed, it was only this year that shorts for tennis were considered acceptable, and these only when worn with a tennis shirt, the collar of which was turned up at the back, the neck unbuttoned and tie-less, leaving the throat 'fully exposed to the air'. For cricket, it was becoming increasingly evident that shorts would never be accepted. Mr Arthur Mailey, the famous cricketer, said, 'When shorts come in at the door, romance flies out of the window.'

By 1937, thanks to the Reformers and the Prince of Wales, men of all stations were more conscious of their dress than they used to be. The time of the Depression was over, and with growing prosperity wages were on the increase and the leisure period also on the increase. Following America, where 'the country is now impinging upon the town in matters of dress', not only flannels, tweeds and pork pie hats were worn, but the business suit was being cut in sporting style, with yokes at the back, pleats, belts and patch-pockets with pleats. There was a clear call for more manly styles in men's clothes, and corduroy sports suits had large bold bellows pockets and stitched belts. Materials were heavier, styles tailored and colors in browns, fawns and coffee tints. 'The women follow us with their mannish styles, but at least they cannot accuse us of being effeminate!'

"THE TAILOR & CUTTER," MAY 6, 1938
(Registered at the G.P.O. as a Newspaper)

PRICE FOURPENCE WEEKLY
ANNUAL SUBSCRIPTION 25/6 POST FREE

THE TAILOR & CUTTER

AND OUTFITTING NEWS

VOLUME 73   NUMBER 3733

S.B. Sports Jacket G.1060 is made in Messrs. G. & G. Kynoch's Cloth No.64056 and the Button Three, Yoke Back Sports Coat G.1061 is from Messrs. S. A. Newall's No.1287

147

1938

clothes, it appeared, were experiencing a boom in trade because thousands of people were having their first holidays, thanks to the new 'holidays with pay' campaign. This was reflected all over the country in a demand for brightly colored and novel styles in sportswear, especially those in an American design; 'bright snappy sports shirts, gay ties, lumber-jackets of novel design, anything that was unusual, and the wilder and gayer they were the better.' The leisure jacket came in green with a yellow design, and had a heavy belt and bellows pockets with flaps. Striped sports suits came with striped shirts and striped ties to match. The sports shirts had the American trend of collars with long points to them, and were regarded as utility garments as they could be worn on the beach and in town. Lisle beach shirts started to appear with brighter designs than their woollen predecessors. They had half-sleeves and were fastened with a tab and single button at the neck (see page 144). Colors were blue-gray, gray, navy, maroon and white or with horizontal stripes.

In underwear a new revolutionary design, having tremendous success in the United States as well as Canada and Australia, was introduced into Britain. This was the 'Y-front', which needed no buttons. It was hoped that the older men would stop wearing the long-sleeved vests and long underpants and take to wearing these athletic pants already popular with the younger generation.

While in England the university men no longer set the standards of dress, in America students of Yale and Harvard, together with filmstars of Hollywood, set all the fashions. Their sports jackets were now strawberry-colored and often collarless. An American influence showed itself in bold designs on sports jackets, which were striped or checked with two or more designs and colors together. One could choose from single, double or even triple inverted pleats to the back, or have pleats from the sleeve, or insets to the waist. Patch pockets, too, could be with or without inverted pleats. The back and front were often yoked with knife-pleats down to the waist where a fitted half-belt was stitched. The shoulders were square and had a wide back stretch. Trousers to wear with the jacket were either made of the same material, usually a light saxony, cheviot, worsted or serge, or made to contrast in gaberdine or flannel. It was estimated that 70 per cent of men chose to wear flannels throughout the year. Douglas Fairbanks Jnr. was 'at his best' in gray flannels and an open-necked shirt. Frank Sinatra and Bing Crosby wore shirts buttoned at the neck, but no tie.

Back in England there was no doubt that the King was having a considerable influence on the sartorial taste of the community, and at events like Ascot, dressed in a manner that was 'wholly to serve as an example to all his subjects', he wore a black morning coat with double-breasted lapels, a black waistcoat and dark striped trousers. His topper was gray with a pronounced curl to it; his shirt was gray with a

The threat of war was looming nearer, making it increasingly necessary to produce protective clothing 'against certain poisonous gases'. Already the oilskin manufacturers were working to capacity providing such materials, and firms were now able to produce protective suits to sell to the public for less than £2. The Government, too, had ordered sufficient gas-masks to provide one each for the entire nation. As it was going to be difficult to induce the children to wear the hideous gas-masks without there being 'serious panic' at the time of a raid, their masks were made to resemble Mickey Mouse or other humorous characters to make them more likeable objects.

By April, serious setbacks in the tailoring trade were being felt. 'Trade during the last few months has failed to make anyone very much richer unless he is engaged in armaments.' By June, *The Tailor and Cutter* stated that the general war scares and exaggerated talk of air-raid precautions were causing considerable depression in sales, *except for sports clothes*. Sports

handkerchief to match, and it had a double collar with a wide opening which housed a gray tie with narrow black stripes woven in a criss-cross fashion—but he forgot his gloves (as his father would never have done) and two out of every three other men followed his example. At Eton and Harrow, shepherd's plaid trousers dazzled the eye, monocles flourished and fancy waistcoats predominated. Waistcoats were now considered neater-looking than a pullover and the majority of men found the pockets an advantage. 'The small boys looked perky in their top hats, Eton collars and jackets, dark or light blue ties, button-holes and tasselled canes.' At Cowes most people, like the King, came attired in a double-breasted 'reefer' in navy blue. This was worn with white flannels, white socks and white buckskin shoes, which looked and felt cool, with a yachting cap. The Duke of Sutherland and several other smart men came dressed in a double-breasted reefer with chalk stripes. This jacket had an outside ticket pocket, a fashion that was enjoying a tremendous vogue.

For semi-formal town wear, many of the younger men, like the Duke of Kent (Prince George), had taken to wearing a quieter outfit of double-breasted reefer, smart gray trousers and a Homburg or bowler hat. With such an outfit a stiff white collar was correct. A new shirt from Austria had the shirt collar made of double material so that when the collar showed signs of fraying, the wearer merely cut off the upper layer to reveal a new layer beneath.

As political anxieties grew, the politicians sometimes allowed their sartorial standards to slip. Sir Samuel Hoare, the Home Secretary, wore a 'Foreign Office' hat, but never with the charm that Anthony Eden infused. Even Eden himself, whose black Homburg was so well known that it was often called the 'Anthony Eden' hat, was now having anxious periods, when his garments suffered, and Winston Churchill was always a target for the sarcasm of the best tailors, who thought that he never got anything right.

Most men were tending once again to buy a safe four-piece saxony suit in darker colors of ox-blood, bottle green or royal blue. If possible, to this would be added a double-breasted sports jacket in check cloth

Bing Crosby and Frank Sinatra

designed to harmonize with the quieter pattern of the
lounge. Mr Owen Nares stated that 'no matter how
expensive or how well made a man's clothes were, if
they were too conspicuous he was not well dressed'.

Shirts came in pleasing, quieter designs. Distinctive-
ness without dazzle was the keynote. Striped shirts
had the stripes set wider apart and were less bold in
color. They appeared in browns, grays and blues in a
mercerized cotton. The 'Fusex' shirt had a self-
stiffening collar. This was exceedingly popular as
when it was laundered at home it retained its stiffness.
Excessive imports of cheap shirts from Japan were
causing concern, as there seemed to be difficulty in
restricting their entry into Britain and they hindered
British goods. As there was an increasing demand for
cheaper garments, craftsmanship was bit by bit giving
way to the standard work of machines. The riotous
designs in knitwear were steadily losing their appeal.
Neatness, good taste and a sense of restraint were
considered more pleasing on a pullover. Knitted waistcoats appeared in quiet but unusual patterns, and the
new continental sweaters were extremely heavy. Some
of them had shawl collars and buttoned on the left side,
some zipped just at the neck, others all the way down.
Colors were plain and dark.

Suddenly, in October, the war scare was over, and a
great feeling of relief swept over the country. The
Government's call to the nation to become physically
fit had encouraged the taking up of all kinds of sporting
activity; riding, hunting, polo, shooting and golf were
all suggested as part of the campaign. Riding was
especially popular and no longer 'the privilege of the
very wealthy'. It was one of the hobbies of tens of
thousands of people of moderate means. For hunting,
the 'pink' coat and the white breeches were worn, but
for everyday riding a four-buttoned hacking jacket
was worn, preferably of Harris tweed. This was cut
longer than the lounge with a back seam and slits at the
side. The fronts were rather straight with rounded
corners, and the skirt part of the jacket cut easy. There
were two pockets cut on the slant and breast pockets
with flaps. A fancy canary waistcoat or slip-over, a
shirt of the collar-attached style and a toning tweedy
tie were worn with the jacket, or a chunky pullover
usually of a closely knit cable stitch, and with a roll
collar. These came in a variety of colors; maroon, wine,
navy, delphinium, canary, green and black and white
were favorites. Jodhpurs or breeches were the correct
nether garments to wear, and a pair of hand-knitted
woollen gloves in a pale color, or knitted string gloves.
On top, a black or brown bowler or even a snap-
brimmed felt hat completed the outfit.

Although some wore gray flannels and others even
wore shorts for the shoot, either the kilt or a tweed for
'The Glorious Twelfth' was considered correct, and
knickerbockers with gaiters were more appropriate
than plus-fours. Most jackets were on the plain side,
and in a dark inconspicuous shade of cloth, for if a
light or vivid kind were used this would generally
'cause the birds to turn, and the whole drive might be
spoiled'. Special 'pivot' sleeves for 'strenuous work on
the moors' were a feature and so were deep, wide

bellows pockets. The majority of the jackets buttoned three and had notched lapels, and some were almost as close-fitting as a lounge. The smartest set, when shooting, wore a new collarless coat with a yoke and sewn-on belt. This was with trousers of a narrow-shaft corduroy, and on their heads a soft felt snap-brimmed hat with the crown slightly pinched at the front and the sides gracefully curved, the back artfully dented.

For the golfer, rich browns, orange and a touch of green were recommended. A new blouse-backed shirt provided ease and comfort by means of a narrow stitched belt over which the top draped loosely; alternatively, the new cardigan shirt which buttoned to the neck and had a knitted waistband, storm-cuffs and two large buttoning flap pockets. For riders and motorists as well as golfers was designed the 'Vestover', a garment specially made for the man who demanded

the warmth of wool but felt a little dubious about the pullover's informality. It was shaped like the waistcoat but without buttons, and came in a heavy stitched rib with a yoke in a contrasting check effect.

'Nowadays, bank clerks, the insurance agent and even the typist and book-keeper can afford ten days in Switzerland during the winter.' White was popular at St Moritz, and men, women and children wore trousers with heavy white woollen pullovers with crew necks or fleecy-lined zip-fastened windjammers, white knitted skullcaps or peeked caps, white stockings and gloves, and strong stout boots. Stylish dark brown corduroy jackets with patch pockets on the breast and bellows pockets with flaps were worn with a new shirt to match in a velvet called 'needlecord'. Skating was popular too, and as plus-fours were considered 'too untidy' on the ice, the skaters generally wore . . . lounge suits.

1939

With the temporary feeling of optimism owing to the avoidance of war, and with town and country styles converging, the suits were all cut in sporting style and had pointed lapels and jetted or patch pockets. These clothes looked slick enough for town and comely on healthy out-of-doors men even on London pavements, and tweeds were seen in Mayfair. A new range of slip-overs to wear with the suits had been treated with a special process, the result of which was that not only did they match Harris tweed but even had the same odour. Germany, obviously envious of the smart tweed suits, tried to produce an artificial tweed coat from cellulose wool; it was dearer and 'not as good'.

For suiting there were new angora cloths with tiny checks and red over-checks, blue-black hopsacks with patterns of white stripes or blue-gray herringbones, and most popular of all were saxony and worsted cloths which had Glen Urquhart checks or large window-pane squares. In America, where the latest fashion was for husbands and wives to dress alike, if the husband wore Glen Urquhart checks, the wife had to follow suit. To wear with the suits, slip-overs, ties and socks patterned with the design that picked out the dominant weaves in the suit or its accompanying shirt were very fashionable.

There was a wide choice of overcoats, in both style and pattern. The fashionable coat for town was cut in country style, and displayed bold Glen checks or window-pane squares in green and brown, as shown opposite. A smart new reversible coat with tweed on one side and gaberdine on the other was designed so that the lapels on each side showed the contrasting material. A pork pie hat and a pair of suede or reverse hide shoes were worn with these coats, though Mr Winston Churchill was noticed to prefer zip-fastened shoes. There was a call for military and cavalry-styled

raincoats, especially among the younger men, and one could acquire a Japanese raincoat for the equivalent of only 44 pence.

Every third German now wore a uniform, and though Herr Hitler had decided that most Germans should be content to have clothes made from artificial wool his own personal attendants, chosen for their height and bearing, wore white silk stockings, satin breeches, and gold frogged coats cut from English cloth imported for the purpose. The silk stockings, however, did not need to be imported, as the latest German achievement was to make 'silk' stockings out of castor oil.

By April 1939 conscription was at last announced in Britain, and two hundred thousand young men were called up. Contracts for cotton, wool, khaki and serge for Army clothing and equipment were placed by the War Office all over the country. Both Oxford and Cambridge voted in favor of conscription, and issued official blazers for their Officer Training Corps; Oxford produced a dark blue blazer with a crown in silver wire over red velvet, the University arms and a new motto, 'Militia Nobis Studium' (our study is the art of war).

The King, whilst on tour in June in Canada and the United States, wore all his jackets double-breasted. In Canada he wore his double-breasted lounge with large chalk stripes and the sleeves invariably showing about half an inch of shirt cuff. When in the States he wore a double-breasted dinner jacket with wing collar and stiff shirt. Double-breasted styles were soon worn

by all men, 'for the style boasts an impressive front and looks well on sports clothes as well as lounge, blazer or D.J.'. In former days, three or four buttons on each side with the jacket fully fastened was usual, but now one, two or three buttons were correct. Flannel suits became double-breasted, buttoning two but showing three, and they had fashionable wide-set stripes to give character. The jackets, cut with wide back and chest, now measured in length from 29 to 30 inches and the trousers 19 to 19½ inches at the hem. Dinner jackets came in midnight blue with a small herringbone pattern in the cloth. The fronts buttoned one but showed two and a button-hole of a red carnation was in vogue.

Men's dress tails showed all the 'glossy perfection of a penguin and, in the mass, just as much originality'. Their tails had grown in length and in London were up to 2 or 4 inches longer, and the bold lapels were faced with black silk. Buttons were ivory, and in the button-hole, a white carnation or gardenia.

At Ascot in June, a morning coat, duly styled in the double-breasted cut, made its appearance and was worn with 'sponge-bag' checked cravats. At the Derby in June, while the Duke of Gloucester and Mr Hore Belisha, Minister for War, appeared in black morning coat with gray top hats, Americans came in brown checked tweed plus-four suits with red over-checks, and with them pork pie hats, golf stockings and brown shoes.

Having disposed of collars and even lapels to their jackets, some Americans were now attempting to reduce pockets in men's clothing. It was felt that the lines of well-designed clothes had been lost by 'man's habit of stuffing his pockets with junk. Now clothes are streamlined like cars.'

Two-piece sports suits with collarless jackets and contrasting trousers in cheviots, saxonies or corduroy became fashionable in England and the 'intelligentsia were going into corduroy as fast as they could'. Pullovers were still heavy but stylish. They had narrow stand collars, heavy raglan sleeves and were knitted in shetland wool, often of a mustard color. Canary yellow slip-overs came in cable stitch and waistcoats were fashionable, either with long plain color sleeves, or reversible and sleeveless.

By July the tailors were snowed under with orders for clothes for officers of the regular and territorial forces. The War Office decided that the greatcoat or 'British Warm' should be issued to each man of the Field Army, as well as one complete uniform, one suit of overalls, two pairs of boots, one pair of canvas shoes and a complete set of underclothes. It was thought that a military outfit ought to possess fitness for purpose as well as style and a touch of swagger, but the new battledress for commissioned officers and the rank and file was heralded as 'ugly, clumsy, unhealthy, expensive and very difficult to make ... especially in a hurry'. The battledress consisted of a two-piece suit made up of a blouse cut on very easy fitting lines over

the shoulder, and the back cut without a center seam. The trousers buttoned at the ankle, where the old-fashioned puttees had been replaced by small ankle gaiters of webbing. The two garments were joined together by means of hidden buttons, the tunic part pouching over a 3 inch wide belt fastened on to the trousers. A patch pocket was set high on the right side of the trousers for field dressings, and one lower on the left for rations or maps. Two patch pockets on the breast had flaps and the fly-front was finished at the neck with a Prussian collar. The dress was made in

TWO-WAY PULLOVER

You Can Make it with a Polo Collar or with a V-neck Opening

SOME men find a polo-necked pullover a most comfortable garment to wear when motoring, riding, cycling or playing golf. Others like a pullover to have a simple V-necked opening.

Here are given the instructions for making a warm pullover in whichever style is preferred. The polo collar and neck inset can be omitted in favour of a simple ribbed band at the V neckline. The patterned surface of the garment gives it distinction.

MATERIALS REQUIRED

11 oz. Baldwin and Walker's 4-ply Ladyship Scotch Fingering.

1 pair knitting needles, No. 8.

1 pair knitting needles, No. 11.

Measurements. — Length, from shoulder to lower edge, 21 inches. Length of sleeve, from shoulder, 25 inches. Length of sleeve seam, including cuff, 21 inches. Width all round below the underarms, without stretching, should be 38 inches.

To fit a 38 to 41 chest measurement.

Tension.—Pattern on No. 8 needles, before pressing, seven stitches to 1 inch in width; 8 rows to 1 inch in depth.

Alteration in Size.—For a larger garment use thicker needles, or a size which produces fewer stitches to the inch. For a smaller garment use finer needles, or a size which produces more stitches to the inch.

Abbreviations.—K, knit; P, purl; sts., stitches; tog., together; pat., pattern; inc., increase; dec., decrease; beg., beginning.

THE BACK.

Using the No. 11 needles, begin at the lower edge of the back by casting on 126 sts., and work in the rib of K 1, P 1 for 2¾ inches, working into the back of all the *knit* sts.

Change to the No. 8 needles and the pat., as follows :—

1st row.—* K 9, P 9. Rep. from * to end of row. Rep. this row 8 times more.

10th row.—* P 9, K 9. Rep. from * to end of row. Rep. this row 8 times more.

These 18 rows form the pattern.

Continue in the pat. until you have worked 5 patterns in all, when the work should measure 13¼ inches from the cast-on edge.

To Shape the Armholes.—Keeping the pattern correct throughout, cast off 3 sts. from the beg. of each of the next 8 rows.

Continue in the pat. on the remaining 102 sts. until the armhole measures 7 inches on the straight, *i.e.*, from where the first 3 sts. were cast off.

To Shape the Neck.—Work in the pat. over 42 sts., cast off 18 sts., pat. 42.

Work on the last 42 sts. in the pat., casting off 3 sts. from the beg. of every neck edge row until 30 sts. remain.

To Shape the Shoulder.—Cast off 10 sts. from the beg. of each armhole end row until all are cast off.

Join the wool to the neck edge of the remaining 42 sts., and work to correspond with the first shoulder.

THE FRONT.

Using the No. 11 needles, begin at the lower edge by casting on 126 sts., and work in exactly the same way as stated for the back, until the armhole shaping is completed and 102 sts. remain on the needle.

Work in the pat. over 51 sts., and place the remaining 51 sts. on a spare needle.

Work on the first 51 sts. in the pat., decreasing 1 st. at the neck edge on every alternate row, until 30 sts. remain, then work without dec. until the armhole measures the same as for that of the back, *i.e.*, 7 inches on the straight.

Shape the shoulder by casting off 10 sts. from the beg. of each armhole end row, until all are cast off.

Join the wool to the neck edge of the remaining 51 sts., and work to correspond.

THE SLEEVES (both alike).

Using the No. 11 needles, begin at the cuff edge by casting on 63 sts., and work in the rib of K 1, P 1—working into the back of all knit sts.—for 2¾ inches.

Change to the No. 8 needles and the pat., as follows :—

1st row.—K 5, * P 9, K 9. Rep. from * to the last 4 sts., P 4.

2nd row.—K 4, * P 9, K 9. Rep. from * to the last 5 sts., P 5.

Rep. these 2 rows 3 times more, then the 1st row again.

10th row.—P 4, * K 9, P 9. Rep. from * to the last 5 sts., K 5.

11th row.—P 5, * K 9, P 9. Rep. from * to the last 4 sts., K 4.

Rep. these 2 rows 3 times more, then the 10th row again.

These 18 rows complete 1 pat.

Continue to work in the pat., increasing 1 st. at both ends of the needle on the next, then every following 9th row, until the sts. are increased to 91, taking care to work the increased sts. in the pat. as the work proceeds.

Continue in the pat. without increase until the sleeve seam measures 20 inches, then cast off 2 sts. from the beg. of every row until 15 sts. remain.

Cast off.

THE INSET COLLAR.

Using the No. 11 needles, begin by casting on 130 sts., and work in the rib of K 1, P 1 for 4 inches, working into the back of all knit sts.

To Shape Inset. — *1st row.*—* Rib 6 (K 1, P 1, K 1) all into the next st., rib 6. Rep from * to the end of row. (150 sts. on the needle.)

Work in the rib for 7 rows.

9th row.—Cast off 36 sts., rib to end of row.

10th row.—Cast off 36 sts., rib to end of row.

Continue to work on the remaining 78 sts. in the rib, decreasing 1 st. at both ends of the needle on every alternate row until 6 sts. remain, then dec. 1 st. at both ends of the needle on every row until all the sts. are worked off.

FOR "V" NECK.

If the garment is preferred with the ordinary "V" neck, omit the instructions for the Inset Collar, and, in place of these, work as follows :—

Using a set of four No. 11 needles, with the right side of work towards you, work up 51 sts. down the left side of front neck opening, beginning at the shoulder seam. With a second needle, work up 51 sts. up the other side of neck opening ; and, with a third needle, work up 54 sts. from shoulder to shoulder across the back of the neck, making 156 sts. in the round.

Work in the rib of K 1, P 1—working into the back of all knit sts—and, on the first round, pick up and P 1 st. at the centre "V" of neck. (This st. should be purl on every round.)

Work 11 rounds in the rib, decreasing 1 st. on each side the centre "V" st. on every round.

Cast off loosely, still continuing to work in the rib.

TO MAKE UP.

Press on the wrong side with a hot iron over a damp cloth, but do not press any of the ribbed parts, or you will find that they slightly stretch and lose their neat appearance and good fit.

Sew up the shoulder seams, and sew the sleeves into the armholes. Press these seams, then sew up the side and sleeve seams.

Neatly sew in the "Inset" and the collar to the neck, and carefully press the seams.

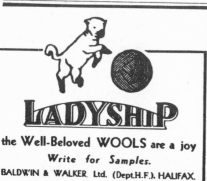

A Smart Pullover

This Neat-fitting Garment Should Please the Most Exacting Man

MOST men are glad of the extra warmth of a pullover when the weather gets chilly. This easily made design is knitted in a wool which will enable the garment to keep its shape and wear well to the very end.

Lister's "Poplar" wool is available in a number of attractive colours, so that you can, if you like, forsake the more ordinary greys and fawns and make the pullover to match a fleck in a favourite tweed jacket.

MATERIALS REQUIRED

For small or large size: 7 oz. Lister's "Poplar" 4-ply knitting wool; 1 pair Lister needles, No. 11; 1 pair Lister needles, No. 9.

MEASUREMENTS

Small size.—To fit 36-38in. chest.

Large size.—To fit 38-40in. chest.

Length from shoulder, 22in.

To knit large size, follow figures in brackets [] when working the back. The front is the same for both sizes.

Tension: 7 st. and 9 rows equal 1in. (No. 9 needles).

Abbreviations: k., knit; p., purl; st., stitches; in., inches; tog., together; cable 4=slip 2 st. on to short needle *behind* work, k. 2, then k. 2 st. from short needle.

BACK

Using No. 11 needles, cast on 110 [122] st.

Next row.—*, k. 1, p. 1. Repeat from * to end of row. Repeat this row for 3in.

Change to No. 9 needles and pattern as follows:—

1st row.—*, k. 2, p. 2, k. 6, p. 2. Repeat from *, ending k. 2.

2nd row.—*, p. 2, k. 2, p. 6, k. 2. Repeat from *, ending p. 2.

Repeat these 2 rows twice more.

7th row.—As 1st row.

8th row.—P. 3, *, k. 2, p. 4. Repeat from * ending k. 2, p. 3.

9th row.—K. 3, *, p. 2, cable 4, p. 2, k. 4. Repeat from *, ending p. 2, cable 4, p. 2, k. 3.

10th row.—As 8th row.

11th row.—K. 3, *, p. 2, k. 4. Repeat from *, ending p. 2, k. 3.

Repeat these 2 rows four more times.

20th row.—As 8th row.

21st row.—As 9th row.

22nd row.—As 2nd row.

Repeat these 22 rows until work measures 13in.* *.

To shape for armholes (keeping pattern unbroken):—

Cast off 5 st. at the beginning of the next 2 [4] rows, then k. 2 tog. at each end of every row until 82 [88] st. remain.

Continue in pattern on these st. (but with 2 st. less at each end) until work measures 22in.

To shape for shoulders.—

Cast off 7 st. at the beginning of the next 8 rows.

Slip remaining 26 [32] st. on to spare needle and leave on one side.

FRONT

Using No. 11 needles, cast on 122 st. and work exactly as back as far as * *.

To shape for armholes (keeping pattern unbroken):—

Cast off 5 st. at the beginning of the next 4 rows, then k. 2 tog. at each end of every row until 92 st. remain.

To shape for neck. With right side of work facing:—

Next row.—K. 2 tog., k. 43 st. in pattern, slip the next 2 st. on to a safety pin. Turn. Work back.

Continue in pattern on these st. for 6 more rows, but knitting 2 tog. at neck edge on the 4th row, and knitting 2 tog. at armhole edge on every row. (37 st. remain.)

Now, keeping armhole edge straight, continue knitting 2 tog. at neck edge every 4th row until 28 st. remain. Continue on these st. until work measures 22in.

To shape for shoulder. Commencing at armhole edge:—

Cast off 7 st. at the beginning of alternate rows, four times.

Return to remaining 45 st. on needle, joining wool at centre edge, and work to match first side.

NECK BAND

Join right shoulder seam, then, with right side of work facing, and using No. 11 needles, pick up and knit 70 st. down left side of neck, then with wool behind work, slip the 2 st. from safety pin on to needle, pick up and knit 70 st. up to right shoulder, and finally knit across 26 [32] st. of back from spare needle. (168 [174] st. now on needle.)

Next row.—(Wrong side of work is facing):—P. 1, k. 1 forty-eight [fifty-one] times (96 [102] st.), p. 2, then k. 1, p. 1, to end of row.

Next row.—K. 1, p. 1, to within 4 st. of centre 2, k. 1, p. 3 tog., k. 2, p. 3 tog., k. 1, then p. 1, k. 1, to end of row.

Next row.—P. 1, k. 1, to centre 2 st., p. 2, then k. 1, p. 1, to end of row.

Repeat the last 2 rows once more.

Next row.—K. 1, p. 1, to within 4 st. of centre 2, k. 1, p. 3 tog., k. 2, p. 3 tog., k. 1, then p. 1, k. 1, to end of row.

Cast off neatly in rib.

ARMBANDS

Join left shoulder seam, then, with No. 11 needles and right side of work facing, pick up and knit 152 st. round armholes.

Work in k. 1, p. 1 rib for 6 rows, knitting 2 tog. at the beginning of every row.

Cast off neatly in rib.

TO MAKE UP

Pin out to required measurements and press carefully under damp cloth, avoiding k. 1, p. 1 rib welts. Join side seams, then press all seams.

drab serge, and the metal helmet, which fastened with a leather chinstrap, was painted in a similar tone. When the helmet was not worn, headgear was a field service cap. Mr Hore Belisha referred to this 'ski-suit' type of battledress as 'the most practical and comfortable ensemble'.

Meanwhile, back on the beaches in the heat of August, men were going gay in vivid beach gowns with Aztec designs, in blue and white Terry Towelling with an oil-skin lined pocket for tobacco and cigarettes. There were swim suits in a laced honeycomb effect, trunks with fly-front zip and a money pocket, and 'Limpet' trunks which came without a belt or side seams, as they were made from Lastex yarn and botany wool to give maximum grip over the hips. On 25 August the Secretary for War was on holiday on the French Riviera without coat, waistcoat or braces. His trousers were held up by a belt and his sports shirt had short sleeves and was open at the neck. Sports shirts were now all made of Terry Towelling rather than rayon or artificial silk and retailers announced that 'those of artificial silk are so dead that we cannot give them away'. The House of Commons issued a text saying that there should be a distinctive marking on all imported goods. Goods from Italy, Germany and Japan had to have definite indication of this fact; goods from any other foreign country must be termed 'foreign' and those from the Dominions should be termed 'Empire'.

Cossack pajamas were now patterned in Paisley or tartan or had animals and birds like peacocks embroidered on the front. Scarves and squares came in Paisley or a willow pattern design, but instead of the old school tie a regimental tie was now preferred, these being sold in their thousands.

By the end of August, factories were working at full pressure on contracts for the militia. In early September Mr Chamberlain, the Prime Minister, was seen in a dark lounge suit, umbrella held under the arm at an acute angle, and a black Homburg hat that was suffering from lack of modelling, looking 'stubborn and intractable'. At 11.00 a.m. on Sunday 3 September Mr Chamberlain announced that the nation was at war with Germany. At Savile Row tailors found a new use for their skills. They made blankets from remnants and splints for their local shelter from cloth-boards. Gas-masks, hitherto kept in the background and regarded as a curiosity, now became a vital part of one's apparel. 'The gas-mask must be taken with you wherever you go, from home to shop, shop to restaurant or wherever you may call, shop or office to back home. The wearing of gas-masks has a tremendous effect in bringing home to everyone the fact that war exists, that we are all in it.' It was found that the children, instead of being frightened of the masks, actually enjoyed playing with them.

To conform with the blackout regulations on night lighting, a 'ghost-coat' was devised with a white proof finish that presented a ghost-like surface in car headlights. Other safety garments suggested were an inflatable waistcoat in case of shipwreck and a bullet-proof waistcoat made of steel tape and silk, 'for the day may yet come when every well-dressed man will consider his wardrobe incomplete without at least one bullet-proof waistcoat which will weigh only a few ounces.'

The war had put large numbers of men back into khaki, navy and air-force blue, but there was an acute shortage of cloth and, although great pressure was put on the manufacturers, they were unable to guarantee delivery for five or six weeks, even though their mills were working night and day. Regimental buttons, too, were almost unobtainable. Probably for economy, the War Office announced that Full Dress, Undress and Mess Dress would no longer be worn by officers and other ranks, and that Service or Battle Dress would be worn on all occasions and by all ranks except when on leave or when undertaking athletic exercise. Newly appointed officers, except those of horsed units, could no longer provide themselves with a sword. The Scots were exceedingly indignant about the War Office's ban on kilts. 'The kilt', it was stated, 'was not suitable for travelling on the mechanized units.'

In November, after a brief stay in England, the Duke of Windsor flew to France to take up a staff appointment with the British Expeditionary Force. As he left the War Office, he was wearing the rig of a Major General, a guard's service jacket, reverse hide shoes on his feet and a service cap on his head. He had a Sam Browne belt, and carried a cane under his arm.

In November the latest picture of him from The Front showed him standing with his hands deep in the pockets of his trench coat, which was powdered with snow.

157

A cyclist with gas mask and syren

Sailor's Knitted Mittens

Miscellaneous Service Garments, all using the simplest stitches. The instructions are particularly clear and easy to follow. Just the thing for children who wish to do their bit.

Materials required :—

3 ozs. **Baldwin & Walker's LADYSHIP 4-PLY KONORT FINGERING.**
1 Pair Knitting Needles, No. 8.

Measurement :—

Length, from cast-on to cast-off edge, 8 inches.

Tension :—

8½ stitches to 1 inch in width ; 8 rows to 1 inch in depth.

*Abbreviations :—*K, knit ; P, purl ; sts., stitches.

Begin at the lower edge by casting on 68 sts. and work in the rib of K 1, P 1 for 8 inches.

Cast off still working in the rib.

Make a second piece in the same way.

Press lightly on the wrong side with a warm iron over a slightly damp cloth.

Neatly join together the side seam, beginning at the lower edge, for 4 inches. Leave a space of 2½ inches for the thumb to pass through, then join together the remaining 1½ inches.

Knitted Shaped Body Belt.

Materials required :—

4 ozs. **Baldwin & Walker's LADYSHIP BED-JACKET WOOL.**
1 Pair Knitting Needles, No. 8.

Measurements :—

Width, all round unstretched, 20 inches.
Depth at widest part, 10½ inches.

Tension :—

6 stitches to 1 inch in width ; 11 rows (5½ ridges) to 1 inch in depth.

NOTE :—If the needles stated do not produce this tension, try different sizes until you get it correct.

*Alteration in size :—*For a larger garment, use thicker needles, or a size which produces fewer stitches to the inch ; for a smaller garment, use finer needles, or a size which produces more stitches to the inch.

Begin at the centre back by casting on 40 stitches and knit 40 rows (20 ridges).

Now begin to shape as follows :—

1st row. Knit 6, K into the front and back of the next st., K to end of row.
2nd row. Knit without shaping.

Repeat these 2 rows 19 times more, when you should have 60 sts. on the needle.

Knit 60 rows (30 ridges) more, finishing at the shaped edge.

Next row. K 6, K 2 tog., K to end of row.
Next row. Knit without decrease.

Repeat the last 2 rows 19 times more.

Knit 40 rows (20 ridges) more.

Cast off.

Press lightly on the wrong side with a warm iron over a slightly damp cloth. Sew up neatly the centre back seam.

Knitted Skull Cap.

(For use under Steel Helmet or for Sleeping)

Materials required :—

2 ozs. **Baldwin & Walker's LADYSHIP 4-PLY KONORT FINGERING.**
1 Pair Knitting Needles, No. 8.

Tension :—

6 stitches to 1 inch in width.
6 ridges (12 rows) to 1 inch in depth.

NOTE :—If the needles stated do not produce this tension, try different sizes until you get it correct.

Measurements :—

All round the head, unstretched, 20½ inches.
Depth from centre crown to cast-on edge 6 inches.

*Abbreviations :—*K, knit ; P, purl ; sts., stitches ; tog., together.

Begin at the lower edge by casting on 126 sts. and work in the rib of K 1, P 1 for 3 rows.

Change to garter st. (i.e. every row knit) and work until you have a depth of 3 inches from the cast-on edge.

TO SHAPE THE TOP.

1st row. * K 2 tog., K 12. Rep. from * to end of row.
2nd and every alternate row. Knit without decrease.
3rd row. * K 2 tog., K 11. Rep. from * to end of row.

Continue to decrease on every alternate row, working 1 st. less between the decreases until 18 sts. remain.

Break off the wool, leaving an end a few inches long, thread through a wool needle and pass the remaining sts. to the length of wool, then pass the needle through the sts. again and draw up. Do not break off, but continue with the same length of wool to sew up the centre back seam and fasten off securely.

If the back seam is joined stitch to stitch there is no need to press the Cap.

Knitted Knee Cap.

Materials required :—

3 ozs. **Baldwin & Walker's LADYSHIP BED-JACKET WOOL.**
1 Pair Knitting Needles, No. 8.

Begin by casting on 56 sts. and work in the rib of K 1, P 1 for 4 inches, knitting the last 2 sts. on every row.

TO SHAPE FOR KNEE.

1st row. Rib 34 sts., turn, slip 1, K 11, turn.

3rd row. S 1, P 12, turn, S 1, K 13 turn.

Continue to work in this way, taking up 1 st. more before turning on every row until there are 11 sts. left unworked at both ends of the needle.

Next row. S 1, P 32, turn, S 1, K 31, turn.

Work in stocking st. leaving 1 st. more unworked before turning on every row until there are 22 sts. left unworked at both ends, turn.

Next row. S 1, P 11, * pick up a st. from the space left when turning, place on the left hand needle, then P 2. tog. Repeat from * 10 times more, rib to end of row.

Next row. Rib 12, K 22, * pick up a st. from space left when turning, place on left hand needle and K 2 tog. Rep. from * 10 times more, rib to end of row.

Continue to work in the rib of K 1, P 1 over all the sts. as before for a further 4 inches. Cast-off.

Sew up the centre back seam.

Make a second Knee Cap in the same way.

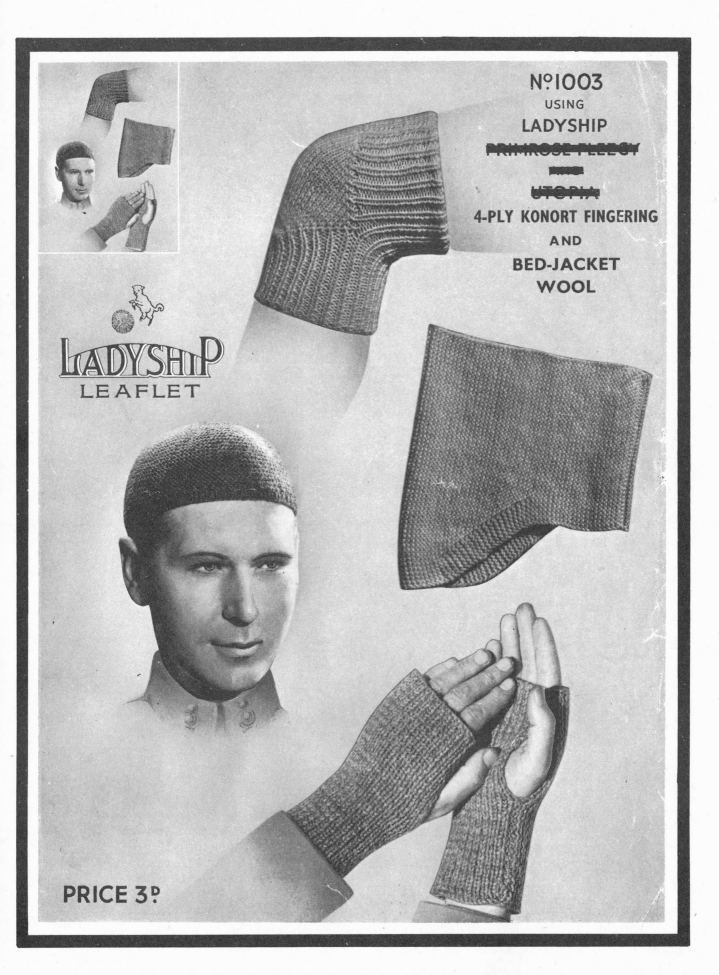

No. 1003

USING

LADYSHIP

~~PRIMROSE FLEECY~~

~~AND~~

~~UTOPIA~~

4-PLY KONORT FINGERING

AND

BED-JACKET
WOOL

LADYSHIP
LEAFLET

PRICE 3ᴰ

Knitting Notes

Yarns have changed a great deal since these patterns first appeared. Some kinds, such as the artificial silk of the 20s, have disappeared altogether. Real wool has also tended to be replaced with wool and nylon mixtures and nylon yarns; they are more practical, though the garments are more authentic knitted up in real wool. No modern yarn will be exactly equivalent to the one given in the pattern, so it is *essential* to test tension before starting on a garment; if you knit with the tension given in the pattern, the garment will come out the right size. An easy method of testing tension is given below.

Many of the patterns recommend 2-ply and 3-ply yarns, which are now very difficult to find. The old 2-ply and 3-ply were thicker than modern 2-ply and 3-ply, and these patterns can be knitted in 4-ply or even Double Knitting if the needle size is adjusted to keep the tension the same. The garment comes out the right size, but with a slightly heavier texture.

However, for those particular patterns, 2-ply and 3-ply yarns do reproduce best the soft, silky feel and fine texture of the original garments. If you can find 2-ply and 3-ply yarns, use them, on the needle size given in the patterns; only remember to check your tension first. If the ply is changed up, you will need more wool; slightly more if you use a 3-ply for 2-ply, quite a lot more if you use 4-ply or Double Knitting for 2-ply or 3-ply.

To test tension

Work a sample 3-inch square, before starting on the garment. If the tension count in the pattern is, say, 8 stitches to the inch, count 8 stitches and mark them off with pins. If the distance between the pins is exactly 1-inch, your tension is correct. If the distance is more, the stitches are too loose — try a smaller needle size; if it is less, they are too tight — try a larger needle size. A more attractive garment is produced if the knitting is kept fairly tight and even.

You can often use tension to alter the size of a garment without altering the pattern. For a garment one size larger, use needles one size larger, giving less stitches to the inch. For a garment two sizes larger, use needles two sizes larger.

Knitting Needle Sizes

British	Continental	American
1	9.25	13
2	8.00	11
3	7.00	10½
4	6.00	10
5	5.50	9
6	5.00	8
7	4.75	7
8	4.50	6
9	4.00	5
—	3.50	4
10	3.25	3
11	3.00	2
12	2.50	1
13	—	—
14	2.00	0

Acknowledgements

Thanks are due to the editors both past and present of the following magazines: *Beehive Knitting Booklets* (Paton and Baldwins Ltd), *'Best Way' Series* (IPC), *Farmer and Stock-Breeder* and *Farmer's Home* (IPC), *Film Pictorial* (IPC), *The Ford Times*, *Good Housekeeping* (The National Magazine Company), *'Help Yourself' Annual*, *Home* (IPC), *Home and Country* (IPC), *Home Making* (IPC), *Hygiene of Life* (British Books Ltd), *The Ideal Home* (IPC), *Ladyship* (Paton and Baldwins Ltd), *Miss Modern* (IPC), *Modern Home* (IPC), *Mother* (IPC), *Mother and Home* (IPC), *My Home* (IPC), *Nash's Magazine* (National Magazine Company), *Saturday Evening Post*, *The Strand Magazine* (IPC), *The Tailor and Cutter* (United Trade Press Ltd), *The Story of 25 Eventful Years in Pictures* (IPC), *Weldon's Ladies Journal* (IPC), *Wife and Home* (IPC), *Woman and Home* (IPC), *Woman's Journal* (IPC), *Woman's Magazine* (Lutterworth Press), *Woman's Pictorial* (IPC), *Woman's Weekly* (IPC). The editors cannot be held responsible for any errors in the original patterns and cannot enter into any correspondence.

My thanks are also due to Tony and Leslie Birks-Hay of Alphabet and Image; to Mik Dunn for all his help; to Stream & Associates for the photographs from *The Tailor and Cutter*; and to Alphabet and Image Photograph Library, Associated Press, Keystone Press Agency, John Mennell, National Film Institute and P & O Photographic Library for additional photographs.

Instructions for knitting the jumper worn by the Prince of Wales on page 53 can be obtained by post from Norah Dunn, 36 Newton Road, London, W.2 for 60 cents (35 pence), inclusive of postage.